LIBERAL LANDSLIDE
The General Election of 1906

ELECTIONS AND ADMINISTRATIONS SERIES
General Editor Michael Hurst

In preparation
Elections and Administrations 1603–1660 by Vernon Snow
Elections and Administrations 1826–35 by Richard W. Davis
Elections and Administrations 1841–46 by Travis Crosby
The Khaki Election of 1900 by Richard Rempel
Disraeli's Great Ministry 1874–80 by Peter Durrans

LIBERAL LANDSLIDE
The General Election of 1906

A. K. Russell

DAVID & CHARLES *Newton Abbot*
ARCHON BOOKS *Hamden Connecticut*
1973

This edition first published in 1973 in
Great Britain by David & Charles
(Holdings) Limited, Newton Abbot,
Devon and in the United States of
America by Archon Books, Hamden,
Connecticut 06514

ISBN 0 7153 5662 3 (*Great Britain*)
ISBN 0–208–01389–X (*United States*)

Set in eleven on thirteen point Imprint
and printed in Great Britain
by Latimer Trend & Company Ltd Plymouth

For Simon
and all those children
like him for whom politics (happily) will
not signify;
and
for Christopher and Emma
who needs must make
their way

Contents

Page

List of Illustrations

Foreword

The general election of 1906 remains one of the most fascinating events of twentieth-century British politics, not merely because the reversal of fortunes it brought about was so great, nor even because the Labour party in effect made its first appearance at that time; but also because it marked (a) the culmination of the two issues which in one form or another had, with Home Rule, been dominating British politics for the previous twenty years—imperialism and the problems of domestic social reform—and (b) a new determination of the working-class majority to bring its electoral influence to bear more self-consciously than before.

The election may not have been—indeed certainly was not—won and lost on lofty considerations about Britain's place in the world, or about the type of Britain the voter wanted to see at home; but these themes ran strongly throughout the years before the election and during the election period itself; and the Liberal victory undoubtedly played its part, not only in determining certain transient issues, but also in creating the kind of commonwealth, and the kind of empire-less welfare state in Britain, that have emerged in the years since the end of World War II.

The book begins with a brief recapitulation of the franchise and its effects in the period before 1906, and proceeds to an examination of the parties, their programmes and their presentations. In view of the large literature that has already accumulated on a (then) small Labour party, it concentrates, without apology, on the Liberal and Unionist parties. But following chapters on Edwardian electioneering and the press, and on the poll, it includes the 'labour vote' among the three or four major movements of opinion—fiscal, religious/nationalist, and social—on which the Liberal and Labour successes were based. The thesis expressed in it, briefly, is that the Liberal party was both wise *and* fortunate in its response to the major political opportunities with which it was—almost gratuitously—present d between 1902 and 1905; wise in its recognition of the Labour movement and of the need to emphasise *domestic* social, rather than fiscal (or any other) reform, but fortunate in the unrepeatable depth of support that it received from Free Trade Unionists, dissenting English, and Catholic Irish. No clear-cut conclusions emerge about the future of the Liberal and Labour parties, though—for what it is worth—the evidence of 1906 points as strongly to Liberal absorption of Labour as to Labour supersession of the Liberal party; but, far more important, surely, than sterile argument about the might-have-beens, is the fact that, at a crucial moment in 1906, a political philosophy obtained a hearing —a policy which, in its ideas and acts, influences all of us still today.

My thanks are due to the Warden and Fellows of Nuffield College, Oxford, for supporting the research on which the original doctoral thesis on the general election of 1906 was based and for making it possible for the story to be told, to a considerable extent, through contemporary sources; and to the many others—too numerous to name—who have encouraged its presentation, in this shorter form, to a wider audience.

Glossary of Terms Used and of Abbreviations

Conservative   of or appertaining to the Conservative party
conservative   cautious, concerned to preserve
Labour   of or appertaining to the Labour Representation Committee
labour   of or appertaining to the labour movement in general
Liberal   of or appertaining to the Liberal party
liberal   concerned with freedom
Nationalist   of or appertaining to the Irish Nationalists
nationalist   support for or supporter of nationalism
Unionist   of or appertaining to the Conservative and Liberal Unionist parties
unionist   indicating support for the union between England and Ireland, and opposition to Home Rule

CCO	Conservative Central Office
CLEC	Croydon Labour Electoral Committee
FTL	Free Trade League
GFTU	General Federation of Trade Unions
ILP	Independent Labour Party
ITC	Imperial Tariff Commission
LCA	Liberal Central Association
LLF	London Liberal Federation
LL and RU	London Liberal and Radical Union
LPD	Liberal Publication Department
LRC	Labour Representation Committee

LUA	Liberal Unionist Association
LUC	Liberal Unionist Council
LUP	Liberal Unionist Party
NEC	National Executive Committee
NFCC	National Free Church Council
NLF	National Liberal Federation
NUCA	National Union of Conservative Associations
NUWSS	National Union of Women's Suffrage Societies
SDF	Social Democratic Federation
SLA	Scottish Liberal Association
TRL	Tariff Reform League
UFT	Unionist Free Trade(r)
UIL	United Irish League
WLF	Women's Liberal Federation
WNLF	Women's National Liberal Federation
WSPU	Women's Social and Political Union

1 BACKGROUND: THE FRANCHISE AND ITS EFFECTS

THE FRANCHISE

Between 1885 and 1918, the British electoral system remained virtually unchanged. The Liberal party was committed—by its (1891) Newcastle Programme—to the introduction of full manhood suffrage, but owing to Irish and other preoccupations failed to bring forward legislation between 1892 and 1895; and the Unionists who succeeded the Liberals in office, from 1895 to 1905, showed little inclination to steal their clothes. Despite an ongoing Radical commitment to fairly wide-ranging reform, and the presentation of over one hundred parliamentary petitions (1901–5) on women's suffrage alone, no major changes were effected. Anxious to eliminate some of the grosser disparities in constituency size, and to cut Ireland in the process down to size, Gerald Balfour appointed a parliamentary committee on constituency boundaries, and brought forward a bill in 1905 to redistribute seats (to Irish disadvantage). But even this modest initiative fell by the wayside, and the 1906 election was consequently fought on the basis of the 1884–5 legislation. Aptly described as 'the last of those rearguard actions whereby the Whigs sought to control, direct and dilute the forces of British democracy',[1] this legislation was not only less democratic than has commonly been supposed, but less democratic even than the ferment of the age.

Au fond, the franchise represented a theory of property rather than of individual rights, and in 1906—as twenty years before— 9–11 per cent of votes were based on specific ownership, or fancy

borough, franchises. Even the broader household, occupation and
lodger franchises were based on the occupation or use of
property, including—as one of its obligations—payment of poor
relief. Subject to notoriously inconsistent rulings in the courts,
they failed to make any provision whatsoever for the multi-
occupation of property (for example by adult sons, relatives, or
men-servants). Since in 1906 there were approximately 8 million
recorded households and lodgings compared with nearly 11 million
adult males, it is fairly clear, not only that between 2 and 3

Table 1

FRANCHISE AND VOTES
(Totals 1906, and percentages 1885, 1901, and 1906)

Type of seat	Owners	Occupiers and householders	Lodgers	Others	Totals
Counties:					
England	479,443	2,578,859	57,073	—	3,116,339
%	20:16:15	80:84:84	–:1:2		68:69:73
Wales	31,910	192,314	3,719	—	227,943
%	21:15:14	79:84:84	–:1:2		5:5:5
Scotland	60,112	346,937	14,276	—	421,325
%	15:14:14	85:84:82	–:2:3		9:9:10
Ireland	8,362	560,476	4,228	—	573,066
%	2:2:2	98:98:98	–:–:1		18:15:13
Total counties	579,827	3,591,989	79,260	—	4,279,153
%	16:14:14	84:85:84	–:1:2		62:60:59
Boroughs:					
England	—	2,216,894	119,513	23,247	2,359,654
%	—	94:95:94	4:4:5	2:1:1	81:82:83
Wales	—	92,943	8,416	877	102,236
%	—	97:93:91	1:6:8	2:1:1	3:3:3
Scotland	—	259,971	16,819	30,610	307,400
%	—	89:87:84	–:3:5	11:10:10	11:11:11
Ireland	—	108,423	2,183	2,989	113,595
%	—	93:96:96	3:2:2	4:3:2	5:4:4
Total boroughs	—	2,678,231	146,931	57,723	2,882,885
%	—	94:94:94	3:4:5	3:3:2	38:40:41
Universities					45,150
Total UK	579,827	6,357,817	226,191	57,723	7,266,708
%	10:8:8	88:88:88	1:3:3	1:1:1	100

million men were disenfranchised by this shortcoming alone, but also that—given the desperate urban overcrowding of the poor (40 per cent or more living two to a room in London)—the majority of them were working-class.

In its provision for the registration of voters, the law suffered from a second major limitation. Under the terms of the Registration Act of 1885, all local authorities were bounden to keep their rate books (or valuation rolls) up to date, to enquire each April and May if anyone other than the ratepayers was entitled to vote, to receive claims for ownership and lodger votes and to publish lists of registered electors by 1 July each year. Individuals (and political parties) then had until 20 August in which to object to votes already registered and to claim votes not yet registered. The revising barristers considered their representations in August and September, and the electoral register as revised by them became effective in the new year. As a system it was certainly a great improvement on the earlier requirement of electors to make individual claims; but it nevertheless remained 'so replete with technicalities, complications, and anomalies' that 'every obstacle' was put in the way of getting on the register whilst 'every facility' existed for getting struck off.[1] It made it particularly difficult for people changing their addresses to ensure that they remained on the voting lists in consecutive years and—with about 5 per cent of county electors and between 20 and 30 per cent of many borough electors (more in London) moving each year—this bore especially hard on the working classes, and on the million or so 'shopkeepers, office workers, superior factory foremen, the less successful professional men . . .'[2] who formed the backbone of the Edwardian lower middle class.

Subject to continuous uncertainty of employment and to still relatively expensive public transport, working men were always on the move to find, or to be near, their work, and in his survey of London (re-issued in 1902), Booth estimated that 'in one fairly representative district in Bethnall Green over forty per cent of families had moved in a single year'.[3] Writing on the *Government of England* in 1908, Lowell similarly recounted the

B

case of a school teacher who had never been able to vote in a general election because 'his very success in his profession, by involving changes in residence, had always cost him his vote';[4] and it is certain that the great majority of the 400,000 or so serving soldiers, sailors, and merchant seamen—for whom no special arrangements were made—were in very much the same position. The battle for registration was consequently an important part of the electoral battle, placing a high premium on effective party organisation. In the belief, unproven but reasonable, that the majority of removals were potential supporters of theirs, the Liberals were always anxious, wherever possible, to avoid fighting an election on an old register.

Including paupers, who were automatically disqualified on receipt of poor relief, there were, altogether, about 4 million adult males excluded from the vote by the electoral and registration laws (Table 2).

Table 2

ESTIMATE OF ADULT MALES WITHOUT THE VOTE IN 1906

Soldiers, sailors and seamen (also including lunatics, criminals and peers)	400,000
Paupers	250,000
Single men and others in joint households	2,000,000
Removals, including (perhaps primarily) lodgers	1,350,000
Total	4,000,000

In addition, moreover, to this *dis*enfranchisement, on a property basis, of a large number of people, the complex range of ownership and fancy franchises (including the university votes) preserved a substantial element of plurality within the system. The university and fancy franchises were relatively small, but—according to contemporary estimates—60–80 per cent of the (roughly) 580,000 ownership votes in the counties were held in plurality. Assuming contemporary estimates to be right, that there were also about 100,000 pluralists among the borough occupation votes, it becomes clear that the total number of plural votes in 1906 can be put at around 600,000 (Table 3). And even this figure may be modest.

Table 3

ESTIMATE OF PLURAL VOTES IN 1906

University votes	45,100
Fancy borough franchises	57,723
Occupiers	100,000
Ownership votes held in plurality	
(estimated at 70 per cent)	416,000
Total	618,823

The number of plural *voters* was unquestionably smaller; Chamberlain confessed in 1885 that he was himself a terrible case of plural voting with six votes, but he cited at least one reverend gentleman with as many as twenty-three. The possibility of actually casting this number was limited by the prohibition of plural voting in any one constituency; but the distribution of polling over two or three weeks until, finally, the 1918 Representation of the People Act confined it to a single day, continued nevertheless to make it possible for many pluralists to vote in adjacent county and borough constituencies.

This combination of disenfranchisement and plurality meant that the franchise was considerably biased against the poorer sections of the community which by any definition included all of the paupers, most of the soldiers, sailors and seamen, a large proportion of those who were disenfranchised by virtue of multiple occupation and the great majority of lodgers disenfranchised by removal and registration. Table 4 suggests that even if it were to be assumed (a) that all plural voters were without exception middle and upper class, and (b) that the disenfranchised were distributed among the electorate proportionately to income groups, the top 11 per cent (and in particular the top 3 per cent) enjoyed very considerably greater voting power, per head, than the bottom 89 (or 97) per cent.

The *actual* discrepancies were almost certainly much greater, not only between the top 3 per cent and the rest, but also between the skilled workers, who with cheap food, beer and entertainment, were able to live tolerably stable, if frugal, lives on £60–£160 per annum, and the unskilled labourers—Robert Tressell's *Ragged Trousered Philanthropists*—who were not only the most itinerant, but the most impoverished group in the population.

Table 4

VOTES AND SOCIAL CLASS[5]

Class	Percentage of population	No of voters (millions)	Estimated no of votes	No of people of all ages per vote
Upper and upper middle	3	0·21	0·46	2·6
Lower middle	8	0·54	0·79	4·4
Skilled working	56	3·78	0·78	6·2
Unskilled working	33	2·23	2·23	6·2

Furthermore, the bias was of political as well as of social significance. Between 1885 and 1906, population movements off the land and away from the county (and also to some extent the smaller borough) seats into the fast-growing suburban (and to some extent urbanised county) seats, meant that the rural areas were increasingly over-represented. Ireland would have lost at least 22 (of its 103) seats in any one of the schemes of redistribution put forward by the parliamentary committee. But even in Great Britain, a county vote had—by 1906—become worth very nearly double the borough average; and, as the following examples show, there were some startling contrasts, in 1906, between the size of electorates in older and in newer centres of population.

Durham	2,580	Hartlepool	14,056
St Georges in the East	3,246	Romford	45,579
Whitehaven	2,945	Grimsby	16,058
East Hull	8,861	Central Hull	20,192
Bath (2 seats)	7,968	Cardiff (1 seat)	27,057
York (2 seats)	13,864	Middlesbrough (1 seat)	20,332
Winchester	2,861	Croydon	78,000

Since the county and smaller borough seats were precisely those in which the plural votes were concentrated (frequently comprising 5–10 per cent of all votes, or more), it is hardly surprising that the Conservatives and Unionists—for whom contemporaries believed 80 per cent of the plural votes were cast—enjoyed a striking predominance in them, throughout the period 1885–1900. Radicals certainly had some reason to feel at an initial disadvantage; but, equally, they had much to gain if, as happened in 1906, a substantial shift in political loyalties could be achieved.

GENERAL POLITICAL RESPONSE

Important, however, as these limitations of property, plural voting, and political bias were, the working classes nevertheless constituted 75–80 per cent of the electorate—ie a majority in one half to two-thirds of all seats (primarily in the urbanised areas) —and in the political generation before 1906 both major parties consequently sought to modify both structure and policy to reflect this fact. Organisationally first in the field, with the NLF, the Liberal party bosses fought valiantly, if with only moderate success, to ensure the inclusion among their candidates of a number of Lib-Lab trade unionists; and—prompted by Randolph Churchill and his Fourth Party—the Conservatives were not slow to follow suit in trying to close the gap between their official and representative organisations. Middleton, who was principal agent from 1885 to 1903, succeeded in creating an excellent working relationship between the NUCA and the CCO, within which the grass-roots Primrose League had its own important role. But the most significant single development of the period was the rapid growth—with the unionisation of unskilled labour in the 1890s—of trade union membership (Table 5), which, with the ILP and Fabian Society, established the basis on which the Labour Representation Committee was built in 1900 and after.

New social and political ideas were not slow, simultaneously, to emerge. 'A few of the abler Liberals (such as Lowe, Fawcett, Morley [and] Auberon Herbert) fought a stern rearguard action

Table 5

GROWTH OF TRADE UNION MEMBERSHIP AND FUNDS,
1890–1904

Year	Membership (hundreds)	Income (£ hundreds)	Funds (£ hundreds)
1892	903	1,462	1,574
1894	924	1,617	1,564
1896	988	1,652	2,151
1898	1,084	1,902	2,644
1900	1,210	1,950	3,733
1902	1,217	2,094	4,139
1904	1,203	2,124	4,426

against such extreme laissez faire' and as late as 1891 a Conservative MP condemned the Bill for Free Education as 'the forbidden fruit of social bribery'.[6] But in the closing decades of the nineteenth century the economists increasingly sought to gather together 'in an orderly fashion and concentrate more attention on the case for state intervention';[7] and, as knowledge of social conditions became deeper and more widespread, so the ideas of the political economists and social analysts—opinion leaders we might now call them—were inevitably adopted, albeit slowly, into the vocabulary of politics.

Influenced by a combination of the Irish issue, the works of Henry George, and the new rural element in the 1884 franchise, the Liberals concentrated very largely at first on issues of land monopoly and reform; but C. E. Montague openly welcomed Rosebery's settlement of an industrial dispute, in 1893, as a break with what he called—significantly—'the bad old tradition of non-interference,'[8] and when—following Mill—Harcourt introduced his redistributive budget in 1894, he laconically justified it with a comment that the only way he knew of gaining the support of the electorate was to earn it. On the other side of the House, Chamberlain—who had made his name in Birmingham with a brand of positive municipal socialism—was an early and vigorous pioneer of old age pensions; whilst Salisbury declared in 1895 that 'the improvement of the daily life of the struggling millions

and the diminution of the sorrows that so many are condemned
to bear is the blessed task [of] Parliaments and . . . the highest
duty of statesmen'.[9] However great their difference of opinion
as to means, even Keir Hardie and Robert Blatchford—author
of *Merrie England*—hardly expressed the increasing social conscience of the time more succinctly.

Table 6[10]

PUBLIC EXPENDITURE TRENDS 1870–1910
(1900 prices, rounded)

	1870	*1880*	*1890*	*1900*	*1910*
GNP (£ million)	790	1,016	1,308	1,944	2,057
Total public expenditure (£ million)	67	82	133	281	264
Main heads (£ million)					
1. National Debt	11	17	24	20	20
2. Military	22	29	36	135	75
3. Civil	34	36	73	126	179
Public expenditure per head (£)	2	3	4	7	6

These growing elements of political organisation and social
commitment—reflecting better knowledge and the wider franchise alike—were not without practical and broadly bi-partisan
effect in the continuing, if often contested, extension of regula-
tory legislation (e.g. Factory Acts and Employers Liability Acts)
and in the slow but sure enlargement of public spending for
public purposes (Table 6). As a result of Forster's Education Act
of 1870, the Technical Education Act of 1889, and the abolition,
in 1891, of all fee-paying in elementary schools, public expenditure on education rose fivefold between 1870 and 1890 (from
£2 million to £11·2 million). The combination of civil service
reform (following the Priestley and Ridley Commissions) and
of local government reform in 1888 and 1894 created an administrative structure *through* which central government was able to
legislate for social services of a local kind (e.g. in the Public
Libraries Act of 1894) and *within* which the newly constituted

local authorities could at last begin to come to grips with the problems of 'gas and water socialism' created by growing urbanisation and advancing technology. With real wages increasing (1870–90) by approximately one-third, the standard of living insensibly improved for many in the population.

But the *political response* to this combination of proven need and electoral pressure was very much muted by the interpolation into the political dialogue of the issues of Ireland and of empire. Beholden as it was to the Irish vote in Parliament, Gladstone's last administration made disappointingly little effort to implement the more progressive items of the Newcastle Programme. As colonial secretary in the Unionist administration that succeeded it, Chamberlain's energies were rapidly diverted into broader fields than pensions. The Unionists, in the short term, gained. Given the sense of national insecurity created by the increasing challenge—commercial as well as political—of Russia, Germany, France, and the USA, the firm imperial policies they pursued in Africa, north and south, were initially popular, and left a legacy of uneasy arrogance in the jokes and songs of the music halls that persisted up to World War I. The Liberal party (and nascent Labour movement) were—on the contrary—deeply divided by the Boer War and, helped by a temporary war-begotten stimulus to trade and employment, the Unionist party was able to secure a renewal of its mandate in the Khaki Election in October 1900 with only minor losses. As, however, victory over the Boers proved elusive and the cost of the war in men (finally 20,000) and money (finally £250 million) mounted, the suspicion grew that it had, in the end, been fought at the expense of more progressive policies at home.

The government's confession in the Queen's Speech to the new parliament in 1900 that the time was 'not propitious for any domestic reforms which involve large expenditure',[11] and its acquiescence in the Taff Vale judgement threatening the financial independence of the trade unions, lent substance to radical accusation—neatly reversing the Unionist platform of 1895—that 'the forces making for unrest abroad [were] found to be the same as the forces stifling progress . . . at home'.[12] It became increasingly clear that whilst some social progress had been made, little enough had been done to meet the still urgent problems of old age and unemployment, or of the poverty of the submerged third of the population, which Rowntree in 1901 showed to be every bit as real as Booth had demonstrated twenty years before. In his aptly-titled treatise on *Riches and Poverty* (published in 1905), the Liberal Leo Money pointed out that, despite all the progress made, the real distribution of national wealth had barely changed in forty years.

> If [since 1867] our national income had but increased at the same rate as our population [he wrote] . . . it would in 1905 amount to but £1,200 million . . . It is in fact about £1,700 million. Yet the Error of Distribution remains so great that while the total population in 1867 amounted to 30 million, we have today a nation of 30 million poor people in our rich country and many millions of these are living under conditions of degrading poverty . . . We have won through the birth and establishment of the factory system at the cost of physical deterioration. We have purchased a great commerce at the price of crowding our population into the cities and of robbing millions of strength and beauty. We have given our people what we grimly call elementary education and robbed them of the elements of a natural life. All this has been done that a few of us may enjoy a superfluity of goods and services. Out of the travail of millions we have added to a landed gentry an aristocracy of wealth . . . [who] striding over the bodies of the fallen proclaim in accents of conviction the prosperity of their country.[13]

With crude but effective calculations, he showed—as accurately as was necessary—that 1 per cent of the population owned 55 per cent of all national wealth, and that the depressed third of the population—casual urban and agricultural labourers—barely existed on less than £60 per year (Table 7).

If, then, the Edwardian era dawned with the feeling that 'not only a new reign but also a new social era had begun',[14] it marked less a recognition of reform achieved, than a determination— significant to each and every party—to ensure that neither Ireland

nor imperialism should impede more significant social advances
in the years to come.

Table 7

DISTRIBUTION OF EDWARDIAN OWNERSHIP AND INCOME

Class	Total number	Percentage of the population	Percentage of national wealth	Income per year (£)
(i)	300,000	1	55	1,000–1,500 (or more)
(ii)	600,000	2	25	400–1,000
(iii)	2,500,000	8	11	160–400
(iv)	16,500,000	56	8	60–160
(v)	11,000,000	33	1	Under 60

(i) rich; (ii) upper middle class; (iii) lower middle class;
(iv) skilled working class; (v) casual and agricultural labour

THE RUN-UP TO THE ELECTION

Balfour, who succeeded Salisbury as Conservative leader in
August 1902, was in some respects a model Tory, who succeeded
during his administration in leading the country out of its Boer
War isolation into agreements with France and Japan, without
showing either weakness towards Russia or hostility towards
Germany, and who sought in bills on education, licensing, immigration, and unemployment, to make an approach, at least, to
pressing social problems. But, hampered by his own innate
rationality, he persistently failed to recognise the importance, as
Graham Wallas put it in his book of that title in 1908, of *Human
Nature in Politics*, and—as his sister-in-law commented in 1903—
'he quite failed to win his spurs among the mob'.[15] He showed
very little *contemporaneous* interest in the rise of a Labour movement dedicated to independent action with which, amid the
debris of 1906, he professed to be so fascinated. And—lacking
any cabinet colleagues except Chamberlain with much gift for
popular presentation or appeal—he too often pursued his policies
with scant regard for their party or popular political effect.

The Education Act that he piloted in 1902 was very much a case in point. Necessitated by the Cockerton judgement, which invalidated the rate support of technical and secondary education by county and borough councils, it was administratively logical and educationally defensible; but by making rate-payers responsible for the support of the 83 per cent Anglican voluntary schools without giving them any choice in the type of religious education to be provided, it rode roughshod over dissenting opinion, split the Liberal Unionist party, and gave a powerful impetus to post-war Liberal reunification. In 1903 Balfour accepted his Chancellor Ritchie's view that owing to its fatal effect in the constituencies, the unpopular corn tax (introduced as a fiscal measure in 1902) should be repealed, but—concerned very largely with Irish land, and army, reform—he failed to put forward any positive programme on which Unionist—and electoral—opinion might be rallied.

For all their imperial squabbles, the Liberal leaders were wiser in their day. Recognising the importance on the one hand of uniting on Asquith's 'step by step' compromise over Ireland, enabling Home Rule to be relegated *pro tem* to a secondary place, they also saw, on the other hand, that without some *modus vivendi* with a Labour party able to 'influence the votes of nearly a million men',[16] they might all too easily find the LRC as real a threat as the Irish Nationalists had been to the independent working majority which they sought (but failed to gain) in 1892. Public opinion did not begin to move strongly against the Unionists until 1903 and 1904, and, struggling to revive both morale and organisation, the Liberal party was not until later in a sufficiently strong position to try 'to strangle the Labour Party in its cradle',[17] even had it wished to do so. It therefore came to terms. This made political as well as practical sense; for there were so many common Liberal-Labour interests—opposition to the war, to Taff Vale, the Education Act and the corn tax—that, as the socialists of the SDF and ILP feared, it was by no means clear, in 1902, how political allegiances would finally divide. This, indeed, was precisely why Hardie and MacDonald had to fight

so hard for their policy of essentially pragmatic Labour independence, enshrined in the 1903 Newcastle Resolution requiring
officials, candidates and MPs to 'abstain strictly from identifying
themselves with or promoting the interests of any section of the
Liberal or Conservative parties'.[18] And it was certainly as reasonable for the Liberals to hope that a constituency agreement along
the lines negotiated by MacDonald and Herbert Gladstone (in
1903) would create the conditions for a *longer-term* understanding
between the two parties, as it was for the Labour leadership to
try to buy time to consolidate its independence.

To Chamberlain (if not to Balfour) the threat to the Unionists
of a joint Liberal-Labour front seemed real enough; and, returning from South Africa shortly before Crooks's capture of Woolwich for the LRC, he viewed the developing political situation
with little short of dismay.

> . . . he found the by-elections going against [them]. He found a
> Land Bill about to be introduced into the House of Commons on
> which he had never been consulted . . . he found . . . Brodrick's
> army schemes a topic of universal criticism running counter in
> some important respects to his own South African projects. He
> found an Education Bill in its most unpopular phase and daily
> alienating valuable supporters . . . [and] above all his one shilling
> duty on corn as a means of obtaining preferential treatment for
> Canada was rendered impossible by the Chancellor of the
> Exchequer's refusal to embody it in his budget.[19]

He thus decided that, for party political and imperial reasons
alike, the time had come to express views that had long been
maturing in his mind (but particularly since the 1902 Colonial
Conference) for the utilisation of imperial preferences for social
as well as imperial ends, and he roundly said at Birmingham, on
15 May, that unless the question of trade and commerce was
satisfactorily settled, he did not believe in 'a continued unity of
the Empire' and that 'without preferential duties it would be
impossible either to raise the money required for social reform
or to lower the rate of unemployment'.[20] His subsequent statements in the House of Commons—which Balfour regarded as a

'quite gratuitous challenge both to his colleagues and the world'[19] —clearly espoused the notion and necessity, in the broader interest, of food taxation, which would fall on rich and poor alike, but claimed that by providing higher wages and more regular employment, farmers, industrialists and workers alike would be better off.

Believing that, 'over-sensitive to temporary [sic] movements of public opinion',[19] Chamberlain had rushed precipitately to unfounded (even if intrinsically desirable) conclusions, Balfour was thus faced with a tactical dilemma of some delicacy. Describing his role as being to state as clearly as he could 'the principles on which fiscal policy should proceed and leave it to friends . . . to say whether they agree . . . or no',[21] he produced his own personal policy statement—his *Economic Notes on Insular Free Trade*—in which he argued equally strongly against insular Cobden-style Free Trade and against the rash introduction of 'insular protection'; and he remodelled his cabinet in mid-September (1903) to exclude Chamberlain (but not Austen Chamberlain) on the one hand and the more extreme Free Traders (but not Devonshire) on the other. He announced that an enquiry into the workings of fiscal policy would be held, and seems to have believed that the majority of the party would rally round his middle-of-the-road policy of retaliation where necessary against foreign tariffs, without any general tariff or preferential scheme.

However, whilst Balfour recognised more accurately than Chamberlain the unpopularity of *any* proposals involving the additional taxation of food, this proved to be an untenable compromise solution. Devonshire resigned within a month, and many of Balfour's 'friends' were not slow to turn to one or the other extremist point of view. Chamberlain launched his first Tariff Reform campaign, in October 1903, and sought, on the basis of a 10 per cent general tariff plus imperial preference, to appeal quite specifically to the working classes. 'You have the majority of votes,' he said at Liverpool, 'the responsibility is yours.'[22] He established the Imperial Tariff Commission and the Tariff Reform League, and early in 1904 he won his battle for control of the Liberal Unionist Association as—henceforth—a committed tariff reform body. On the other side, the Free Food League was formed, and by December 1903 the Unionist Free Traders, led by Cecil, James, and Burleigh, were making preliminary overtures to the Liberals for some kind of *de facto* alliance.

Balfour fought hard to keep his parliamentary majority intact, but as the drift of Unionist Free Traders to the Liberals continued, he seemed consistently unable, as Austen Chamberlain complained with Tariff Reform in mind, to 'raise a great ideal and touch the spirit of the nation'.[23] Indeed, by bringing forward a Licensing Act known to have been drafted in the offices of the Trade Defence League and a measure for the introduction of Chinese coolies into South Africa under semi-servile conditions, he only fortified the movement of extra-parliamentary opinion against his party and strengthened the existing currents of Liberal (and of Liberal and Labour) co-operation. Furthermore, whilst the LRC was less dedicated to Free Trade as a doctrine than were the mass of the Liberals, Ramsay MacDonald privately admitted in 1904 that 'the opposition of organised Labour to Tariff Reform was almost unanimous';[24] and Shackleton voiced a common (Liberal and Labour) point of view when he told the 1905 LRC conference that Chamberlain's campaign had only been 'started for the purpose of drawing the attention of the working man away from the misdeeds of the government'.[25] As the younger Liberals developed an increasingly collectivist and interventionist platform, so Keir Hardie admitted, in August 1905, that the Liberal party appeared 'more and more conscious of the nature and realities of social conditions';[26] and—whilst maintaining its independent line—the LRC tacitly accepted the practical realities of co-operation by signing the Caxton Hall Concordat with the TUC and the GFTU, in February 1905, under which it undertook not to oppose the candidates (including many Lib-Labs) endorsed by the parliamentary committee of the TUC, and agreed to enjoin no more than 'great care' on the part of its members when speaking from what it euphemistically described as 'neutral', i.e. Liberal, platforms.[27]

The government's position was further weakened by the attacks which came from within on even its more traditional policies. Curzon criticised it for appearing to side with the military in India, and the military establishment at home for bringing forward what it regarded as an unworkable plan for separate short- and long-term armies. Wyndham was forced to resign in 1904 for alleged complicity in plans for 'administrative devolution' in Ireland, and Gerald Balfour's Redistribution of Seats Bill served only to facilitate co-operation between the Liberals and the Nationalists on something less than full Home Rule. Initially promising bills on alien immigration and unemployment relief earned further TUC condemnation by taking poverty, and not need, as their criteria of entry and of benefit. And when Balfour frankly confessed to a delegation of unemployed that there would not be any point in recalling Parliament since 'six hundred gentlemen would not be able to help',[28] he seemed finally to confess his bankruptcy in social, as in fiscal, matters. By September 1905 even the *constitutional* propriety of his continuation in office was being seriously discussed.

With the Anglo-Japanese alliance safely ratified that month, Balfour was in fact seriously considering a dissolution, and he was 'motivated or almost entirely motivated' in his decision to go on 'by concern for party organisation'.[29] His private secretary, Sandars, warned him that virtually every party agent in the country had pleaded strongly for 'more time to place and familiarise candidates and improve local organisation',[30] and Acland-Hood, the chief whip, reported on 25 September that since their machinery was 'sadly in need of repair', every month that they could spend upon it would, he hoped, 'produce good results'.[31] In another fatal compromise Balfour took him literally and prepared to act accordingly. He remained convinced, he told Devonshire in October, that it would yet prove possible to rally the party on a programme of opposition to the 'legislative projects of the most dangerous kind' that a radical government would be forced to bring in—'the unjust increase of direct taxation, the taxation of ground rents, the perilous diminution of military

strength, payment of members, Home Rule all round and so
forth . . .',[32] and he therefore anticipated staying only until 'some
major point . . . in the debate on the Address'[33] finally provided
him with an apt pretext, early in the new year: hardly enough
time for any real organisational improvement.

To Chamberlain, long chafing under what he regarded as
Balfour's inability to lead, such tactics were simply not acceptable,
and when on 2 November 1905 Londonderry flatly accused him
of disloyalty to Balfour, he was stung into a reiteration of his
view of Tariff Reform as a guarantee of higher and steadier
employment in such a way that it constituted a direct—and
intended—challenge to the party leadership. Meeting at Newcastle on 14 November, the NUCA gave him explicit—and for the
first time overwhelming—support. Declining to accept Balfour's
renewed plea for party unity on, in effect, the lowest fiscal
common denominator, delegates passed a resolution in favour of
preference and a general tariff by an overwhelming majority;
and the *Morning Post* observed the following day that a party in
which Tariff Reformers were in a majority could not much
longer accept the leadership of a man who 'led his troops up to
but not across the Rubicon of fiscal reform'. When a few days
later the LPD's booklet *Ten Years of Toryism* appeared, with
scarcely a mention of unemployment, and was therefore scath-
ingly criticised by Keir Hardie, Chamberlain seized the opportunity of the LUA's annual conference at Bristol on 21 November
to appeal—for the last time before the election, as it seemed—
to the Labour movement and the Unionist party alike, for what
the *Manchester Guardian* epitomised (on 22 November) as 'a
hot short campaign on unemployment as a product . . . of the
present fiscal system'. Balfour was reported to be so angry that
he was considering immediate resignation not only from office
but also from the leadership of the party and it seemed for a long
day or two that the election might, in the end—and surprisingly
—be fought by Chamberlain on his own terms.

Politics are, however, full of the unexpected, and in November
1905 it was the unexpected that occurred in the sudden—and for

Balfour timely—re-emergence of the emotive Home Rule issue. Throughout the autumn Liberals of divers schools had spoken out—more freely than ever before—on the need for the Liberal party to obtain a majority independent of Nationalist support. Although Campbell-Bannerman was—as always—anxious, and wisely, to do nothing to prejudice the support of either Irish or Liberal stalwarts at the polls, he was aware—as Crewe warned him—that since 'more than ever before the Liberal party was . . . [on trial] as an engine for securing social reforms . . . it had to resist the I.L.P. claim to be the only friend of the worker'. 'Can it do this', Crewe asked, 'and attempt Home Rule as well?'[34] In the third week in November he therefore held discussions with Redmond and T. P. O'Connor to let them know that whilst he could not pledge his party to full Home Rule in the next parliament, he had 'not the slightest intention of embarrassing himself and his friends and all the friends of the Nationalist cause in Ireland, by such self-denying ordinances against a Home Rule proposal as had been uttered by some of his colleagues'.[35] He accordingly promised, as immediate Liberal policy, administrative reform (possibly 'some sort of general assembly elected by the Irish' which Labouchère reported to be 'the main thing that Redmond wanted'); continuing opposition to redistribution (as 'Redmond's chief card against the priests'); and as much moderation over education as was practically possible (in the face of the dissenting interest).[36] He obtained Redmond's vitally important promise in return that—whatever he felt obliged to say in public —he would do everything in his power to bring the Irish on to the Liberal side in the election. After clearing his lines with the more critical of his leading colleagues—Asquith, Grey, and Haldane—he therefore said at Stirling on 24 November that whilst Liberal policy in the immediate future would be devoted to the great social questions, he hoped the Nationalists would thankfully accept 'an instalment of representative control . . . or administrative improvements, provided it was consistent with and led up to the larger policy'.[37]

This formula, like Asquith's earlier 'step by step' compromise,

C

was warmly welcomed by Liberals of all shades of opinion; but it appeared to Rosebery, who was in Cornwall and was out of touch with the leadership, to amount to nothing less than an unrepentant recommitment of the party to the full Home Rule policy; and, speaking at Bodmin on Saturday 25 November, he accordingly said that—to his dismay—Campbell-Bannerman appeared to have 'hoisted once more in its most pronounced form the flag of Home Rule'.[38] On 27 November his words were blazoned in every Unionist daily, and the political situation was altered overnight. Balfour confided his view to the Unionist candidate for Chatham that 'the split between . . . Rosebery and Campbell-Bannerman will alter the result of the General Election',[39] and even the Tariff Reform papers (with the exception of the *Morning Post*) now agreed with the view expressed by Garvin in *Outlook* (2 December) that if Balfour could manoeuvre the opposition into office, he would have rendered 'a brilliant service to Imperial as well as to party interests . . . Ministers unmuzzled would be free to fight with more effect [and] a great Unionist rally would be certain'. Balfour agreed and—in the expectation that the formation of a Liberal administration would in itself bring old Liberal disagreements to the surface—he finally surrendered the seals of office on 4 December.

As events had it, however, the very fact of Rosebery's speech facilitated Campbell-Bannerman's task of forming an alternative —and very temporary—administration, and not only decided him to accept the King's Commission, on the grounds that 'any shrinking or reluctance would be read as inability through dissension',[40] but—finally—persuaded Grey and Haldane, as well as Asquith, that, although they had earlier agreed (at Relugas) to refuse office unless Campbell-Bannerman went to the Lords, they could not now risk jeopardising their party's prospects at the election.[41] Although their acceptance thus remained finely in the balance between 4 and 7 December, Campbell-Bannerman was able in the end to form a cabinet, and a government, which was not only representative of all sections of the Liberal party but was judged *inter alia* by James to be 'infinitely

stronger, man for man, than the late Government'.[42] Whilst
'*Daily News* men' held most of the important home departments
in the Commons, plus Dublin Castle, and were well represented
in the Lords in Ripon, Crewe, and Loreburn (Reid), all four
vice-presidents of the Liberal League came in, and three had
key positions in the Exchequer (Asquith), the Foreign Office
(Grey) and the War Office (Haldane). The inclusion of Burns at
the Local Government Board was warmly welcomed by many
people—from Theodore Roosevelt to Beerbohm Tree. And
although it was ridiculed in *Clarion*, Crooks, Bowerman, and
Isaac Mitchell—all LRC candidates—said in congratulating him
that his appointment had removed 'the last barrier to the workmen of the country to having full responsibility in administering
the affairs of the nation'.[43]

When thus, on 16 December, Campbell-Bannerman announced
the dissolution of Parliament (to take effect on 9 January) and
the election campaign immediately began, the political forces
of the country were intriguingly arrayed. Chamberlain's bid for
the working-class vote on a policy of Tariff Reform—somewhat
eclipsed during the manoeuvres that led to the formation of the
Liberal government—nevertheless remained on the table;
Balfour's anti-radicalism had received an initial setback in the
successful formation of the Liberal government, but had certainly
helped to heal, or hide, his party's divisions; the Liberals seemed
well set to win over a greater proportion of middle-class (and
pluralist) votes than hitherto; and the balance between progressive Liberal and would-be independent Labour forces
remained interestingly poised. A turning-point had arrived more
significant than any since 1885 and 1886, and the nation sensed it.

Notes to Chapter 1 will be found on pages 214–15

2 PARTY ORGANISATIONS AND CANDIDATES

Liberal and Labour

With the by-elections showing an increasing swing in their favour, the Liberals approached the onset of the campaign in a confident mood; but their confidence was as firmly based on an organisational improvement as it was on the fickle evidence of public— and published—opinion. Indeed their organisations were almost certainly in better shape, in 1905–6, than at any time for ten or twenty years. Soon after Carruthers Gould remarked, in 1895, that it would do the party good to 'wander in the wilderness until the soles of [its] feet [were] gritty', Ellis—then chief whip— prophesied that it would take 'ten good years . . . to do the job'[1] of reforming it; and he proved to be almost exactly right. The NLF played an invaluable part in holding the party together during the divisive days of the war, but the revival of the local associations did not begin to gather momentum until 1901–3 and was scarcely complete before 1905. In this sense, timing as well as tactics were on the Liberal side.

Herbert Gladstone, Ellis's successor, wisely involved the party's popular as well as official organisations from the start. In 1899 he appointed a (strictly consultative) committee comprising representatives of *each* organisational level (LCA, NLF, and local associations),

> to go through the whole of the constituencies of the country to consider the position of local organisations, to concert measures for finding suitable candidates and fixing them in constituencies to the best advantage, and generally to consider such other matters and to take such action as may be found desirable;[2]

36

and he set up a separate sub-committee to examine the special problems of the metropolis, where, despite a thriving Progressive policy on the LCC, the Liberal record had—for a decade—been abysmal. In the light of their conclusions he—equally wisely— came to the conclusion that the committee's suggested establishment of three new divisional associations would result only in an unnecessary multiplication of federations and officials and that— given the 'horrible burden of party finance'[3]—he should adopt a distinctly *selective* approach. He thus decided to concentrate the party's tenuous annual resources (of about £15,000) on London, on the Home Counties, and on those other constituencies 'where men of small means but real ability were willing to come forward as Liberal candidates'.[3]

On the basis of the London sub-Committee's proposals he formulated a definitive scheme—substantially implemented between 1902 and 1906—for the adoption of the new (post-1888) boroughs as registration areas, for the creation of a new London Liberal Federation (in place of the moribund London Liberal and Radical Union) to be responsible for registration as well as propaganda work, and for the employment wherever possible of professional agents to act as constituency secretaries as well as registration agents and to make good the lack of organised workers which he rightly diagnosed as the supreme weakness of the party in London. Working with J. R. Seager, who came over from the LL and RU to be secretary of the new London Federation, he divided the sixty-one London constituencies into three categories —twenty-eight that the party was likely to win, ten that it might just possibly win, and twenty-three that it was unlikely to win; and he concentrated both agents and resources on the first of them.

By dint of unremitting personal effort he also improved the financial position of the LCA so that—whilst remaining poor compared with the Unionists—he subtly altered the central/local balance of power and thus was able to adopt a policy of refusing financial help except to already adopted and approved candidates. Where possible he sought a pound for pound matching contribution; he operated a sliding scale equating the size of central

Table 8

LIBERAL REORGANISATION IN LONDON, 1902–6

Constituencies	Gladstone's *priorities			Agents to be appointed	
	A	B	C	Scheme 1†	Scheme 2‡
Poplar (2)	2	–	–	1	⎫
Hackney (3)	2	1	–	1	⎬ 1
Stepney (5)	5	–	–	2	1
Bethnal Green (2)	2	–	–	1	⎫
Shoreditch (2)	2	–	–	1	⎬ 1
Finsbury (2)	2	–	–	1	⎫
Islington (4)	3	1	–	1	⎬ 1
St Pancras (4)	3	1	–	1	1
Camberwell (3)	1	1	1	1	⎫
Lambeth (4)	1	1	2	1	⎬ 1
Bermondsey (4)	4	–	–	1	⎫
Southwark (2)	1	1	–	1	⎬ 1
Deptford (1)	–	1	–	1	⎫
Greenwich (1)	–	1	–	1	⎬ 1
Kensington & Paddington (4)	–	2	2	1	–
Other London seats	–	–	18	–	–
Total	28	10	23	16	8

* A—Likely to be won; B—possibles; C—unlikely to be won
† Estd cost—£4,975 pa. ‡ Estd cost—£3,300 pa.

contributions to the size of the electorate (e.g. £2,330 for Romford with an electorate of 29,316 and a mere £380 for Winchester with an electorate of 2,681); and in many cases he used the promise or refusal of funds as a way of ensuring as far as possible that the right candidates were placed in the right constituencies and that the electoral agreement with the LRC was honoured. C. W. B. Prescott was one of several candidates forced to resign (in his case from Kent St Augustines) because the LCA either could not or would not provide the funds he wanted and when, for example, the Medway Association asked for £1,500 plus £1,000 per annum, W. M. Crook, Secretary of the Home Counties Liberal Federation, was far from sympathetic: the proper way to cure them, he said, 'would be to run a Labour man there'.[4]

Many Liberal associations were indignant at the degree of central intervention that this policy inevitably involved; and at its 1905 Annual Conference the NLF saw fit to reaffirm the autonomy of the local men. But the shortage of funds was felt even more acutely in many constituency associations than it was at headquarters (in Leeds, for example, in 1905 the party obtained three-quarters of its income from a mere twenty people) and—Pease told the NLF Conference—although the Conservative government's unexpectedly long retention of office imposed a 'great strain'[5] on Liberal organisations up and down the country, it also served to strengthen Herbert Gladstone's hand. In May 1905, for example, a Hampshire Liberal wrote to ask with something like desperation for more money to continue employing a party worker, adding that he 'would lament a fiasco after so much labour for the sake of a somewhat larger grant called for simply by the delay . . .';[6] and many similar requests for support were received, in 1904 and 1905, at the LCA in Parliament Street and the Scottish Liberal Association in Edinburgh. Where candidates and associations wanted funds they were forced to accept the measure of central control involved.

Up to a point, therefore, the party's relative financial weakness was turned to good effect. With R. A. Hudson, Secretary of the NLF, and Hon Secretary of the LCA, relations between the official and representative wings of the party remained generally close and cordial, and they made it possible for optimum results to be achieved in the constituencies, with the available resources. Henry Norman, one of Herbert Gladstone's assistants at the LCA, reported at the time of the Brighton by-election in April 1905 that the Liberal agent had 'done marvels for the organisation' and a month or two later wrote enthusiastically of similar organisational improvements wrought at Wolverhampton and in the Black Country. About the same time, R. V. Wells reported to Crook from Fareham in Hampshire that the local party was doing 'splendidly in organising the constituency . . .', whilst— unsparing in his own travels round the country—Herbert Gladstone wrote of a 'wonderful Liberal revival' in Shropshire.[7]

In Scotland, a special general election committee was formed to represent and co-ordinate the activities of the SLA with those of the Liberal League, the Young Scots Society, and the Scottish Reform Club, and the SLA reported in 1904 that the party had appointed a special organiser in virtually every constituency.[8] The provision of speakers (and incidentally of cars) was organised with thoroughness; the organising committee for East Scotland reported in 1905 that—despite some shortage of money—its branches had been very successful with ordinance and lodger claims; and Hector MacPherson had good reason therefore to report, in the *Daily News* on 6 December 1905, that Liberal organisation there had never been so good.

In London, similarly, the seven or eight new agents appointed under Herbert Gladstone's reorganisation scheme effected something like a revolution in the organisation of Liberal registration and propaganda work, and in Croydon—which was in this sense typical of the *outer* London constituencies—the Liberals made substantial net gains (often running into hundreds) in claim and counter-claim before the Revising Barristers in 1904 and 1905. Acland-Hood wrote, significantly, to Balfour in September 1905 to say that the old register was 'not the advantage it used to be', as he happened to know that the Radical agents had been 'most active in tracing removals',[9] and the *Daily Express* commented on 19 January 1906 that by employing 'a far more intelligent, enterprising and altogether better type of agent', the Liberals had 'honeycombed the constituencies with centres of work'.

This improvement in constituency organisation was significantly supplemented by the rise of the large number of ancillary Free Trade organisations that were formed between 1903 and 1905. Whilst Campbell-Bannerman refused to compromise with the parliamentary Unionist Free Traders over education, Ireland, or other Liberal policies, he consistently took the view that 'everything should be done to make things easy for them'.[10] The Free Trade Union which was formed in 1903 (with McKenna and Hobhouse as directors, and Whiteley as treasurer) provided a particularly important non-party organisation, ancillary to the

Liberals, which made it possible for Unionists—who (as one of them said) were 'reluctant to face the odium of leaving the Unionist Club and go[ing] straight over to the Liberals'[11]— nevertheless to play their part in the Free Trade movement. Herbert Gladstone bemoaned the fact that (so he believed) the Tariff Reform League spent £5–£10 for every £1 spent by the FTU. Sidwell Shotton, of the North of England Free Trade League, likewise complained that Free Traders did not back their opinions with cash like Tariff Reformers. But this was, perhaps, because they did not have the need; for, thanks to a combination of pressure from Herbert Gladstone and from events, a countrywide network of Free Trade associations of various kinds was not slow to emerge. After the by-election at Barkston Ash in October 1905 Sandars ruefully complained that 'the Radicals practically had two armies . . . their usual political army [and] the Free Trade Union with its own special staff and workers . . . bringing none of its election expenses into account and operating as a voluntary organisation'.[12] At by-election after by-election the Free Trade associations provided the Liberal, and sometimes also Labour, candidates with the men (and women, e.g. through the Women's Free Trade Union) necessary for registration and canvassing.

The Liberal party's own ancillaries were also at a peak of efficiency and activity. The National League of Young Liberals— which from its inception in 1903 was an active propagandist on social as well as fiscal issues—already had three hundred branches by 1906. The Women's National Liberal Federation (concentrating on canvassing and persuasion) and the Women's Liberal Federation (rather more on registration) brought a combined team of about 100,000 into action in its interest. Heading a delegation from them, just before the election, Lady Aberdeen (the WLF's President) wrote to assure Campbell-Bannerman that he had 'no more devoted and loyal supporters' and that they would 'give a good account of themselves during the election'.[13] And they did just this.

All this organisational effort and improvement was underpinned by early action to place Liberal candidates, and to obviate incipient Liberal—and Liberal/Labour—constituency divisions.

In the first place Herbert Gladstone successfully arbitrated in all but two of those constituencies where the miners were standing (for their last election, as it turned out) as Lib/Labs within the Liberal party. In Yorkshire he persuaded the Hallam Liberal Association to nominate as their candidate Wadsworth, the President of the Yorkshire Miners Association, and thus held off the potentially disruptive and largely ILP-inspired pressure for more seats for Yorkshire miners; and in Durham he similarly secured the seat at Gateshead for a second candidate of the Durham Miners Association, despite some local constituency objection. In South Wales where—after the Glamorgan coal dispute—the South Wales Miners Federation had originally hoped to put up as many as twelve candidates, Herbert Gladstone eased a difficult situation by arbitrating at South Glamorgan in favour of Brace, the Federation's Vice-President, and by persuading the Liberal Cornelius Warmington to give way to Thomas Richards (General Secretary of the Miners' Federation of Great Britain) in South Monmouthshire. Chester-le-Street was something of a special case, since the Durham Miners Association nominated a member of the ILP (J. W. Taylor) who refused to make *any* concession to the Liberal Association and was consequently opposed by a Liberal as well as a Unionist candidate. Apart from this, outright Liberal opposition to a Lib/Lab candidate arose only at Gower, where Herbert Gladstone's effort to dissuade the Liberal Association from a last-minute nomination of T. J. Williams against J. Williams, the General Secretary of the Amalgamated Society of Colliery Workers, proved unavailing. In securing—thus—the continued placement of a number of working-class Lib/Labs in—largely—areas of traditional strong Liberal support, Herbert Gladstone and the Liberal associations made an important contribution to the preservation of a united front against the Unionists.

By similarly tactful handling, Herbert Gladstone also obviated any fears that the Liberal League might set itself up as a rival organisation within the party. As late as mid-1903 Campbell-Bannerman was complaining that the League was also rushing in where it was not wanted, but despite the inter-party rivalry epitomised by the 1905 Relugas compact of Liberal Leaguers against Campbell-Bannerman and by Rosebery's *démarche* at Bodmin, the League operated in 1905-6 within the structure of the party's organisations. In the City of London, for example, the local branch of the League co-operated closely with the London Liberal Federation in the choice of the two Liberal candidates for the City (Schuster and Ridgeway) and all forty-one League-supported candidates received the full support of their local associations. Nearly half of them, furthermore, received financial help from the Liberal Central Association. The result was that—in addition to Chester-le-Street and Gower—there were only two constituencies where for personal and particular reasons local Liberal parties went into the election in a divided state. The first of these was North Lambeth where Dhabadai Naorojii (President of the London Indian Association and one-time colleague of Hyndman's in a campaign to raise Indian living standards) persisted in standing despite his failure to have the support given him by the moribund London Liberal and Radical Union confirmed by the London Liberal Federation. And the second was South Hackney where the flamboyant Horatio Bottomley stood, curiously enough with the support of the Hackney Free Church Council, against the honest, narrow-minded, and aptly nicknamed Nonconformist 'call-from-God Riley'.

The Liberal leaders were thus able to counter the complaints of central interference, voiced at the 1905 conference of the National Liberal Federation, by pointing to the full and harmonious constituency coverage achieved which—as Table 9 shows—was instrumental in achieving a dramatic fall in the number of seats which their opponents could expect, without opposition, to win.

Such indeed was the change in the Liberal constituency organisation and confidence that, even in Ireland, they trebled their coverage from six in 1900 to twenty (including the Russellites) in 1906; effecting thus—with the Nationalists—a complete coverage of the country's 103 parliamentary seats. At the conference, Pease rightly paid tribute to Herbert Gladstone's '. . . quiet and unostentatious work [which] had enabled candidates to be selected in constituencies not previously fought'. It was no secret, he added, that 'arrangements had been made to fight every seat, with possibly one or two exceptions, in the favour of Free Trade Unionist members of Parliament . . .'[14]

Table 9

NUMBER OF UNOPPOSED RETURNS, UNIONIST AND LIBERAL, 1885–1906
(England, Scotland, and Wales)

Year	Total no of seats	Total no of unopposed returns	No of Unionist returns unopposed	No of Liberal returns unopposed (inc LRC)
1885	567	26	7	19
1886	567	153	114	39
1892	567	51	33	18
1895	567	135	123	12
1900	567	176	153	23
1906	567	37	5	32

The last—and significant—element in achieving this very full (and united) coverage of seats was the constituency agreement which Herbert Gladstone and Jesse Herbert negotiated with the LRC in England and Wales (though not Scotland, which was outside the LRC's jurisdiction) in the early part of 1903. Against the background of the party's then still serious financial difficulties, Jesse Herbert saw the LRC's £100,000 election fund as 'the most significant new fact in the situation',[15] which held out the possibility of fighting the Unionists on a common front, at—to some extent—the LRC's expense. But Herbert Gladstone believed that 'many Tory working men . . . would vote for a Labour but not for a Liberal candidate,[16] and he was as much concerned to maximise the solidarity of the vote against the Conservatives and the Unionists, particularly in areas where the Liberal party had traditionally been weak, as he was to relieve the burden on his party's funds. With a membership by 1905 of 158 trade unions (with 921,280 members), 73 trades councils, two local LRCs, the Fabian Society and the ILP, Snowden not unreasonably described the LRC as the 'largest and strongest political organisation in Britain . . .',[17] and Herbert Gladstone was determined to ensure that its power and influence were not used to prejudice Liberal chances at the election. At the same time, on the Labour side, Ramsay MacDonald knew well that, for all its paper independence, the LRC would make small headway against combined Liberal and Unionist opposition. He therefore undertook, in the negotiations, to do his best to obviate LRC opposition to the Liberals in the country at large, in return for a free run, so far as possible, in forty or fifty seats in double-member constituencies and in largely Unionist-dominated areas.

In the two to three years that followed, both party leaders did their utmost to make the agreement stick. Many (but not all) Liberal associations objected; but—as MacDonald himself testified—Herbert Gladstone did 'his best to coerce rich Liberals who wanted to place Liberals in the field in opposition' to LRC candidates;[18] and although he was not always successful the *Daily News* noted on 26 December 1905 that his handling of delicate situations was invariably adroit. Since the LRC was—in a sense—the creature of the independent and representative organisations of which it was composed, MacDonald's task was even more difficult. But by means of circulars, candidates, conferences, and personal influence, he strove to establish the authority of the National Executive Committee as at least a clearing house for candidates and sought—with considerable success—to check the uncontrolled proliferation of LRC candidates by placing financial responsibility for them firmly on to the affiliated organisations. Many of these (like the Liberal associations) were loud in their complaints that candidates were 'sent down from London'[19] and in 1904 at the annual conference of the LRC saw fit (like the NLF a year later) to reaffirm the autonomy of their local branches. Between 1903 and 1906 there was, however, 'a gradual but nevertheless unmistakable tendency to concentrate power in the hands of the LRC leadership' and there were some signs at least of union recognition of LRC sovereignty over the selection—and by implication the placement—of candidates.[20] The result—broadly speaking—was that, although subject to a fairly continual element of change, the two parties succeeded in ensuring that the—still secret—concordat was observed.

In Lancashire where Unionists had so long been ascendant that, notwithstanding strong support for Free Trade, the outlook for the Liberals in 1903 was not so promising as it was elsewhere, local agreement was negotiated in Manchester, whereby the LRC nominated candidates for the North Eastern and South Western Divisions and left the Liberals with a straight fight in the remaining four; and when the Bradford and Salford ILP proposed nominating Bramley as a Labour candidate against Balfour (Unionist) *and* Horridge (Liberal) in the Eastern Division, they were sternly reminded that they were 'in honour-bound to work with the local LRC'.[21] In Liverpool—*per contram*—the local Liberal Association happily accepted, and supported, Sexton's late nomination for the LRC, in a division (West Toxteth), which might otherwise have been left unopposed, and there was —finally—only one Lancashire constituency (Eccles) out of the thirteen where LRC candidates were put forward, where a Liberal also stood. Like Chester-le-Street, however, this was something of a special case, since although in Ben Tillett the LRC had a nationally known figure as its candidate, Tillett was away in the West Indies not only for some months before the election but also for most of the actual election period itself; and the local Liberal Association not surprisingly wished to be able to fight the Unionist in a somewhat more active and evident way. Subject to this exception, there was only one Liberal seat (Grimsby) outside London and more traditional Liberal areas, where neither local associations nor leaders were able to prevent the onset of a three-cornered (Liberal, LRC, and Unionist) fight.

Of the more traditional Liberal, or Lib/Lab areas, the cities of the West Riding of Yorkshire—which between 1885 and 1900 had averaged a 75 per cent return of Liberal candidates—constituted the most difficult case. The Liberal associations were strong. They had in many cases made gestures towards the acceptance of working-class Lib/Lab candidates, and that seemed to them to be enough. By the end of 1903 they had already selected the great majority of their candidates. However, as they were opposed by several affiliated branches of the LRC, in which the ILP was the preponderating influence, the result was a degree of failure on both sides. Herbert Gladstone's efforts to reach an understanding over the three Bradford seats came to grief on the refusal of the local Liberal Association in the Western Division to give way to Jowett for the LRC, which was in turn influenced by the independent candidature of the Social Democrat, Hartley, in the Central Division; and he was similarly unsuccessful in his efforts to persuade Runciman to stand down for Turner at Dewsbury.

In Sheffield an awkward situation was largely redeemed (for the Liberals) by the self-cancelling rivalry of the ILP and the Lib/Labs, but in Herbert Gladstone's own city of Leeds, a carefully worked out compromise (whereby the LRC's O'Grady was given a clear run in the Eastern Division and the Liberal candidates in the Southern and Western Divisions) nearly came to grief when the Society of Locomotive Engineers decided—late in 1905—to nominate Fox, as LRC candidate, in the Southern Division. Only MacDonald's personal intervention saved Herbert Gladstone from Labour opposition in his own Western Division; whilst at nearby Huddersfield Asquith described T. R. Williams's candidature for Labour as nothing less than 'an act of aggression'.[22] However, neither in Yorkshire nor in the other traditionally Liberal areas where LRC candidates stood—mainly Durham and Wales—was the aggression all on one side, and Henry Radcliffe— nominated for Merthyr long after Keir Hardie—flatly refused to stand down despite Herbert Gladstone's persistent entreaties that he should do so. In much the same way a second Liberal was nominated against the LRC's Wilkie at Dundee—which stood outside the formal agreement—despite the fact that the first Liberal to be nominated in this double-member constituency took the line that his views were reasonable, moderate and acceptable.

It was perhaps in London, however, that the difficulties in negotiating and maintaining the agreement were most acute. This was due primarily to the striking contrast between the capital's national and local political affiliations. Although returning an average of only one Liberal to Parliament for every three or four Unionists between 1885 and 1900, Londoners voted the (joint Liberal and Labour) Progressives into *municipal* power at every election following the establishment of the LCC in 1888. And—perhaps because of the increasing intrusion of their municipal issues into the national arena—found it difficult to decide which of the two, to some extent opposing, parliamentary parties might best defend them there. Different local associations took different views, at different times, in different places. Walthamstow, for example, passed easily enough from a Liberal-supported Labour to a Labour-supported Liberal candidate (John Simon) but in Deptford the Labour, and in Croydon the Liberal, party did not find it possible to behave quite so flexibly.

In Deptford, the Liberals were the first to put a candidate in the field and they complained bitterly, at the 1904 annual conference of the NLF, about the LRC's action in nominating Bowerman against him and—as they put it—in 'supporting extreme Socialists against duly chosen Liberal candidates'.[23] Later when, despite the inauspicious beginning, all the more active Liberal forces, including the Nonconformist churches, rallied round the Labour candidate, a hard core of Liberals continued—despite his evident loss of support—to support the Liberal, against the Labour, candidate. In Croydon, where there was a not dissimilar division of opinion within the Liberal association, many Liberals were attracted to the idea of a Liberal/LRC co-operation along lines suggested by some of the by-elections, and wanted to select a candidate who, as they put it, 'knew the desires and experiences of the people by personal experience';[24] but they came into conflict with officials of their own association whose best idea in 1903 (predictably rejected by Labour) was to invite Labour representatives to a conference to consider joint action 'especially as regards the selection of a Liberal candidate for Parliament'.[25] Attitudes thereafter hardened and the secretary of the Croydon Labour Electoral Committee (CLEC) went out of his way to emphasise that 'in Croydon the . . . difference between Liberals and Labourism [was] essentially an economic one . . . and not by any means a matter of sentiment, as was to a certain extent the case at Battersea' (where John Burns was standing).[26] By the time the Liberal caucus had expressed its willingness, after all, to support a Labour candidate, provided only he was a man 'of the Will Crooks, John Burns, or Bell type',[27] the Newcastle Resolution had been passed and the CLEC decided to follow the precedent set at Woolwich and to run their own independent candidate. Not without regret among its members, the Liberal association then decided to nominate its own candidate, and relations between the two parties thereafter went from bad to worse.

The Liberal dilemma in such circumstances was neatly expressed at Hammersmith where a (non-LRC) Labour candidate was nominated *whilst* the local Liberal association was still bargaining with Herbert Gladstone for financial support for a Liberal candidate. One Radical declared that 'if Hammersmith on the whole [was] more like Deptford or Woolwich than Chelsea or Marylebone',[28] then they should clearly desist from nominating a candidate of their own and join with Labour in supporting the Labour candidate. This kind of sociological line was not always easy to draw, and was not always drawn in the same way by the two parties involved. But although the electoral agreement worked less well in London than in the other predominantly Conservative areas, Table 10 shows that it was, by and large, successful in serving its double purpose of obviating Liberal/LRC conflicts and ensuring that the Unionist candidates would be opposed, by LRC if not by Liberal candidates, in those areas where Conservatism was strong.

D

Table 10

THE CONSERVATISM OF THE AREAS WHERE LRC CANDIDATES STOOD

Area	No of seats	Conservative held in 1900	Degree of con-servatism (percentage)	No of LRC candidates	No of Liberal/ LRC contests
Birmingham and Wolverhampton	3	3	87	3	–
Lancashire etc	20	17	83	15	1
London and the south	8	7	74	7	4
The remaining Conservative areas	5	4	60	3	1
Durham etc	9	6	24	7	2
West Riding	10	6	22	8	4
Wales	3	1	13	2	1

Thanks to the combination of Herbert Gladstone's and Mac-Donald's good management, a certain amount of luck (apparent in, for example, the withdrawal of LRC candidates from Taunton, Swansea, and Whitehaven), and the existence of the double-member constituencies—which provided twenty-one out of forty-five LRC seats in England and Wales and eighteen out of thirty-three straight LRC/Unionist fights—the electoral agreement produced a final constituency arrangement which was almost certainly advantageous to both sides. Out of the forty-five English and Welsh seats where LRC candidates were standing, only six had been Liberal in 1900, and Labour had a clear run against the Unionists in three out of every four of them. Although last-minute appeals in the *Daily News* (26 December) and *Daily Chronicle* (1 January) for the settlement of the three-cornered situations by the withdrawal of Liberal as well as Labour candidates fell on deaf ears, the general result was very satisfactory, and contrasted greatly with the situation of the diverse collection of other independent or socialist Labour candidates. These included eight Social Democrats and two independent Socialists —'the only candidates who could really expect to convince the electors that they stood entirely apart from the Conservative-

Liberal struggle'[29]—five candidates of the Scottish Workers Representation Committee, and six 'others'. Taken as a group, they mostly (60 per cent) stood in Liberal-held seats.

Table 11

SUMMARY OF LIB/LAB, LRC, AND SOCIALIST CANDIDATES

Party affiliation				Sponsored by							Membership of	
	SDF	ILP	LRC	TU/ LRC	TU/ TC	TC	TU	Min-ers	Ind	Totals	SDF	ILP
Liberal							3	13	11	27		2
LRC		10	2	1	2	2	31	2		50	2	31
SWRC								5		5		5
Independents (incl J. W. Taylor)	9		2			2		1	1	15	9	3
Totals	9	10	4	1	2	4	34	21	12	97	11	41

UNIONIST

While the Liberals were busily refurbishing their organisations, selecting their candidates and, with the LRC, working to sustain the electoral agreement, the Unionists were struggling with the combined effects of apathy, inexperience, and division. In many areas of the country, where success had been won too easily for too long, the party's agents had, said one Conservative MP, become 'virtual freeholders of their posts interested in £sd rather than politics',[30] and after the Brighton by-election a Conservative supporter wrote to the *Daily Telegraph* (on 14 April 1905) to suggest that Sussex might have a better chance of becoming solid again 'if all the local agents were to vanish into space'. After Barkston Ash (October 1905) even Sandars wrote to Balfour in criticism of the 'solicitor-type of agent'[31] commonly employed, and the Vice-Chancellor of the Primrose League hardly exaggerated when—speaking at the League's December 1905 conference—he said that the whole Unionist organisation had become 'distinctly rather sleepy'. He added that there were a great many districts where the League itself had become 'inactive and required to be re-organised',[32] and it was perhaps symptomatic of the general Unionist weakness that as late as 2

January 1906 it was still appealing for volunteer workers to help
to canvass out-voters. With the exception, indeed, of a handful
of constituencies where—as Acland-Hood said—by-election
disaster had 'opened the eyes of the local organisers to the collapse
of their electioneering machine',[33] the state of local Conservative
organisation was at a lower ebb than it had been for many years.

The replacement of Middleton by Wells at the Conservative
Central Office, in 1903, led to an equally serious situation at the
centre. *The Times* remarked wistfully some years later (on 23
January 1911) that although he was 'successful in pulverising . . .
Middleton's organisation', Wells 'left no trace of his constructive
ability at the Central Office'. As a Conservative journalist,
Iwan-Muller, said, 'incapacity, jealousy, disloyalty, and want of
discipline' were conspicuous at Headquarters, and it had become
obvious that whilst the Central Office 'in the days of Wells did
a great deal of officious meddling and put many backs up . . . it
did no quiet inspection worth noting'.[34] Little was done, in
consequence, to remedy the revealed weaknesses of the local
Conservative associations, and the good personal relations were
removed—just when they were most needed—on which the close
co-operation not only of the CCO and NUCA but also of the Conservative and Liberal Unionist parties so largely depended.

Throughout 1903 and much of 1904, this lack of co-ordination
in the double-headed party was at least disguised. Balfour
succeeded in keeping NUCA unrest at bay and Chamberlain was
preoccupied with his fight to secure a base for his Tariff Reform
campaign in the organisation of the Liberal Unionist party. In
the twelve months following his Birmingham speech of 15 May
1903 he fought a tenacious and in the end successful campaign
against those who, like Devonshire, wished to keep the party
neutral on the fiscal issue so that it could remain committed and
effective in its original objective of maintaining the Union.
Expressing the early confidence of the Tariff Reformers, Powell
Williams—chief agent of the LUP until his death in February
1904—told Devonshire in October 1903 that he believed that
Chamberlain was 'going to carry all before him with the country';[35]

and that if the Liberal Unionist party did not recognise that fact, so much the worse for it. And Fitzroy calculated, and recorded in his diary, that by November 1903 Chamberlain had already captured two-thirds of the Liberal Unionist party's organisation and personnel. Devonshire made one last attempt, through a correspondence published in *The Times* in January 1904 to argue his case, but at meetings of the Liberal Unionist Council, which Chamberlain pushed through in February and May 1904, he finally had to admit defeat. *The Economist* commented on 4 June 1904 that, as an organisation for the defence of the Union, the Liberal Unionist party was 'broken and shattered' and suggested that in future it would (in words picked up by Lowell) be 'in effect ancillary to the Conservative party'. In actual fact it became a powerful and largely independent organ of Tariff Reform opinion and—as James said—its effective machine was thereafter 'unblushingly worked'[36] in that interest. Even Victor Cavendish, the Hon Secretary of the Liberal Unionist Council, complained to Sandars, late in 1905, that at one of the council's meetings he had found himself in 'a perfect hothouse of Protection',[37] and, so far from becoming ancillary to the Conservative party organisations, it became something of an *imperium in imperio*. Its publicity department became as much a rival as an ally of the Conservative Central Office, and at constituency level it often created as much confusion as confidence in the important works of registration and canvassing. As Iwan-Muller aptly observed a short time after the election:

> The dual control both overlapped and left gaps. In some cases it created an absurd overconfidence for the same voter was claimed by Liberal Unionists and by Tories and was counted *twice* in the reckoning of prospective strengths. Even in Manchester, under the unfailing eye of Maltby, examples of this occurred again and again, though the error was corrected then by that unsleeping guardian. And in this respect the LUs [*sic*] were to blame. Animated by a natural desire to magnify their own strength they *frequently* canvassed *Tories*, asked if they were 'Unionist' and on receiving an affirmative reply, put them down as Liberal Unionists. More than a dozen such cases were brought to my notice in

Manchester by employees in the service of the *Manchester Courier*. Cases have been known and I daresay they have not been rare where Tories and LU registration agents 'objected' to voters who were really 'Unionists' but had declined to tell the Tory or the LU canvasser, as the case might be. The joint system [thus] made canvassing sometimes redundant, sometimes inefficient, and in both cases dangerous . . .[38]

The mischief done to Conservative and Unionist organisation did not, however, end with apathy and overlap, for, thwarted in their efforts to convert Balfour to their point of view, the Tariff Reformers not only built up their own Tariff Reform League (250 branches and 40 women's association branches, plus the Imperial Tariff Commission in Birmingham) but increasingly mounted—as 1904 drifted into 1905—a general assault on local Conservative caucuses, on the NUCA, and even on the Conservative Central Office itself. Sir Gilbert Parker frankly told the second annual conference of the Tariff Reform League, in July 1905, that whilst 'they had got machinery which was working quietly and effectively', they 'wanted more machinery—the whole machinery of the Conservative Party' and 'it rested with them to get it';[39] and—neither disinterested nor alone—James warned Balfour later in the year that the efforts of the Tariff Reformers and Protectionists to capture Unionist organisations were on the increase.[40] As Acland-Hood told Sandars, Chamberlain himself tried in a variety of ways to break into the Central Office: 'he tried first of all to seduce the cook (me), then he tried it on the kitchen maid (Wells) and . . . [finally] with the lady of the house (AJB)'.[41] In the event, he failed on each of these occasions, but his effort to get a Tariff Reformer into the CCO were a cause of persistent—and mounting—anxiety to the official leadership. Some time after the special NUCA conference held in June 1905, when the tenor of most speeches was in favour of a bolder line of policy than Balfour's, Sandars told Balfour that the 'organisation trouble' was 'causing much disturbance' in their ranks, that—tired no doubt of fighting his unequal battle—Wells had 'practically put his resignation in

Alec's [i.e. Acland-Hood's] hands', and that there would be 'great difficulty in keeping that most undesirable topic for discussion out of the programme at the [NUCA] conference at New-castle . . .'[42] He was right. Wells did resign, and, in addition to its fiscal criticisms, the conference passed a strong resolution—reminiscent of the days of Randolph Churchill—that it had 'become desirable to strengthen the central management of the business of the Conservative party by the addition of a popular representative element in close touch with the constituencies . . .' Acland-Hood rather lamely promised to work for improvements, and Balfour was reduced to pleading the 'unprecedented difficulty' of the previous two-and-a-half years.[43]

These circumstances of division, dispute, and disagreement were widely reflected in many local Conservative party associations with the result that—whilst the Liberals were sorting out a mere handful of seats in which there were difficulties over Labour or Lib/Lab candidates—the Conservatives were involved in a widespread reshuffle of their candidates across the country. The nine sitting Unionists who crossed the floor between 1904 and 1906 either found new constituencies as Liberals (like Churchill—Oldham to North-West Manchester; Ivor Guest—Plymouth to Cardiff; and J. E. B. Seely—Isle of Wight to Liverpool Abercrombie) or stayed on to fight freshly selected Unionist opponents from the other side, no doubt taking much of their previous party support with them (e.g. Dickson-Poynder—North-West Wiltshire; Foster—University of London; Wilson—North Worcestershire; Leonard Courtney—West Edinburgh; Lionel Holland—Birmingham Edgbaston; and David Erskine—West Perthshire).

But many of those who remained within the Unionist party found it necessary to move to constituencies with fiscal views more congenial to them—like the Free Traders, Goschen and Lucas, who moved from the Home Counties to Lancashire, and the Tariff Reform candidates who were forced out at Hertford and Accrington. Yet more (ninety-seven in all) simply decided to retire, quietly but finally, from political life. These divisions between local leaders undoubtedly did the party a great deal of harm and Sandars reported to Balfour well into 1905 that there was 'a dearth of good candidates' since many were 'refusing to come forward until the position [was] more fully developed . . .'[44] As late as 5 January 1906 the *Evening Standard* reported—with some exaggeration, no doubt, but significantly nevertheless— that there was a formidable list of seats for which no Unionist candidates had yet been found. Although there was a late surge of Conservative candidatures, between September 1905, when Balfour decided for just this reason to hang on to office for a little longer, and the election in January, a high proportion—perhaps between a quarter and a third—of all Conservative and Unionist candidates had all too little time to even begin to combat the disadvantages of long tenure of office, unpopular measures and proposals, and party divisions.

Despite the game of political musical chairs, moreover, there were eleven constituencies in which—in the election—rival Unionist candidates stood opposed to each other, in an unprecedented manner, entirely or largely on the fiscal issue. Noting that in eight of these the Tariff Reform rather than Unionist Free Trade candidates had the official support of their local associations, Acland-Hood took the view that, in this respect at least, 'the free food kettle was . . . blacker than the Tariff Reform pot'.[45] But two of the eight—Elliott at Durham and C. H. Seely at Lincoln—were sitting members, two enjoyed official Liberal support—Richard Cavendish, who reported from North Lonsdale that he had had to promise to support the Liberal government, as the only organised support he got came from the Liberal Association,[46] and Elliott at Durham—and two refused to stand down for reasons that were as much personal as fiscal. At the University of Cambridge Sir John Gorst declined to give way to suspicions—aroused by his presence at two meetings in which secularist resolutions were passed—of unreliability on the education issue, and at King's Lynn, Gibson Bowles chose to combine his advocacy of Free Trade with attacks on Balfour of an unremitting and highly personal kind.

There were thus only three seats in which Unionist Free Traders deliberately interpolated themselves against more or less extreme, and officially nominated, Tariff Reformers—St Loe Strachey and W. R. Smith in the Scottish university seats of Edinburgh and St Andrews, and Glasgow and Aberdeen, and at North Paddington. In this constituency a group of Unionist Free Traders chose to question the procedures whereby a Tariff Reformer—George Strauss—came to be nominated in place of the sitting (but retiring) Unionist Free Trade member, Sir George Aird, and—shamelessly exploiting prejudice against Strauss's Jewish race and wealth—ran Sir Henry Burdett against him as an Independent Unionist and international Free Trade candidate. These three cases were matched on the Tariff Reform side by Tradeston in Glasgow, by South Islington where the League ran its own candidates against official, and more moderate, candidates enjoying the support of their local associations and of the Central Office, and by the much publicised Greenwich where, angered by Hugh Cecil's outspoken and personal criticisms of Chamberlain, Tariff Reformers went so far as to form a new association (the Greenwich Conservative and Unionist Association) and—with Chamberlain's specific approval—to nominate T. H. Benn as Tariff Reform candidate. More importantly, there were a number of other cases where Tariff Reformers made unsuccessful, but still divisive, attempts to oust sitting candidates, which all added to the uncertain situation with which so many constituency associations were faced.

In East Marylebone, for example, Chamberlain fully intended to put up a candidate against Robert Cecil and was defeated only by the refusal of certain leading local Tariff Reformers to support him. However, as late as December 1905 he expressed his *intention* of fighting Bob Cecil in Marylebone, and the publicity attending the case served to advertise Unionist divisions right to the end. At Norwood in South London the Tariff Reformers made a similar move against G. S. Bowles (Gibson Bowles's son) which collapsed only when Bowles appealed directly to Balfour; and in South Nottingham (which Acland-Hood described as a

similar case) the attacks of Tariff Reformers on Henry Bentinck
so angered Portland, one of Chamberlain's earliest supporters,
that he threatened to sever his connections with them. Wyndham,
by no means wholly unresponsive to Tariff Reform ideas,
reported from Dover that a branch of the League was being
formed against his express wish, and added that whilst he felt
confident that he could defeat them in his own constituency, he
feared that they could 'only wreck the Party . . . where [it was]
fighting a sitting Liberal with a young candidate . . .' He said
that he was convinced that such manoeuvres were 'being widely
practised',[47] and Sandars wrote ruefully to Balfour in October
1905 to warn that Chamberlain's activities could only be disastrous
to the moderate wing of the party; even in Austen Chamberlain's
East Worcestershire constituency, he added, there were 'mutter-
ings and grumblings . . . [about] having too much of the Tariff
Reform League'.[48] The general attack on the seats of the Unionist
Free Traders rumoured in the Liberal press in December 1905
never quite materialised; but the contribution of the League to
divided and delayed candidacies was certainly as great as—or
greater than—that of the Unionist Free Traders. The significant
factor, of course, was the deleterious interaction and effect which
the squabbles of the two groups of extremists had on the placement and preparation of party candidates of all shades of
opinion.

In addition to these constituencies in which Unionist candidates were actually, or nearly, divided over fiscal policy, there
were a further five seats where for other miscellaneous reasons
the local Unionists were divided on the eve of the election: South
Lambeth, where the local Conservative and Unionist Association
disavowed their first choice of candidate, F. W. Horner, following
bankruptcy proceedings against him, but failed to make him
stand down; Thanet, where a breakaway group decided to
nominate M'Cormick Goodhart against Marks, the official (and
Tariff Reform League) candidate, whose financial reputation
was, to say the least, unsavoury; Birkenhead, where—despite an
Orange Lodge appeal for his withdrawal—one of the more

curious candidates, Kensit, stood as a Protestant zealot; and—
in Ireland—South Belfast and Antrim, where T. H. Sloan and
Colonel Verschoyle stood for moderate Unionist policies against
Ulster extremists.

As well, therefore, as the lateness of many of their nominations,
the Unionists were handicapped by an unusually high number
of divisions within the party itself, whilst the Liberals were able
to advance towards the election campaign in the knowledge of
vastly improved constituency coverage, greater unity, and better
preparation.

Table 12

CANDIDATES AND CONSTITUENCY COVERAGE BY PARTIES

Party	No of candidates England, Scotland and Wales	Ireland	Total	No of party divisions	Seats covered total	As percentage of English, Scottish and Welsh seats
Liberal	529	10	539	4	535	92·6
LRC	49	1	50	—	50	8·8
Nationalist	1	86	87	3	84	na
Unionist	546	28	574	19	555	93·3
Others	23	—	23	1	22	4·0
Total	1,148	125	1,273	27	1,246	na

In observing the large number of candidates introduced by
the Liberal Central Association, Acland-Hood wrote—a little
scornfully—to Balfour in the autumn of 1905 that the Liberals
had 'manned the constituencies with a tribe of "carpet
baggers" ';[49] but, as Augustine Birrell told the NLF Conference in 1905, their 'excellent candidates' had 'in the great
majority of instances been a long time before their constituencies',
were well known and had 'held an unparallelled number of
meetings'.[50] If delay was costly to Herbert Gladstone, it did give
the new Liberal candidates time to make both themselves and
their views known in their constituencies, and in the circumstances—with the reaction against the Unionist continually
gaining momentum—this almost certainly worked to their advantage.

TYPES OF CANDIDATE

Whilst it is impossible to generalise about the *type* of candidate presented to the electorate by the various parties, there was some justification for Birrell's use of the word 'excellent' at the NLF conference. Although only the Labour and Socialist groups were predominantly working class (Stanton Coit, LRC, and H. M. Hyndman, Social Democrat, were the exceptions) and Keir Hardie never tired of saying—in the midst of much practical Liberal-Labour co-operation before and during the election— that the two older parties alike consisted of landlords, wealthy men, and lawyers, the Liberal candidates certainly presented a much more varied spectrum of classes, religions, occupations, and ages than did the Unionists.

Not surprisingly, there were few industrial interests that went unrepresented among the candidates of both major parties. Whilst, for example, the majority of brewers and distillers were Unionists (e.g. the Guinnesses, the Walkers, and the Longs) the Dewars and Whitbreads were Liberals. Whilst the founders of what was to become ICI were Liberals (Sir J. D. Brunner, Northwich, and Ludwig Mond, Chester), Colonel Pilkington, across the county border at Newton, making glass, was a militant Tariff Reformer. And whilst the chairman of Harland and Wolff was a Unionist (H. Wolff, North Belfast) his manager (A. M. Carlile, West Belfast) was a Liberal. Including over fifty KCs and over thirty solicitors, lawyers, similarly, were fairly evenly divided. However, the Conservative and Unionist parties had drifted into a very much more specific representation of finance and the land; whilst the Liberal party had at least begun the progression of the radical way of politics towards a broader base that included more teachers, writers, journalists, and other professional men.

The Unionists certainly had several distinguished academic supporters, but most of these were standing for university seats; for example, Sir William Anson, whom the Liberals decided not to oppose, at Oxford, on the grounds that as a distinguished

Table 13

THE OCCUPATIONAL BACKGROUND OF CANDIDATES[51]

(percentage, rounded)

	Unionists	Liberals	LRC	Nationalists
Landed interests	40	15	—	*
Farmers	*	*	—	40
Industry	30	30	—	5
Finance	55	35	—	*
Commerce	10	15	—	15
Transport and shipping	10	20	—	—
Working men	—	5	95	—
Lawyers	30	30	—	22
Services	25	5	—	*
Academics	5	10	5	—
Newspaper proprietors and journalists	5	15	—	22
Miscellaneous	15	15	—	—

* Indicates 1 per cent or less

university teacher and scholar he would be a good person to represent university interests. The Unionists also had among their candidates Sir Arthur Conan-Doyle (Hawick Burghs). But most of the politically active academics, like G. P. Gooch, the young historian (Bath) and Bryce (South Aberdeen), were standing in the Liberal interest, as were most of the serious writers like Hilaire Belloc (South Salford), Charles Masterman (West Ham North) and A. E. W. Mason (Coventry), and nearly all of the relatively few ex-government servants, including—at Exeter— the ex-Secretary to the Board of Education (Sir George Keke-wich). The Liberal candidates were also notable for the large number of well-known responsible journalists among them, including Percy Alden, ex-editor of the *Echo* (Tottenham), Llewellyn Williams, ex-editor of the *Star* (Carmarthen District); and Herbert Paul (Northampton), A. Grove (South Northamp-tonshire), H. Cox (Preston), R. C. Lehman (South Leicester-shire) and T. J. Macnamara (North Camberwell), who wrote for a miscellaneous collection of journals ranging from the *Daily News* to *Punch*. Interestingly, they also commanded the support of a sizeable handful of newspaper proprietors, including R. L. Harmsworth (Caithness-shire) and C. Harmsworth (Droitwich) who were connected with the Amalgamated Press, Sir George Newnes (Swansea) and Frank Newnes (Bassetlaw) who controlled the *Westminster Gazette* and *Titbits*, and G. W. Agnew (West Salford), the proprietor of *Punch*. The Liberal candidates also included among their number twenty-seven manual workers and two members of the ILP. Thus whilst among the Unionist candidates the land, industry, finance, and the army still predominated, Liberal candidates undoubtedly presented a broader spectrum—of industry, the professions, and—if marginally—the working-classes.

The Liberals were also far less predominantly 'Oxbridge Anglican' than their opponents. Whereas between 50 and 55 per cent of the candidates of both main parties had been to a university of one kind or another, nearly half of the Liberals—compared with less than a quarter of the Unionists—had attended provincial universities; one-third of the Liberal candidates (compared with a mere 10 per cent of Unionist candidates) had been to state secondary schools; and nearly 40 per cent of Liberal candidates (compared with 15 per cent of Unionists and 66 per cent of LRC candidates) belonged to one or other of the dissenting churches. Since—incidentally—the Liberal candidates also included well over half of the Catholics and Jews who stood (including perhaps the best-known Catholic candidate—Hilaire Belloc), Anglicans were very nearly in a minority among them. Yet Anglicans accounted *per contram* for nearly 90 per cent of their Unionist opponents. Finally, it may be mentioned, that the Liberal candidates were also somewhat younger than their Unionist rivals, with the majority of them (62 per cent) falling—like the LRC candidates—into the 30–50 age group. The majority of the Unionist (56 per cent) and Nationalist candidates (52 per cent) were, on the other hand, over 50 years old.

Whilst therefore the two older parties continued to have much in common in terms of their representation of industry, finance, and commerce, there were significant differences between them

in terms of educational and to some extent occupational background, and in terms of age; and these differences pointed (a) to
the greater catholicity of the Liberals, and (b) to some considerable areas of common interest between the Liberal party and the
LRC, which came across clearly enough in the programmes that
these two parties placed before the electorate.

Notes to Chapter 2 will be found on pages 215-17

3 PARTY PROGRAMMES

INTRODUCTORY

With the exception, only, of the SDF, LRC, and UIL (United Irish League) party policies were not presented to the electorate as formal, published party programmes. Pressure group manifestoes were legion, which the older parties saw as protestations, to be nailed like so many Lutheran theses on the portals of their eternal principles. But it would be difficult to find anything more definitive among Conservative or Liberal publications than the CCO's *The Record* and LPD's *Ten Years of Tory Government*. The memory of Newcastle had bitten deep, and, as Bryce told Campbell-Bannerman in November 1905, and as Balfour well knew, programmes could be 'embarrassing'.[1]

However, the Unionist and Liberal organisations more than made up for this by flooding the electorate with propaganda leaflets on all the major topics of the day. The *Morning Post* estimated, on 3 January 1906, that the Unionists were issuing leaflets at the rate of two-and-a-half million a day; in the campaign period alone the LPD issued about twenty-two million leaflets and three million booklets; and the *Daily Mirror* aptly commented on 22 December that 'days of bewilderment are in store for the conscientious elector, for political leaflets are simply raining upon the country'. Moreover, most of the thousand or so candidates (except some Irish Nationalists) issued their own personal manifesto or election address. These were not always very forthcoming. Henry Lucy, as Toby MP in *Punch* (on 27 December), advised candidates to remember that they

> are filed and may at later epochs be brought up to your discomfiture. Get in as many political topics as the current day affords.

64

Use capital letters in introducing them. Whilst appearing to be emphatically saying something be as little definite as possible in declaration of opinion. For this purpose a study of Mr. Balfour's speeches will be invaluable.

But they were fuller than has now become the case, and, with the party leaflets, presented a kind of programmatic choice to the electors that was clear enough.

LIBERAL

The Liberal programme was characterised by two main features —by unanimous agreement on the major fiscal issue of the day and by the selection of a wide spectrum of social, and other, supporting issues. David Davies (Montgomeryshire)—later described by Herbert Gladstone as one of the party's only two

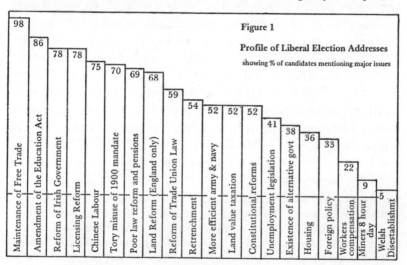

Figure 1

Profile of Liberal Election Addresses

showing % of candidates mentioning major issues

Whigs—was quite alone in supporting quasi-Tariff Reform measures for the rearrangement of the existing tariffs designed to improve British trade and strengthen the bonds of union between the colonies and the mother country; and slightly more than two-thirds of all candidates included proposals for social

E

reform, in their election addresses, that went beyond the traditional Nonconformist issues. Whatever the merits or limitations
of these policies, this combination of fiscal unity and breadth of
view undoubtedly gave the Liberal programme a significantly
greater strength and flexibility than that of their opponents.

Its major thrust was, undeniably, the maintenance of Free Trade
policies and the argument—in 40 per cent of leaflets and 98 per
cent of election addresses—that Chamberlain's proposals for
imperial preferences would impoverish and divide. Despite his
close shadowing of Chamberlain between 1903 and 1905, Asquith
chose to dissect Balfour's more modest policies, in his election
address; but Augustine Birrell more typically advised his North
Bristol electors that they need not try to 'distinguish between
Mr. Chamberlain's well advertised policy or Mr. Balfour's half
hearted proposals', because if the new ministry were beaten,
protection would follow 'as the Night on Day'. Churchill said
in North-West Manchester that whatever were 'the precise
relations, personal or fiscal between Mr. Balfour and Mr.
Chamberlain', it was certain that the victory of one would be the
victory of the other; that the victory of either would be the victory
of both; and that the victory of both involved 'in one form or
another, upon one pretext or another the introduction of a retaliatory, preferential, or protective tariff'. And, in an election address
which Margot Asquith laconically described as 'good but not as
good as Robespierre's',[2] Campbell-Bannerman himself emphasised the same point.

> Let me only add [he said, after a short, summary criticism of
> Chamberlain and the Unionist record], in case I am told it is
> unfair to identify the late Prime Minister . . . with the extreme
> proposals of his leading colleagues, that I understand Mr. Balfour
> to be agreed in principle with Mr. Chamberlain and also that
> the Unionist Party is committed to the programme of tariffs and
> preferences put forward by Mr. Chamberlain. This being so I
> conceive that the minor fiscal policy indicated by Mr. Balfour
> occupies, in the estimation at any rate of the majority of our
> opponents, little more than a nominal place in the contest . . .

The gist of Campbell-Bannerman's criticisms, and of the

Liberals in general, was that Chamberlain's policy was an un-
realistic attempt to turn back the clock to a narrow and injurious
protective system, which might help a few specialist producers
but would certainly hit the consumers and damage the economy
as a whole. Liberal leaflets were packed with figures of the trade
revival and figures comparing the volume—*per capita* and overall
—of British and foreign trade; and Liberal election addresses,
almost without exception, described cheap food and cheap raw
materials as the very foundation of British manufacturing supremacy. They argued that tariff would beget tariff, and retaliation
an endless chain reaction, and many candidates warned of the
damage that tariffs would do to the ship-building, textile,
chemical, heavy engineering, and other import-processing industries.

However, their central appeal was undoubtedly to the consumer
interest in cheap food—to the cabmen and domestics in Finsbury,
the commuters in Croydon, the railway workers in St Pancras
and Derby, the farm labourers in the rural areas, and to all those
who, whether working in productive industry or in services like
transport, made up the lower two-thirds or three-quarters of the
electorate. 'You know how difficult it is to provide for your
families', said one Liberal leaflet, significantly directed at their
women-folk.

> If [Mr. Chamberlain] succeeds, you will find it more difficult to
> pay for the food for your families and the clothes that they wear
> . . . Think what it will mean when all these things will cost you
> more—Bread, Ham, Tea, Cheese, Butter, Eggs, Furniture, Oil,
> Candles, Books and Clothes . . . If you want to stave off HARD
> TIMES, have nothing to do with Mr. Chamberlain or Protection
> . . . but urge your husbands and sons to vote for Liberals and Free
> Traders.[3]

Or as half a million copies of another leaflet more tersely said, 'If
you want your loaf, you must shut up Joe.'[4] In nearly three-
quarters of Liberal election addresses, the candidates added a
warning against Unionist calculations, as either hypocritical or
irrelevant, setting off reductions in those war taxes, which only

their own folly had made necessary, against the new taxes and higher prices that Tariff Reform would bring.

But while saying this, the Liberals were careful, in this election, to avoid striking anti-imperial attitudes. To some extent, no doubt, they were trimming their sails to the winds, but to a much greater extent they were expressing a profoundly different philosophy of empire, and they did so in terms which besides being positive and definite, have a recognisable and even modern ring about them. Simply stated, the Liberals believed that the *commercial* federation of the empire was impossible. 'Our self-governing colonies have', submitted Cawley (Prestwick), ' . . . informed us that they always intend to place such a duty on articles coming from the United Kingdom as will amply protect their own manufacturers'; and—thus—so far from creating common interest, he and others argued that Tariff Reform could only be divisive.

> What we are asked to approve [said Lionel Holland (Edgbaston)] is not Free Trade within the Empire—a proposal more worthy of serious consideration—but a plan of tariff bargaining which even includes the imposition of duties against those of our Colonies who fail to give us a preference, and offers endless occasion for friction and misunderstanding.

Liberals stressed that they were not hostile to empire as such, but only to Chamberlain's idea of its evolution, and they envisaged both its future and its strength as a commonwealth of free—and it was to be hoped Free Trade—nations, enjoying in peace a common sovereignty and the common protection of the British navy. If Cobden had in his day expressed anti-imperial views, so too, the LPD was fond of pointing out, had Disraeli and Salisbury in theirs.[5]

The Liberals sought, furthermore, to turn the Conservative flank by enlisting tradition, history and even patriotism in the service of Free Trade. At Northampton J. G. Shipman and Herbert Paul described it in their joint address as 'an English policy framed by Englishmen for England, in British interests alone, especially the interests of the poor', and, along with many others, they saw it as a safeguard of what was traditionally the United Kingdom's greatest contributions to the empire, its economic strength, its capital, and its power. Others stressed the social and economic importance of Free Trade to the United Kingdom as the heart of the empire. So far from being the patriotic policy, they said, Tariff Reform was but one more example, on the grand scale, of Unionist willingness to favour minority interests at the expense of both the United Kingdom and the empire, which they argued was very evident in the Education and Licensing Acts, in the war peculation revealed in the Butler Report, in the attack on the trade unions, in the 1902 sugar convention (providing bounties for West Indian producers), and above all in the introduction of the Chinese into South Africa after the war.

One widely distributed leaflet (also used as a poster) showed a line of Chinese being shepherded along by a fat plutocrat, whilst Tommy Atkins, from the shades, asked a sleeping John Bull 'is THIS what we fought for?' and C. G. Greenwood (Peterborough) was one of many to condemn the degradation of the empire 'in the interests of an insatiable gang of cosmopolitan financiers'. The ex-government, said John Burns (Battersea), in one of the most colourful, and quoted, of election addresses, had made itself 'a mere register for the desires of sordid, pushful, colonial capitalists', and—referring to Tariff Reform—he appealed to the electorate not to be 'misled be a fiscal pervert who has abandoned all he wisely knew, to advocate that which he . . . does not understand, in the interests of those who already possess too much, to the detriment of those who have too little'.

It was against this background that the Liberals rejected a Unionist tendency to claim a unique sense of responsibility in foreign affairs as, in the words of J. F. L. Brunner (Leigh), 'a piece of vulgar and impudent affectation'. The prolongation, and price, of the South African war gave them a rare chance to paint their belief in arbitration and rationality in international affairs on the canvas of alleged Unionist irresponsibility and war, whilst—at the same time—pledging continuation of existing foreign policy commitments and agreements. Adopting the slogan of 'Defence not Defiance', they claimed that a more prudent conduct of foreign affairs and a more efficient organisation of the country's defences would keep Britain strong, keep the peace, *and* make retrenchment possible, and they sought to ridicule the doubts cast on their own reliability by attacking their opponents' record. Campbell-Bannerman wrote of four years of 'costly and confused' War Office 'experiments', and Haldane (who made a point of maintaining that his views on defence and foreign policy were equally consistent with Campbell-Bannerman's *and* with Rosebery's) said in his election address that 'wavering minds' and 'divided counsels' had produced their expected effects. Grey was similarly critical. Foreign affairs, he said, 'are not at present a matter of controversy'; but it would be necessary to halt the 'spendthrift increase in expenditure and to secure that the Public Service shall receive full value for the money which has to be spent in the future'. Thus was the circle squared, of imperial responsibility and retrenchment.

It was also against this background that many Liberals, especially these younger Liberals who, as Trevelyan told Campbell-Bannerman in 1903, were 'not content to be passive Free Traders', proclaimed the need for a new attack on social problems at home. Durham Stokes (Stepney) said that, as 'an imperial race', their 'first and finest imperial effort' must be to maintain and raise the standard of living and housing, to charge themselves 'with the proper education and well-being of the children, and . . . by a system of Old Age Pensions to wipe away the lasting reproach to a great country, that one third of its aged citizens [were] paupers'.[6] Runciman, Burns's Parliamentary Private Secretary, said that he and Burns had 'already been at work in the Department' and hoped 'through its instrumentality and within the limits of its powers to promote many urgent social reforms'. Charles Trevelyan expressed confidence that 'a new era of financial and social reform' was about to begin, and four out of every ten candidates said that the very composition of the cabinet (and in particular its inclusion of Campbell-Bannerman and

Burns) betokened Liberal determination in this field. And although the need to repeal or amend the Education and Licensing Acts of 1902 and 1904 came first in many Liberal minds, pledges made to other social reforms amounted to a recognisable and extensive commitment. The combined pressures of younger men and of political circumstances had had their effect.

In the first place, nearly two out of every three candidates (59 per cent) drew attention to the need to bring legislation for old-age pensions. Few candidates were as specific as Leo Money who suggested in his book, *Riches and Poverty*, a pension of 5s od per week, *claimable* by all over 65 with less than £1 a week income, or with property rated at less than £250, and estimated to cost £15 million per annum; but a significant minority pledged themselves in clear terms. Scott Robertson (Bradford Central) declared that he was 'in favour of Old-Age Pensions payable out of national funds'; T. J. Lennard (South Bristol) wrote that he 'need not reiterate' his views on this question, which was 'a national duty'; and even the cautious Maddison (Burnley) said that whilst 'the wasteful expenditure of the Tories' had made it more difficult to deal with the question, it should be dealt with 'during the life of the next Parliament'. Chamberlain's failure to fulfil his many promises of pensions was continually recalled, and since, in both LPD leaflets and candidates' addresses, this was associated with opposition to his new promises of benefits from Tariff Reform, so—subtly—a linkage between Free Trade and social reform was inferred.

With varying degrees of commitment, nearly two-thirds of the Liberals also pledged themselves to reform of the law relating to trade unions. Most Lib/Labs, and Liberals fighting LRC or socialist candidates (e.g. Enoch Edwards—Mid Wales, Stuart—Sunderland, Anderson—North Ayrshire) categorically affirmed the need to put right what Isaac Mitchell (Labour) called 'the injustice resulting from the judge-made Trade Union Law', by returning to the *status quo ante*, including legal immunity for trade union funds. For the majority, Percy Alden (Tottenham) more typically declared that the Taff Vale decision would have to be reversed, but by the introduction of 'such a Bill as that introduced by Mr. Shackleton'—which (unlike Whittaker's 1905 bill) would have left the unions still responsible under law for certain misdemeanours and for breach of contract. However, these differences were hardly significant when, as more than one leaflet said, the Liberal party as a whole was 'pledged to legislation to secure in the interests of the community as a whole that working men . . . [should] have restored to them rights of combination, without which they were powerless'.[7] Given Unionist opposition to either degree of reform, the overwhelming Liberal commitment came over clearly enough.

Liberal policy on the vital issue of unemployment showed a similar spectrum of opinion; but it was, broadly, based on two agreed propositions—that protection was a quack remedy, and that—as Masterman (West Ham North) said—since Free Trade maximised wealth but did not look after its distribution, what was really needed was wise legislation which would 'correct the errors of . . . distribution, spread the national wealth more evenly, and give every man and woman—and every child—a chance'. Taking their cue from Henry George, many Liberals argued that the remedy for maldistribution lay primarily in the land-owning system: and that the people did not reap the full advantages of Free Trade only because land monopoly withdrew from the producers so large a share of the wealth created. They therefore proposed to take back that part of the share through the taxation of land values. 'I am satisfied', said Joseph Dobbin in his election address in the Ayr Burghs, 'that the Taxation of Land Values is the best alternative to a policy of restriction of trade, not only as a means of diminishing non-employment, but as a source of revenue calculated to relieve the onerous burden of taxation at present pressing on the industrial community'. Some Liberals, however, went further and demanded the taxation of mineral as well as landed wealth, and a few like Masterman (West Ham North) and James Branch (Enfield) openly accepted the case for the municipalisation or nationalisation of monopolies. 'All monopolies should be municipalised or nationalised', Branch wrote, 'the object being the development of industry under fair conditions of Labour, and the convenience of the public, while the profits are applied in reduction of rates.'

It was, with some additions, this same group which—like Lionel Holland (Birmingham Edgbaston)—unequivocally stressed the duty of the state to enable 'the industrious man' at all times 'to face the world from a secure and independent footing', and accepted the desirability of state-sponsored schemes of road-building, afforestation, and farm colonies. Masterman said he was 'in favour of National Schemes for dealing with the unemployed', and—stressing the need for schemes of land development, and state scholarships 'for all who fit themselves'— Richardson (Aston Manor) said that 'the Workshops, Universities, Farms and Factories thus set up would form a safe and certain step towards the State ownership and organisation of the means of Production by which alone the *Problem of the Unemployed . . .* [could] be solved'. The more cautious—like Maddison—said merely that 'the organisation of works of public utility might mitigate the evil of unemployment' but warned that anything in the nature of permanent works would but aggravate it and suggested instead a combination of retrenchment, licensing reform, improved technical education, and above all of agrarian reforms to stimulate the resettlement and recultivation of the land (e.g. greater security for tenants, farm rent courts, value for improvements, state credits, and powers of compulsory purchase).

Other social reforms—housing, workers' compensation, the eight hour day, and so on—had a lower priority; but over half the Liberal candidates pledged substantial constitutional reforms designed to place more effective political power in the hands of the poorer strata of society. Thirty-three per cent pledged the ending of disqualification for receipt of poor relief, and the introduction of shorter qualifying periods for voters, 29 per cent the abolition of plural voting, and lesser numbers the payment of MPs, procedural reforms, and reform of the Lords. And John Burns created a sensation, which penetrated even the Palace, by promising 'the abolition of . . . *all* hereditary authorities'; but, as he later explained, he was referring only to the House of Lords.

In the light of these commitments to Free Trade and to social and constitutional reform, the Liberals did their utmost to shelve the issue which had above all prevented effective reform in the last Liberal government—Home Rule. Edmund Lamb (Leominster) declared that 'no measure of Home Rule . . . [could] be brought forward to the next Parliament', which should devote itself to 'large measures of social reform', and—having said that he would oppose a Home Rule bill if brought in—C. H. Corbett (East Grinstead) concluded that Ireland would have to wait, because it was 'time for England and Scotland to have their turn'. For some, indeed, the situation presented a golden opportunity openly to declare their long-felt hostility to their party's whole Gladstonian inheritance on Ireland. Charles Henry (Wellington) said categorically that 'Mr. Gladstone's Bills of 1886 and 1893 have been rendered obsolete by the march of events in Ireland', and Russell Rea (Gloucester) wrote off Gladstone's Home Rule as 'a matter of past history and not of present policy'. Agar-Robartes (South-East Cornwall) and Sir Edward Strachey (South Somerset) both said that they were 'opposed to an independent Parliament for Ireland, or *anything that* . . . [*might*] *lead up to it*', and William Thompson (Wick) maintained, more strongly still, that the idea of a separate and independent Parliament for Ireland had been 'finally and definitely abandoned'. Including ex-Unionists, like Poynder, Schuster, and Churchill, and the Russellites in Ireland, there were fifty or more Liberal candidates (or 10 per cent) who were openly and clearly opposed to Home Rule, in the accepted sense.

The great majority of the party, however, combined an honest commitment to Home Rule with an equally sincere wish to place their electoral priorities elsewhere. They therefore confined their pledges to some form of administrative devolution, arguing either like Bryn Roberts (Eifion) that 'the surest and speediest method' of obtaining Home Rule was 'to go step by step', or, notably in

Scottish and Welsh constituencies, that there should be a general scheme of administrative devolution in the United Kingdom. Halley Stewart (Greenock) declared:

> The House of Commons has become feeble for general legislation owing to the growing claims on it for purely local business, due to an ever-increasing population. If legislation is to be effective, Parliament must be relieved of all work that can be better discharged in the provinces. Scotland rightly demands that it should have the control and management of purely Scottish affairs. To Ireland equally should be given local control in the spirit which animated Tory legislation . . .

Some took refuge in rather vague formulas such as that presented to his electors by Burns, who said that he favoured 'such legislative independence' as would enable Ireland to 'revive her industries, maintain her population, and stimulate her social and agrarian prosperity in accordance with Irish ideas'. But Herbert Gladstone spoke for most in suggesting that if any measure passed by a Liberal government was held to be 'a step towards Home Rule' he was entitled to ask the electorate to consider it 'solely from the point of view of justice and sound policy', and at the subsequent election it would be the electorate's duty to decide whether or not 'any further step' was required.

There were, thus, many variations of view, but the major theme was common to most, and strong throughout—namely that, whilst some form of Home Rule remained a Liberal objective, legislative independence for Ireland was not part of Liberal policy in the election; that any Unionist endeavours to show that it was were only an obfuscation; and that the Liberals simply sought to continue the policies started—but abandoned—by Balfour and Wyndham. Those candidates, who, like Richard Cherry (Liverpool Exchange), claimed that the Prime Minister *had* declared for Home Rule of the old kind, and that there was no reason why the Liberal belief in self government should not be given effect in Ireland as elsewhere, amounted to no more than one in fifteen candidates, and most of them were standing in those constituencies in England where the Irish vote was strong enough

to exert a very special influence. The Liberal programme for
Ireland was thus a careful balancing act between personal belief
and political expedience; an Achilles heel, in short, which the
Unionists were not slow to attack.

In brief summary, the Liberal *programme* consisted of the
maintenance of Free Trade and of sound finance; of peace
through strength and understanding; of land reform, old age
pensions and other social reforms; and of a highly qualified
approach to Irish government. The Liberal *appeal* rested on a
combination of these items, and of condemnation of the Unionist
record when dealing with them.

'Don't be hanky-panky'd a third time', read a pithy and typical
LPD leaflet:[8]

(1895)
In 1895 the Tories promised *Old Age Pensions* and got a large
majority in the House of Commons
WHERE ARE THOSE OLD AGE PENSIONS?

(1900)
In 1900 the Tories went to the Country on the Khaki issue. They
again got a large majority . . . (But) did you know or think in 1900
that you were voting for the *Education and Licensing Acts*, for
snubbing the Volunteers and for *Chinese Labour in South Africa*?

(1905)
A third time the Tories want your *vote*—this time on the cry of
"*No Home Rule*"
DON'T LET THEM GULL YOU AGAIN

This cry is intended to take your attention off the issue of *Free
Trade and Protection*, and off the Black Record of *Ten Years of
Toryism*.

But haven't you had enough of
MR BALFOUR'S GOVERNMENT
AND
MR CHAMBERLAIN'S PROMISES?

With typical hubris and hyperbole, Churchill well summarised both the programme and appeal—and the confidence with which they were put forward. He wrote in his election address:

> A majority elected under the spell of patriotic emotion, upon a national issue, in the stress of an anxious war has been perverted to crude and paltry purposes of party. It has spent public money with unexampled profusion. It has hurried to place retrograde legislation upon the Statute Book. It has consented to every abrogation or infringement of liberty, constitutional or personal, at home or abroad, that was suggested to it. Under its hand the procedure of the House of Commons has been mutilated, and respect for Parliamentary institutions has been notably and notoriously diminished. Jealous of nothing save the leisure of its members it has bartered Parliamentary rights for longer holidays and easier hours of session, and shirked urgent public business at the promptings of personal indolence. Viewy, intolerant, dilettante, lax, the tool of Whigs and wire-pullers, the lackey of private interests, the Parliament of 1900 has grudged the freedom of speech, conspired against the freedom of trade, parodied the freedom and dignity of labour. Lastly, by accepting every humiliation and stooping to every artificial manoeuvre that its master might require, it has enabled a Minister to maintain in office himself and a small clique of favourites—mostly incompetent—and to rule in default of national esteem and in defiance of popular authority for upwards of two whole years.

Churchill concluded:

> The hour is propitious for a Liberal Administration . . . Not since 1868 has such a chance occurred. Many questions formerly disputed are settled. A lively sympathy with the Colonial Empire, a vigilant care for our vast Indian dependency, the maintenance of an undisputed and indisputable Naval Supremacy, loyalty to the Crown and to the Government are not to be claimed as the perquisites of faction. They belong to all the people. In the defence of Free Trade, in the Temperance movement and many grave social questions connected with large cities, Liberal principles have gained and are gaining the support of moderate and reasonable men beyond the limits of our regular political organisation. After more than thirty years as I read history the Liberal Party advances once more as the true representative of Great Britain. Our cause is more than a party cause. Our victory will not be merely a party victory, it will be a national victory . . .

LRC AND INDEPENDENT SOCIALIST

If Churchill and the Liberals seemed concerned, primarily, to secure the return of Liberalism from the wings of time, LRC and other Labour candidates were concerned to assert the right of the working man—for the first time, in effect—to occupy if not the centre, then at least a larger part, of the political stage.

In ideological terms the LRC's manifesto was as reformist as most of the candidates' election addresses, and followed Liberal policies almost as closely, as did the TUC's. It laid slums and high rates at the door of spiralling and untaxed land values. It associated both the war and introduction into South Africa of Chinese labourers with the enrichment of a privileged minority. It described the Unemployment Act as worthless and protection as a red herring and stigmatised protection as a policy—irrelevant to poverty and unemployment—that could only serve to hinder the workers 'from dealing with the land, housing, old age and other social problems'. It reflected only marginally the 1905 conference resolution passed—without discussion—in favour of 'the overthrow of the present competitive system of capitalism, and the institution of a system of public ownership for the means of production distribution and exchange,[9] and was scarcely revolutionary either in tone or in detail. About two-thirds of the election addresses of LRC candidates contained some reference towards some aspect of socialisation, but the corporate vision expressed in them was not socialism but social justice, and much of the language used was strangely (or perhaps not so strangely) reminiscent of Liberalism. Keir Hardie (Merthyr), for instance, wrote of the creation of 'an era of freedom, fraternity . . . equality . . . [and] national righteousness', and T. F. Richards (Wolverhampton West) of 'a sober people when the days of Privilege and Monopoly have passed'. Indeed, as Figures 2 and 3 show, the LRC addresses had more to say about Taff Vale and Chinese labour, education and licensing reform, and even Free Trade and Home Rule, than about socialism; and the only candidates to subscribe to socialism

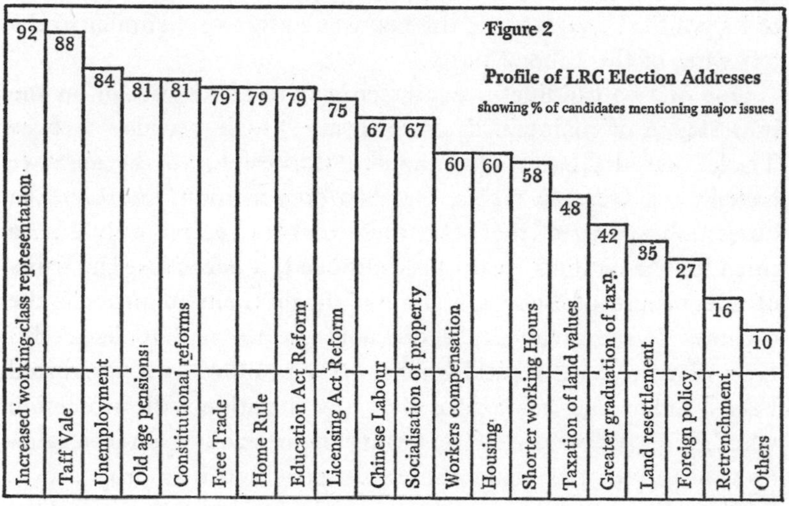

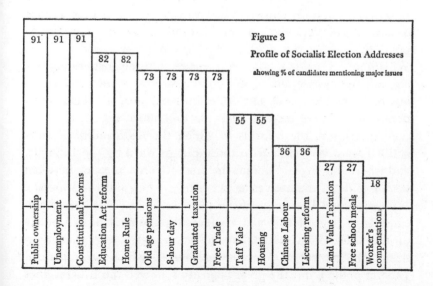

Figure 2

Profile of LRC Election Addresses

showing % of candidates mentioning major issues

92 — Increased working-class representation
88 — Taff Vale
84 — Unemployment
81 — Old age pensions
81 — Constitutional reforms
79 — Free Trade
79 — Home Rule
79 — Education Act Reform
75 — Licensing Act Reform
67 — Chinese Labour
67 — Socialisation of property
60 — Workers compensation
60 — Housing
58 — Shorter working Hours
48 — Taxation of land values
42 — Greater graduation of tax^n.
35 — Land resettlement
27 — Foreign policy
16 — Retrenchment
10 — Others

Figure 3

Profile of Socialist Election Addresses

showing % of candidates mentioning major issues

91 — Public ownership
91 — Unemployment
91 — Constitutional reforms
82 — Education Act reform
82 — Home Rule
73 — Old age pensions
73 — 8-hour day
73 — Graduated taxation
73 — Free Trade
55 — Taff Vale
55 — Housing
36 — Chinese Labour
36 — Licensing reform
27 — Land Value Taxation
27 — Free school meals
18 — Worker's compensation

as their major political objective were the Social Democrats and one or two of the other independent Labour candidates. In terms of its political programme, the LRC was in fact very similar to the left wing of the Liberal party.

One or two candidates expressed a note of scepticism on the importance of maintaining Free Trade. 'Is it because of Free Trade', asked Glasier (Birmingham Bordesley), 'or because we haven't got German tariffs, German conscription, and German horseflesh sausages [that] the wage earners receive only . . . a third [of the nation's wealth]? No, indeed, it is because the fruits of the people's labour are drained from them to provide the fortunes of the great idle landowners and the monopolists.' But Keir Hardie more typically took up a position as a convinced Free Trader who was 'opposed to any flirtation with protection whether disguised as preferential tariffs or a zollverein or retaliation, or any of the many aliases under which it is proposed to foist . . . [it] upon the nation'. He went on to indicate with all the abandon of the novitiate that he 'would abolish the customs house altogether and do away with all forms of indirect taxation, save the excise duties upon spirits'. Even the manifesto of the ILP (which as a body tended to be far more critical of Free Trade) described protection as but 'one form of the same thing [monopoly] that keeps the workers poor'.[10] What was needed, said Winstone (Newport), was not protection against foreigners abroad, but protection against monopolies at home; and seven out of every ten of his LRC colleagues included a specific condemnation of food taxes in their election addresses.

Furthermore, the reforms to which the LRC candidates subscribed were very similar to those put forward by the Liberals, and where they were different the line often ran as much between LRC candidates themselves as between the LRC and the Liberals. Education and licensing reform were cases in point. Some LRC candidates (e.g. Hardie and Henderson) adopted the ILP policy of secularisation of education and some again (e.g. Snowdon) municipal control of licences (neither of which were part of Liberal policy), but the great majority followed the Liberal lines on both. Similarly LRC candidates put forward a number of remedies for unemployment—ranging from the allocation of public funds to make a reality of the Unionist Act, to municipal and public works, to land resettlement, and to the redistribution of taxation. Although both Labour and Socialist candidates tended to show a *greater* awareness of the link between unemployment and the maldistribution of income—'the rich have more than they can spend and the poor are too poor to buy. That is why there is lack of employment and the shopkeepers have bad trade' (Kennedy, SDF)—no clear line could be drawn across the political spectrum to coincide in any way precisely with party labels. Isaac Mitchell (Darlington) was perhaps less adventurous than some of his colleagues in the LRC, but the review of unemployment and reform presented in his election address was nevertheless typical of most of his party and showed how close in spirit this lay to—at any rate progressive—Liberalism.

> Unemployment and bad housing are caused by Land Monopoly which prevents the people having access to that which is their natural heritage, by the absurd tax upon our national industries, resulting from the excessive burden of Royalty Rents, by the lack of organisation in industry, by the huge taxation of industry and labour for the benefit of the privileged few which results from the constant appreciation of Land Values in our populous centres, by the depreciation of our credit as a nation owing to the disastrous and profligate expenditure of the Unionist Government; and by the Unionist Government's own action in discharging over 15,000 workers from their own establishments during the last 2½ years.

The Speaker commented—quite reasonably—on 20 January that Ramsay MacDonald's own election address might equally well have been written by a member of the Liberal party.

The publication of a separate LRC manifesto was nevertheless an event of some significance, not merely on account of the terseness and urgency of its language, but because of the common determination to which it bore witness 'to create a driving force in politics which will overcome the inertia of politicians in regard to social reforms'.[11] Hardie and MacDonald worked hard—

F

through the candidates' conferences arranged in 1903, 1904, and 1905—to facilitate an exchange of views and iron out differences; and although Ben Tillet and J. N. Bell moved at the 1905 LRC conference that the party should adopt the TUC's manifesto—on the grounds that it seemed 'a little foolish for the great proportion of the delegates to attend the Trade Union Congress and formulate a programme there and then to gather together again at the LRC conference for the purpose of laying down another programme'[12]—the NEC finally commissioned Hardie and MacDonald to prepare a specific party alternative. Time justified its decision. Whilst, in the event, the TUC's manifesto merely besought electors to 'vote for Labour and other candidates' who were prepared to support certain policies which it felt to be in the interests of its membership, the LRC manifesto opened with a hard-hitting statement that the election was to decide whether or not Labour was to be fairly represented in Parliament. 'The House of Commons was supposed to be the people's House and yet the people is not there', it continued. 'Landlords, employers, lawyers, brewers and financiers are there in force why not Labour? . . . You have it in your power to see that Parliament carries out your wishes.'[13]

This was the appeal from the hard centre of nine out of ten of the election addresses of LRC candidates. Figure 2 shows that it was closely supported by their determination to see the Taff Vale decision reversed, and to obtain constitutional reforms that would remove many of the anomalies and disabilities built into the electoral system. But, as the ILP's manifesto reiterated, the labour voters already held the key to their own success. 'We desire it to be plainly understood that the fault lies at the door of *you*, the working classes', it said. 'You have been content to leave your political thinking to be done for you by party politicians, and your opinions to be formed for you by their hirelings in the press.'[14]

The reformist programme of the LRC—and to a lesser extent of the ILP and SDF also—was not greatly dissimilar from that of the Liberal party; but it was supported, and distinguished, by constant reiteration of the views that only by increasing working-class representation could the vigorous prosecution of the programme be guaranteed, and that this could—in 1906—be finally achieved.

CONSERVATIVE AND UNIONIST

Compared with both the Liberal and LRC programmes, Unionist policy—as formally expressed through party leaflets and election addresses—was characterised by a very much narrower spread of issues. The TRL naturally concentrated on the fiscal issue, but well over half the leaflets issued by the CCO were also devoted to it, and there were only four other issues that 50 per cent or more of the candidates found worthy of specific mention in their personal election addresses. This compared with 11 among independent Socialist and Labour candidates, 12 among Liberal candidates, and 14 among LRC candidates. Significantly, these four issues were the mainly traditional issues of defence of the union, management of foreign policy, maintenance of strong defence forces, and safeguarding of the Education Act.

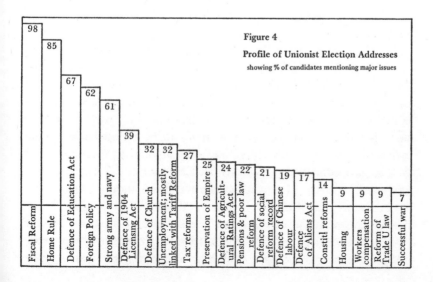

Figure 4

Profile of Unionist Election Addresses

showing % of candidates mentioning major issues

To this extent, then, Chamberlain had cause to be satisfied with the effects of his two-and-a-half years of solid campaigning: in that the vast majority of Unionist candidates (and organisations) were united not only on the need for fiscal change, but also on the presentation of this need as the first and most important element in the Unionist programme. As a result of defections, retirements, and other pressures, the proportion of out-and-out Free Traders was reduced from around 10 per cent of the parliamentary party in April 1903 to a mere 3 per cent (15–20) of the candidates standing in the election; and although their importance was far greater than their numbers, there were consequently few Unionist candidates to appeal to their electors— as did Goschen, to the industrial classes of Bolton—'to return to Parliament a Free Trader who would uphold his opinions in the Unionist Party'. The vast majority of candidates were quite content to echo the point of view put forward by the National Union that, since the existing state of economic affairs no longer resembled Free Trade as conceived by Cobden and Bright, 'mere strumming upon the shibboleths of the days of Cobden and Bright—true at the time they were uttered will not save the country'; and both the cco and TRL argued that action was required to secure some kind of 'fairer trade'.[15] In its *Short Handbook for Speakers*, the Tariff Reform League listed twenty-five industries and trades which, it said, were in absolute or relative decline owing to unfair foreign competition, and many candidates, to whichever wing of the party they belonged, emphasised the consequent need for action. H. L. W. Lawson, a Chamberlainite standing in the Mile End division of the Tower Hamlets, said that they must have 'a free hand to beat down the hostile tariffs of foreign countries which refused [British] manufactured goods, particularly those for which East London [was] famous', and C. A. Moreing (another Chamberlainite standing at Gainsborough in Lincolnshire) wrote—and spoke—at length of the unfair competition of German metalwares. Similarly Naylor (Caernarvon District) and Black (South Aberdeen), who were both more moderate, said that it was essential to protect their

British quarrymen constituents against Norwegian competitors. Even in Lancashire where 80 per cent of Unionist candidates were careful to avoid any suggestion of the taxation of raw materials, most of them (following Balfour himself) wrote of the need to protect and re-open markets for cotton goods, by the threat or act of retaliation.

There was a general consensus, furthermore, that *some* degree of fiscal reform, retaliatory or protective, would prove to be essential if the problem of unemployment were to be solved; and here again Chamberlain's influence could be perceived. Leaflets of the CCO, as well as of NUCA and TRL, recalled the resolution passed at the National Union's 1905 conference that Tariff Reform would secure 'more employment and steadier wages for workers';[16] and virtually all of the (30 per cent or so) candidates who specifically mentioned unemployment in their election addresses, not only proposed some degree of fiscal reform as the remedy, but also poured scorn on the Liberal remedies of land reform and land value taxation. There were a few—like J. W. Spear at Tavistock—in country districts who said they would support any steps just to other sections of the community which would check the evils of urban over-population and rural stagnation by making it more worthwhile for the rural population to remain in the country districts; and Balfour admitted that, unlike state-managed industry, it might just be possible to make farm colonies pay. But the majority of candidates who referred to the issue at all agreed with Herbert Davies, the Australian Unionist candidate for East Hull, who maintained that since the farmers had great difficulty in competing with overseas produce as it was, any new settlements would aggravate rather than solve the unemployment problem. Describing farm colonies as 'tree planting and swamp filling', Sir John Nutting similarly held that they could never be more than a temporary palliative.

Generally campaigning on the slogan of 'deeds not words', Unionist candidates condemned Liberal proposals as undesirable, unworkable, or extravagant. Defending the 1904 Licensing Act as a measure which would promote temperance whilst doing justice to the licence-holders, they pictured the Liberals as fanatics who wished to replace the pub with 'the cold comfort of the Temperance Hall'.[17] They attacked the taxation of (at least rural) land values as a form of taxation which was bound to be passed on in the form of higher land prices, and maintained that it was a pipe dream to suppose that the Liberal policy of retrenchment could be combined with sound defence and great schemes of reform. Sir Vincent Caillard, the Tariff Reform Unionist candidate for East Bradford, rightly pointed out that a reduction of £50 million in public expenditure between 1903 and 1905 had in fact been accompanied by a rising and not a declining level of unemployment.

Tariff Reform Unionist candidates, following Chamberlain, took the argument from fiscal reform to more regular employment a step further by maintaining that 'free imports really defeat the objects of Trade Unionism' and therefore that Tariff Reform was designed to protect workers against sweated goods from abroad, just as trade unionism was designed to protect them from exploitation at home.[18] The Tariff Reform League implicitly rejected the Liberal and Labour attack on trusts and monopolies by posing the choice being presented to the British people as lying between 'trusts in this country, where they employ British capital and British labour, and are amenable to British public opinion and British law; [and] foreign Trusts and Combinations over which we have not and cannot have the slightest control'.[19] The Imperial Tariff Commission neatly caught, in one of its leaflets, the mood of the Manifesto of the London Council of the Trade Union branch of the Tariff Reform League.

> The days when Trade Unionism meant a bitter constant strife between the employer and his working men are passed, and the new Unionism which has taken its place, if it is to succeed, as in justice it should, must resolve itself into a combination of capital and labour in this country in opposition to the common enemy of both which is capital and labour assisted by state aid of the foreigner.[20]

This measure of agreement on the necessity of fiscal change, however, and on some relationship between fiscal reform and the level of domestic employment, was not matched by a comparable unity over means. Sandars reported to Balfour, shortly before the election, that in the reshuffling and selection of candidates most committees 'insist upon a candidate who . . . [is] a Tariff Reformer but who *publicly* . . . will not pledge himself further than the policy [of retaliation]',[21] and several Unionists reported that—as the *Manchester Guardian* said on 12 January, of the Manchester area—'those who were originally protectionists . . . fall back upon Retaliations'. As a result, the 1903–5 trend towards Chamberlainism in the parliamentary party was not carried forward into the campaign period; the proportion of Unionists taking refuge in vague evasive formulas actually increased, from around 45 per cent of *MPs* in April 1905 to 55–60 per cent of *candidates* in January 1906. Very few candidates, even among the Tariff Reformers, came out with a clear declaration for Chamberlain's general tariff and preference on corn; and rather more, on the other hand, went out of their way to make it clear that, although supporters of fiscal reform, they were hostile to anything approaching protection. For example, Major Stewart (East Renfrew) said that he had 'never concealed . . . [his] mistrust of the specious arguments in favour of a general tariff, with its constant temptations to particular traders to agitate for its manipulation in their own favour irrespective of the general welfare. His views were echoed not only by the Free Traders *à l'outrance* but by nearly all of the 13 per cent of Unionist candidates who confined their expressions of opinion, on this issue, to a few cautious words on retaliation. Sandars wrote to Balfour on 13 December 1905 to say that 'two policies are *known* to exist',[22] and, as Table 14 shows, less than half the party (and certainly a smaller proportion than Chamberlain must have hoped) were prepared to go the whole hog.

Within this spectrum of opinion judgement of the commercial potential of the empire, as a trading unit, was equally broad. Chamberlain declared (again) that, in the empire, Tariff Reform would gain an immense new market; Du Pré (Loughborough)

Table 14

ANALYSIS OF FISCAL VIEWS IN UNIONIST ELECTION ADDRESSES
(PERCENTAGE)

Group	Percentage of total number of Unionists	Percentage of Balfourites/ Chamberlainites
A. Free Traders	3	—
B. Balfourites	55	—
(i) Advocacy of the practice or threat of retaliation	13	24
(ii) As (i) but also mentioned impossibility of judging on Empire trade till Colonial Conference	26	47
(iii) As (ii) plus specific opposition to food taxes	7	13
(iv) As (ii) plus specific opposition to food and raw material taxes	6	11
(v) As (ii) plus pledge of 2nd general election after the Colonial Conference	3	5
C. Chamberlainites	40	—
(vi) In general: establishment of trade equality; beginning of a preferential system	24	62
(vii) As (vi) but pledged no overall increase in cost of living	12	30
(viii) As (vi) but pledged no overall increase in the cost of living, or cost of raw materials	2	4
(ix) Clear declaration for 10 per cent General Tariff and preference on corn	2	4
D. Not included (election addresses not available)	2	—

maintained that the empire market, 'certain to expand tenfold', would 'afford an increasing outlet' for British manufactures; and, basing its assertions on a series of comparisons 'between the level of exports in 1871 (a boom year) and 1902 (a year of depression), the TRL issued leaflet after leaflet seeking to substantiate these predictions—which, of course, lay at the root of the Tariff Reform case over unemployment relief. Most Balfourites, on the other hand (like Seton-Kerr at St Helens), were openly cautious or sceptical about the possibility, and even the desirability, of achieving the Tariff Reformer's vision of a self-contained, self-supporting, and federated empire, and just as they tended to present retaliation as a means not to a protective market, but to *freer* trade, so they saw the future of the empire not as a closed British preserve, but as a power system which would protect British interests without seeking to exclude those of everyone else. Like Balfour himself, they often linked the need for strong armed forces and a strong foreign policy to the need for retaliation in trade, and a number of near-Free Traders, like Geoffrey Drage at Blackburn, similarly came out strongly in favour of the creation of imperial institutions which could lead towards what he called 'the accomplishment under Divine Providence of the great mission of the British Empire'. Thomas Studdard— another Lancashire candidate—similarly blamed Radical weakness—from Majuba on—for Kruger's 'unprovoked' attack, and declared that 'the courage and the wisdom of the Conservative Government . . . in fighting and bringing the . . . war to a successful conclusion has brought prosperity to the cotton trade and security to . . . [the] Empire'. He warned his constituents that if they valued their livelihoods they would vote Unionist as the only way of guaranteeing 'the maintenance of the empire and the position of Great Britain as a world power', on which they depended.

Such imperially-minded candidates made it very clear, however, that they did not accept the view put forward—by F. E. Smith and others—that the 'definite rejection of Tariff Reform' would in the course of time reduce the country to 'the position of a second-rate and inexpansive power'. Indeed, they emphasised in many cases that, although prepared to go to a Colonial Conference with open minds, they were by no means clear that great and beneficial results would flow from it. A number of them maintained, with Keith Fraser of Caithness (and their Liberal opponents) that the colonies 'were never intended to form one Empire commercially', and all of them made it plain that they were not prepared to construct imperial unity on the basis of taxation of food in the United Kingdom. Indeed it was just because the imperialism of the Tariff Reformers had—potentially —such a wide appeal that it was, in their view (and Sandars'), 'the greater the pity' that it should have been based on this 'unpopular proposal'.[23]

As Table 14 suggests, it was this aspect of Chamberlain's policies which most clearly divided the party on the fiscal issue, and led the majority to err on the side of caution in presenting their views to the electorate. Chamberlain warned the British farmer that he 'would not get a great deal out of' a 2s 0d corn duty and Jesse Collings denounced the big loaf cry as no more than 'an implied lie'. Other Tariff Reformers maintained that the policy of Tariff Reform would make the colonies the granary of the empire and TRL leaflets were full of statistical demonstrations of the fact, so it was said, that overall prices would not rise. However their promise of price or tax reductions to offset increases in the price of *some* foodstuffs, fed rather than allayed suspicions already aroused by the extremists' view that no sacrifice could be too great if imperial federation were to be achieved; and the general devotion of the Chamberlainites to their imperial dream meant that—for all their innate protectionism—they failed to drive home the more intelligible, but less imperialist, argument put forward by Charles Booth (no less), that whilst prices and costs would rise this would be offset by the benefits of increased industrial activity and therefore of wages too. If to some extent Tariff Reform should have the effect of increasing prices, Booth wrote, 'it would not affect my opinion of [the] proposals, since the well being of the poorer classes, not less than that of

the more regularly employed and the well to do, depends very
much more on general conditions of prosperity and the fluctua-
tion of employment than on changes in the level of prices . . .'[24]
Since over half the Unionist candidates made it clear that they
could not even begin to consider the possibility of preferences
based on food and raw material taxes until a colonial conference
met to consider the whole question, and a sizeable minority of
nearly a hundred made it clear that they would not consider them
even then, the proposals must in any event have seemed somewhat remote.

The effect, in terms of the Unionist programme, was two-fold.
On the one hand the (very) broad agreement on the commercial
and social advantages (especially in reducing unemployment) to
be gained from *some* measure of fiscal reform meant that, apart
from a fairly widespread, and well argued, defence of the Education Act as an important piece of social legislation, the Unionists
had very little to say compared with the Liberals, and appeared
to be committed to a much narrower band of opinion, on the
major social issues of the day.

The fact, in the second place, that these Unionist candidates
presented such a wide spectrum of opinion on the (fiscal) means
by which social reform was to be implemented, and on the
imperial unity which it was to help promote, meant that—as
Chamberlain had feared all along—the presentation of Tariff
Reform as the necessary basis for a genuine improvement in
the standard of living of the mass of the working people did
not come across in the party's programme with either clarity or
impact.

This was, no doubt, the reason why so many Unionist candidates turned (with an almost evident sense of relief) to foreign
policy and defence issues. Here, predictably, there was complete
unanimity. They discounted the presence of the Liberal im-
perialists in the cabinet as any guarantee of responsible imperial
policies and held up to contempt the claims made by pro-Boer
Little Englander Liberals, that they could better ensure the
security of the realm. As Balfour said:

To the foreign policy of the new Government, we might seem
justified in looking with more satisfaction than to its legislative projects, for apparently it is to be a continuation of our own. But
confident as I am of the capacity and patriotism of Sir Edward
Grey, I doubt the success of his intentions. A foreign policy which
is to be specific, honourable, and consistent, requires not merely a
Foreign Minister of ability, but a Foreign Minister who has two
conditions in his favour. The first is a strong defensive naval and
military force . . . [and the] . . . second . . . is the support of a
united Cabinet dependent on a united Party. . . .

Several Unionist candidates pointed with pride to the creation
of the Army Council and Committee of Imperial Defence, but
it was perhaps significant—in the light of the profound disquiet
expressed in 1904 and 1905 National Union conferences about
the state of the armed forces revealed by the War Commission's
report[25]—that the number of Unionist candidates to make specific
mention of defence issues in their election addresses was, in 1906,
as low as 33 per cent.

Indeed, it was perhaps because they faced so many difficulties
and divisions in presenting many of their other traditional policies
that Unionist candidates placed so great an emphasis on the one
aspect of them on which they were all agreed without reservation,
namely the defence of the Union. Whether they took the view
that the renewed threat of Home Rule would come openly or in
'the more insidious . . . [policy] of instalments' (Edmond Talbot,
Chichester), they agreed with Balfour that the Liberals boasted
'an unrepentant fidelity to the views they entertained between
1892 and 1895', the country had to anticipate 'a return to the
policy they then attempted but were fortunately too weak to
accomplish', and they put about sombre warnings of what it
would cost the country, if attempted. As one cco leaflet said with
somewhat startling logic, Home Rule would mean:

> . . . the importation of thousands of ruined Irish labourers to com-
> pete with the English working men in the already crowded labour
> market . . . the maintenance of a strong fleet in St Georges
> Channel and a large increase in the English Navy . . . the
> commencement of the break-up of the Empire and the eventual

separation of the Colonies . . . and . . . in the end a new conquest
of Ireland.[26]

At the same time, to offset the effect of such propaganda on the
important Irish Catholic vote, many individual Unionist candidates went out of their way to emphasise the importance of
defending the principle of religious education in schools. Indeed,
next to fiscal reform and Home Rule, the education issue loomed
largest in the Unionist election addresses, and a typical cco poster
showed Campbell-Bannerman assiduously watering the radical
plants of 'Imperial Disunion, Home Rule, Crime, Atheism and
Depravity'.

Even on these issues, which were both archetypal and immediate, there were minorities who stood out of line. A handful of
candidates said that they *would* support any well-considered
scheme of devolution to local or regional authorities *throughout*
the United Kingdom, i.e. including Ireland, and a sizeable
majority (of about 50) declared their willingness to accept any
reasonable amendment to the 1902 Education Act in order to
meet nonconformist or other religious objections. But if any
one thread ran through the Unionist programme, it was nevertheless the appeal to national and imperial integrity, within which
Chamberlain—and many other candidates—sought to encompass
their other, and especially fiscal, views. In his election address,
Chamberlain wrote:

I have sought in domestic policy the greatest happiness of the
greatest number, and I have endeavoured at the same time to
uphold the greatness of our common country and the unity of our
Imperial Dominion. In my opinion both these objects are
threatened by the new Government which has lately taken office
pending an appeal to the people. It is essentially a Home Rule
and Little England Government. It seeks by tortuous ways to
compass the disruption of the United Kingdom although it dare
not place Home Rule openly upon its programme. It must
however exist, if at all, by the support of Irish votes and by the
help of those who have openly avowed that separation is their
ultimate object. In its professed anxiety for peace it will not face
the sacrifices necessary to maintain [it] and to enable us, in the

face of ever-growing armaments of other countries to defend ourselves and our Empire against unprovoked attack. [Finally] its members have shown profound indifference to the wishes of our Colonial kinsmen for closer commercial union and have deliberately made a Party question of a great Imperial policy . . .

The Times described this (on 2 January) as 'a clear and trenchant exposition of Unionist policy which . . . may serve as a model to Unionist candidates everywhere', and it well reflected the approach of the Unionist leaders when—as what Sandars called 'the attacking [i.e. opposition] party'[27]—they began the campaign in earnest in the second week in December. 'We have the chance', so Wyndham believed and wrote to Balfour, 'of fighting a magnificent rearguard action';[28] but could they seize it?

Notes to Chapter 3 will be found on pp 217–18

4 THE ELECTION CAMPAIGN

In the opening shots of the campaign, fired whilst Campbell-Bannerman struggled with the problems of cabinet formation, the Unionists did their best to recapture the initiative by laying a pronounced emphasis on Ireland. Speaking at Colchester on the evening of 8 December (after press reports of Grey's refusal of office), Brodrick said that 'the Unionists had to fight in years gone by against Home Rule when it was—*as it must be now*—the first plank in the Liberal platform', and Carson, in London, similarly recommended to Campbell-Bannerman (in the event of his going to the Upper House) the title of Lord Stirling since, he said, it was at Stirling that he had made 'the speech which had been of such assistance to the Unionist cause'. At Ardwick the following evening, in a succinct expression of the Unionist attitude, Balfour added that: 'the forces by which the Radical Party can alone come to power and hold power are of a kind which will compel them, gladly or reluctantly, as the case may be, with triumph or with diffidence, as circumstances permit, but will still compel them to be now, as they have been for twenty years, a party of Imperial disintegration'. When on 13 December Redmond again insisted that the Irish cause did not depend on this government, or that, but on 'the inexorable logic of facts and circumstances',[1] Austen Chamberlain, speaking in Bradford twenty-four hours later, immediately seized on his words. He challenged the four Vice-Presidents of the Liberal League to reconcile their (then known) acceptance of office with their past statements and he said that 'no man who was true to the Unionist

faith would hesitate to take up the gage of battle that the Prime
Minister has thrown down'. The *Daily News* commented, on 15
December, that Unionist tactics were clearly going to consist of
abuse of Campbell-Bannerman and of the new government, and
of exploitation of Home Rule.

The *Daily Chronicle* bluntly stated, on 11 December, that
Liberalism could not 'reduce itself to permanent impotence for
Ireland's sake', and the *Westminster Gazette* suggested, the
following day, that the issue was only one of tactics and accom-
modation, on which the Irish nationalists should not expect far-
reaching legislation in the next Parliament. St Loe Strachey's
Unionist Free Trade journal, the *Spectator*—widely quoted if
not widely read—commented, as the dissolution was announced,
that the new cabinet did not intend, if it commanded a majority
in the next Parliament, to introduce a Home Rule Bill, that the
'essential issue' placed before the electorate would be the maintenance of Free Trade, and that the opposition would be 'given
no excuse for evading the issue or pretending that the issue of
Home Rule had taken its place'; speaking in London on 14 and
19 December, Churchill and Asquith made the same point.

They kept their sharpest barbs, however, for the circumstances
of Unionist resignation. Ridiculing the line being put about by
his opponents, that the Liberals were the enemies of their country, as good enough for an 'Orange mob . . . in Belfast', or for
'suburban notabilities . . . at a Croydon soirée', Churchill—in the
City—compared the Unionists to a bankrupt company whose
director had deserted; and five days later at the Queen's Hall,
where large crowds chanted their determination to 'stamp, stamp,
stamp upon Protection' (one of the commonest Liberal campaign
songs), Asquith commented sarcastically—above the loud interruptions of the suffragettes—that 'the remarkable sequence of
events' leading up to Balfour's resignation would afford 'an
admirable text for a cynically-minded historian'. As Francis
Channing said at Stockburn, not many days later, the Unionists
were asking for a renewal of the greatest of trusts when their
conduct proved that they had no faith in themselves. 'They have

run out of the back door with the cry "the State, the Church, everything is in danger", and have themselves deliberately handed over the machinery of Government to conspirators and enemies of their country, crowning a long chapter of wrong-doing and failure with an act of culpable suicide . . .'[2] Spender commented in the *Westminster Gazette* on 16 December that it was somewhat absurd for the Unionists to claim—as the *Daily Telegraph* did that morning—that they had only resigned to 'find . . . out what the Radicals intended to do with regard to Ireland', and in a widely quoted letter to *The Times* of 15 December, Sir Henry Howarth expressed what must have been as much in Unionist as in Liberal minds. 'The suicide committed by the Conservative Government . . . has produced no adequate justi-fication', he wrote, '. . . and I do not think any person believes that the Prime Minister intends to commit himself to carrying through a Home Rule Bill in the coming Parliament.'

In these circumstances, the Unionist attack shifted somewhat, in the second week in December, on to the failure of the Liberals, to that date, to spell out their own domestic policies with precision. Addressing a delegation of the unemployed on 13 December, Campbell-Bannerman and Burns both said that they could not commit themselves over unemployment relief until the cabinet had had time to consider the matter; and although the *Daily News* commented the following day that just when unemploy-ment seemed to be 'a problem beyond the resources of states-manship, a man of the people—whose views were well-known—[had arisen] to advise the governing classes . . .', the Social Democrat, James MacDonald, told a gathering in Hyde Park that 'their grievances would not be settled by Sir Henry Campbell-Bannerman's "butterscotch" or John Burns's sympathy'. Once again, therefore, Unionists joined with some Labour, and Socialist, speakers in accusing the Liberals of having no positive solutions to recommend. On 15 December, even as *The Times* declared that such confidence as there was in Campbell-Banner-man's administration was purely negative, Austen Chamberlain ridiculed the apparent Liberal belief that with Burns at the Local

G

Government Board unemployment no longer existed, and Acland-Hood spoke in similar vein at Taunton. Two days later, at an ILP rally in Manchester, Keir Hardie demanded a special half-penny on the income tax to provide funds for unemployment relief and—with Mrs Pankhurst speaking for the WSPU—emphasised the need for independent Labour representation if action on unemployment was to be secured. And in his second major campaign speech, at Bristol on 19 December, Walter Long significantly criticised the Liberals not just for their Irish policies, but in other fields for what he now described as their 'abstinence from policies'.

For a few brief days, furthermore, it seemed just possible that the Unionist leaders might (at last) succeed in galvanising their own fiscal reform policies into some kind of demonstrable (and united) alternative to Liberal government. The Tariff Reformer Hewins felt that, in his opening campaign speech at Oxford on 8 December, Chamberlain had been disappointingly vague. He clearly committed himself to some kind of general tariff and some degree of corn taxation but, Hewins wrote,

> he seemed depressed by my account of the position in Canada . . . considered the results of the negotiations rather vague and hoped the Canadian Government would make an optional tariff which we could reject or refuse . . . he began by raising the Home Rule issue and ridiculing the new Ministry . . . [and only in] the latter part of the speech dealt with the Imperial issue rather too vaguely and sentimentally . . .[3]

Whilst still unsure whether Balfour really agreed with him or not, Chamberlain nevertheless—and somewhat provocatively—declared that 'the chapter of . . . political history in which Mr Balfour had been the most important and the principal figure [was] over'. And when, speaking warmly of Balfour, in his speech at Bradford (on 14 December), Austen Chamberlain declared that he could say 'and say with knowledge, that between the leaders of . . . [the Unionist] Party there . . . [was] no difference of principle, [and] no difference of aim or object', Spender seized eagerly on his words to write an editorial in the *Westminster*

Gazette (on 15 December) to prove beyond all doubt that the Unionist party was committed to a policy of Tariff Reform.

'You couldn't have a better text for your [next] speech than the quotation from Austen Chamberlain in this evening's leading article' Asquith wrote to Campbell-Bannerman. 'It shows (1) that the so-called crisis [in November] was a put-up job and (2) that J.C. and A.B. are rowing whole-heartedly if not quite in time and swing in the same boat.'[4] However, as the *Daily News* pointed out, Balfour had not himself made his position clear, especially on food taxes and the general tariff (about which it urged electors to ask all Unionist candidates).[5] Indeed he came under renewed pressure not only from the Unionist Free Traders —Devonshire, James, and Goschen—but also from Acland-Hood and the party—to 'draw the line *between* his policy and Chamberlain's',[6] or at least to define it: as Carson wrote to Lady Londonderry on 17 December, he would have to declare how his policy was to be carried out since he could meet no one who understood it.[7] Balfour therefore determined to use the opportunity presented by the speech he was due to give at Leeds the following day to try to help his brother (Gerald) keep an unsafe ex-ministerial seat, and to present Unionist fiscal policy in a way that would both unify the party and mobilise electoral support.

It was both a good and a typical speech. Referring first to a statement he had made in 1892, in order to establish the consistency of his belief in retaliation based—if necessary—on a general non-protective tariff, he once again poured scorn on what he described as the Liberal policy of one-sided Free Trade as a perversion of Cobden's own views. 'Free Trade is not a virtue which the nation practises as a man practises honesty', he said, but 'a relation between countries', and he likened the need for sanctions in commercial negotiations to the ultimate sanction of war in diplomacy. Whilst again warning that nothing would endanger the imperial idea more than the rash introduction into it of the insular idea of protection, he went out of his way to pay tribute to Chamberlain's long and arduous work in teaching the nation not merely to think but to *feel* about empire; and he said

that no one outside a lunatic asylum would reject a small corn
tax *if* it led to permanent empire Free Trade. But he made the
significant admissions that relations with the colonies were 'far
more complex' than the 'simple interchange of commodities'
seemed to show, and that the colonies had 'never themselves put
forward . . . any plan'; and, commending the notion of a colonial
conference to meet and study the whole question of mutual
preferences, he indicated that—in his view—judgement should
in the meantime be suspended. This was perhaps why he chose
to conclude with the usual Unionist warnings about the dangers
posed to imperial unity, to the integrity of the Welsh church, to
religious education, and above all to the Union. The Liberal
Leaguers, he said, had gone over absolutely to the enemy, leaving
the Unionists as the sole defenders of these vital interests.

The speech was an able reiteration of often-stated views and it
seemed—from press reports—to satisfy all shades of Unionist
fiscal opinion. Leo Maxse ecstatically described it in the December number of the *National Review* as 'an intellectual achieve-
ment altogether above platform oratory'; and of the major
Unionist dailies only the *Daily Mail*—Garvin complained in
Outlook—persisted in thinking that 'those statesmen upon whose
cooperation and efficiency the very existence of the Unionists
depended were divided upon what it calls Protection'.[8] *The
Times* expressed a more or less common view when it suggested
that both leaders wanted to reach a similar point on the fiscal
scale and differed only in seeking to approach it from opposite
ends. As the *Manchester Guardian* pointed out, however, this
only meant that the speech meant all things to all men. 'Mr
Balfour has long been running with the hares and hunting with
the hounds but last night he outdid himself . . .' The imperialist
Hewins thought that it had brought the two sections of the party
closer but—equally—that it had cast unnecessary doubt on the
colonial offer;[9] a Dunfermline moderate wrote to thank Balfour
'on behalf of *many* who want to go *forward quietly* under [his]
leadership . . . [for a] splendid speech at a critical time';[10] and—
at the other end of the fiscal spectrum—Goschen (though signifi-

cantly not Devonshire) felt that it 'differentiates his position from Chamberlain's . . . and points to mitigation of sentence'.[11] Finlay commented—with approval—that it might have been taken straight out of Adam Smith.[12] Thus whilst the speech was welcomed as an emollient, the doubters—like the indefatigable Howarth writing again to *The Times* on 26 December—begged leave to wonder whether it could provide a *battle cry* for an election.

> An election cry must be more effective than can be squeezed out of opposition to 'devolution' or to 'administrative autonomy in Ireland' if the Unionist pulse is to be quickened . . . Free Trade, the Liberals tell us, is to be their war cry; and if it is to be met by merely negative and bewildering circumlocution, the case will be a hopeless one.

All speculation as to whether or not the Unionists could have seized the initiative in the campaign at this point was, however, overtaken by the Prime Minister's first major (and as it turned out pivotal) speech, at the Albert Hall on Thursday 21 December. His central point—vigorously put over and no doubt widely taken—was that in the forthcoming election it would be the Unionists and not the Liberals who were on trial. The Unionists had lived and died on tactics and whilst their leader seemed to think that he could pick and choose the election issues 'somewhat as a holiday tripper . . . might exercise a choice between Ramsgate and Margate', the Liberals would not allow him and his colleagues to escape from responsibility for their past actions, and from the judgement of the country both on their fiscal policy and their conduct of affairs. Describing militarism, extravagance and protection as weeds which grew in the same field, he urged the central importance of Free Trade to all aspects of government— to foreign policy, to the economy, and to social reform alike— and he warned that if once they opened the door to protection, there would be little hope for 'those great objects of reform and economy' on which their hearts were set. He denied that the Liberals were Little Englanders. He said that they would restore sound administration to India and would remove—'forthwith as far as it was practicable'[13]—the black spot of Chinese indentures in South Africa, precisely because they cared greatly for relations between the colonies and the mother country; and he pledged that whilst adhering to the policy of the Entente Cordiale, his government would strive to place the United Kingdom at the head of a 'League of Peace'. Turning to the social matters, about which only days earlier he had been criticised from both right and left, he said that the Liberal party would endeavour to reduce taxation *and* provide more money for domestic affairs by cutting down military expenditure and tapping fresh sources of taxation in land values, liquor licences, and the better *distribution* of wealth. Warned by Dillon that any modification of the Stirling policy on Ireland would have 'the most disastrous results',[14] he undertook to apply the principle of popular control not only to licensing and education but also—as and when opportunity offered—to domestic affairs in Ireland. And he said that since Liberalism could not 'pass on the other side of the way . . . like the Levite', his government would deal with the terrible problems of overcrowding and unemployment, through land and rating reforms, reform of the Poor Law, and experiments (unspecified) in the relief of unemployment. He said nothing on Welsh disestablishment—leaving this for Lloyd George to deal with the same evening in a speech at Caernarvon—and despite frequent interruptions by militant suffragettes, whose pleas for justice were drowned by the Albert Hall organ until the ushers removed them—did not commit himself on votes for women. But he did—explicitly—promise to rectify the Taff Vale decision and 'give freedom and security to the Trade Unions in pursuit of their legitimate aims'.[15]

Liberals hailed the speech with great enthusiasm as 'a challenge to all the interests and monopolies and class privileges that had gathered under the banner of Mr Chamberlain' and a break with the 'triumphant arrogance'[16] of the past years. T. P. O'Connor—Irish Nationalist candidate and eye-witness—recorded that 'the vast hall was filled in every seat, while enthusiasm reigned almost to a frenzy, [and that the] gathering went almost beside itself when Campbell-Bannerman announced that the importation of Chinese labour into South Africa had already been brought to an end'.[17] Morley similarly reported that his wife, 'an old hand at such things, declared that she had never seen such a reception',[18] and when, after the Christmas break, the constituency campaigns began in earnest, every Liberal leader in turn sought to amplify the broad choices presented in it. Fresh from the promulgation of new regulations providing for the maintenance of the dependants of able-bodied paupers in the workhouses, and out-relief for paupers who left workhouses in order to look for work, Burns launched his campaign at Battersea on 27 December by contrasting what he called the slow and solid administration of the new government with the 'orientalised Imperialism' of the old; and, spearheading the campaign in Wales, Lloyd George appealed in Conway, the following evening, for justice for the nonconformists and a fair deal for the poor. The following day, Fowler, Grey, Churchill and others all appealed for a clear verdict on the fiscal issue, judgement of the Unionist record, and the advantage of a clear working majority, such as the Unionists had long enjoyed, to give reforming Liberalism a chance.

Chamberlain, on the other hand, ridiculed the Albert Hall programme as no more than the old Newcastle Programme— 'brought down from its dusty shelf [and] resuscitated once more, in order to disappoint the world which had been expecting something better . . .', but he also said, in unconscious tribute, that it lacked nothing that the Home Ruler, the Little Englander, the Cobdenite, the nonconformist, or the trade unionist could possibly name as the price of his support,[19] and within days of their charge that the Liberal party had no policy, Unionists accused it of having, in effect, too much. The *Daily Telegraph* said on 22 December that the Prime Minister dragged the Liberal Leaguers 'at his chariot wheels', and, speaking in Haldane's constituency on Boxing Day, Balfour said that Haldane's natural moderation had been completely neutralised by it. The *Morning Post*—which had hitherto stood consistently for an election on Tariff Reform—agreed with *The Times* that Liberal policies on

empire, the Union, the armed forces, the church and the land
presented an inescapable challenge, and the *Daily Express* (which
had followed Chamberlain through thick and thin in his tariff
campaigns) now said (on 23 December) that 'Home Rule would
clearly be the chief issue of the election'.

The charge brought further and stronger Liberal disavowals.
Fresh from Christmas with Rosebery, Grey went out of his way
to say, at Berwick, that there could be no Home Rule bill without
a special mandate, and at the start of what his colleague Seely
described as one of the most remarkable electoral performances
of his time[20] Churchill promised, at Manchester, that a Liberal
government would do nothing 'likely to injure the integrity of
the United Kingdom or to lead however indirectly to separation'.
As a result of these strong words, Redmond informed Campbell-
Bannerman that, although he was not now very hopeful, he
nevertheless believed that if he, personally, maintained his
Stirling views the election would be 'got over satisfactorily'[21] and
Campbell-Bannerman was accordingly more circumspect when
he spoke next at Dunfermline on 29 December. Whilst carefully
avoiding any modification of his earlier statement, he emphasised
in answer to a question that 'any legislative body for Ireland that
. . . [he had] ever voted for was to be in subordination to the
Imperial Parliament'. Comparing Balfour's transports of alarm
on the Irish issue to the false fits of professional beggars, he
reiterated that fiscal policy was the outstanding issue and appealed
—again—for a clear verdict against Balfour's obscurities and
against Chamberlain's more intelligible but none the less
objectionable policy of what he called 'limited and obstructed
trade . . . false Imperial instinct . . . and . . . wealth in its most
objectionable form . . .'

In speeches (at the Queen's Hall and in Birmingham) on 29
and 30 December, Balfour and Chamberlain predictably replied
that, so far from obscuring the fiscal issue with Home Rule, they
regarded the election as being concerned with both issues. In a
speech that Hugh Cecil's opponents in Greenwich, and probably
also the Duke of Devonshire, took to indicate specific agreement

with Chamberlain,[22] Balfour described fiscal reform as the 'first great question' to which they would address themselves when they returned to power. Chamberlain reaffirmed his belief in the social and economic as well as the imperial benefits of Tariff Reform. And *The Times* commented that it hardly seemed probable that the constituencies would be content to accept a Liberal leadership by which arguments were 'never refuted but only ignored'. But both leaders concentrated on Home Rule as their major weapon of *attack* and went out of their way to switch the *emphasis* of choice away from that between two fiscal policies to that between Home Rule on the one side and fiscal reform on the other. 'It is now out of the question', commented Garvin in *Outlook* on 30 December, 'that Cobdenism can obtain a majority except by bribing Irish Protectionists with Home Rule' and *The Times* added, in its New Year's Day leader, that it required no particular gift of prophecy to perceive that the coming year would mark a very real parting of the ways.

> The fact is patent to all that a strong Liberal Government, on the one hand, committed to large and far reaching measures of domestic reform and unable to disentangle itself from the meshes of Home Rule, or on the other hand a strong Unionist Government committed to large measures of Tariff Reform, must either of them profoundly alter the course of politics in this country.

But many Unionist speakers, including the two leaders, muddied their own waters by seeking, at the same time, to turn Campbell-Bannerman's announcement on the ending of Chinese labour against the Liberals, as a secondary line of attack, by denouncing it as a mixture of hypocrisy and of economic and imperial folly. On 22 and 23 December (and subsequently) the Unionist press launched a concerted attack on the government's decision to allow the 1,800 December indentures, if it really believed the system to be wrong, and in some cases sought to re-awaken wartime feelings by suggesting that the prolongation of the war which had made the system necessary, had been due to the opposition to the then government of the Little Englanders. Speaking on New Year's Day at Leamington—

where by his own confession he had 'a stormy and rather hostile
. . . reception'[23]—Balfour devoted all his intellectual arts to a
justification of the indentures on economic grounds, and accused
the Liberals of the double hypocrisy of misusing the word
'slavery' and allowing the continuation of a system which they
stigmatised as evil. The *Birmingham Daily Post* simultaneously
described the colonial secretary's dispatch (embodying the
government's decision) as 'a mere electioneering handbill . . . [a]
sop to Exeter Hall', and even Chamberlain—clearly ill-at-ease
defending a policy for which, he said, he was not personally
responsible in the slightest degree—said at Birmingham, on 30
December, that if this dispatch did not mean annulment of
existing contracts it was merely a sop to Cerberus and that if it
was an attempt to govern from Westminster, the colonies would
be lost. But—as the *Manchester Guardian* commented on 1
January—Chamberlain knew, if Balfour did not, that Chinese
labour had 'completed the disillusionment of the country with
the Boer War', and the *Daily News* (simultaneously) said that
Balfour was not the first great Conservative leader to have come
to grief 'through a wrong estimate of the moral conscience of
the nation'. Elgin wrote to Campbell-Bannerman on 28 December that, given the qualification of the word 'forthwith', which
always seemed to him prudent, they could 'state with absolute
accuracy' that they did interfere immediately the law enabled
them to, and that 'for all else' the late government was responsible.[24] As Liberal after Liberal replied publicly on these lines,
it became apparent that the Unionists had made a serious tactical
mistake in seeking to challenge the government's decision in the
way they did.

To the Liberals, indeed, the issue was a great boon in the
answer that it provided to the Unionist anti-imperial cry. By the
New Year pigtailed and manacled Chinamen were already as
familiar on the streets and at Liberal meetings as big and little
loaves, and whilst Lloyd George conjured up the vision of coolies
imported on to the Welsh hills, the London-based Chinese Labour
National Protest Committee swamped the capital with leaflets

indicating that a Tory vote would mean Chinese immigration into London. When in Bermondsey Lord Percy and H. J. C. Cust attempted to link the trade depression with alien immigration and to claim that the Aliens Act was a great piece of legislation against unemployment they were met with cries of 'rot' and 'what about the Chinese?'; and when Percy proceeded—reasonably—to say that the Aliens Act had been designed to keep the Chinese *out*, a brawl ensued. Balfour, who spent most of January fighting a courageous but losing battle in North-West Manchester, met with similar scepticism. Because, he said, he understood that the electorate wanted to hear about it, he devoted several of his speeches almost entirely to it, but raised little interest by his comparisons with the (earlier) British Guiana ordinance (brought in by the Liberals) and much hostility to his claim that the South African compound system was compatible with freedom. His argument of economic necessity invariably provoked references to high dividends, or to the Australian mines, and the rhetorical question 'have we been guilty?' that he put to his audience on 8 January was met with cries of 'yes, you know you have'. Commenting, the *Liverpool Daily Post* said that he had been 'unmercifully but most intelligently heckled, not by Liberals as may have been supposed, but by members of his own party'.

Indeed, it soon became all too apparent in Lancashire that those Unionists in the area—e.g. at South Salford—who admitted Chinese labour to have been wrong, invariably had much quieter meetings than those who (e.g. at Salford West and at North-East Manchester) refused to do so; and that Liberals like Horridge (Balfour's opponent) were able to conduct almost rhetorical conversations with their audiences on the issue confident that they would agree. On 5 January he said it was idle to tell him that white men could not do the work in the Transvaal mines.

Voice: They do it in Western Australia . . .
Horridge: Just what I was going to say . . .
Voice: Yes, but the [Australian] mines pay only 10 per cent . . .
Voice: Is it true that numbered Kaffirs and coloured labourers would work in the mines before the war? . . .

Horridge: No . . .
Voice: I had two relatives in South Africa supplanted by
            Chinese . . .
Voice: I have a son in South Africa engaged in hunting
            [deserting] Chinese . . .

When Cresswell—a visiting South African opponent of the
indentures—spoke in Manchester on 11 January, and there listed
the economic arguments adduced for them, he only confirmed
to enthusiastic and agreeing audiences what Manchester and the
country had already decided to believe. By 7 January when the
Sunday Sun commented that 'no subject attracts more interest
at public meetings', the Unionists had begun to draw in their
earlier accusations to the extent of now charging the Liberals
with exploiting the issue in order to cover up the deficiencies of
their fiscal policy. But the damage had been done.

At the same time, moreover, the Tariff Reform bandwagon
obstinately refused to roll. On 1 January, finally despairing of
Balfour, Devonshire came down off the fence on which he had
for so long been sitting and published a manifesto (in the form
of a letter to the Unionist Free Trade candidate for Durham,
C. H. Elliot) in which he declared that whilst the declarations of
leading members of the Liberal Government made it 'in the
highest degree improbable' that they would introduce a Home
Rule bill, there was a real danger to Free Trade, and two days
later James—who thought Devonshire's advice 'statesmanlike . . .
but not sufficiently specific'[25]—wrote in even stronger terms to
Garnett, the chairman of the (very powerful) Manchester Free
Trade League.

> Throughout the country at every by-election, at every political
> meeting, the relative merits of 'Free Trade and Protection' have
> been most prominently, almost exclusively, discussed. But now
> these assiduous Tariff Reformers, so full of confident assertion,
> seek to change the face of the fight, put the cause for which they
> took the field in the background and demand a pitched battle
> on the question of Home Rule.

Speaking at Bristol on 1 January Walter Long promptly

denounced the Duke for having—as he put it—'thrown the cloak of his great influence and authority over the party who, under the guise of Free Trade, were really fighting the battle of Home Rule', and on 3 January *Punch* showed Balfour as an electoral duellist selecting the pistol of Home Rule in preference to the rapier of fiscal reform. When Campbell-Bannerman's election address appeared on 7 January the *Irish Times* went so far as to describe it as 'impudent [in its] silence on the issue which he had himself raised' and, as reports reached Balfour that 'some Tariff Reformers, leading TRers [*sic*], had lost their nerve and wanted to climb down',[26] more and more Unionist candidates gave the impression of seeking to play down the fiscal issue in favour of what they hoped might be more profitable election issues. Herbert Gladstone said at Leeds on 4 January that the scare was humbug designed to divert attention from the ex-government's record and fiscal policy, and, as Lord George Hamilton and other Unionist Free Traders pointed out, Chamberlain's open opposition to Cecil's Unionist Free Trade candidature at Greenwich showed how seriously he himself took it.

But perhaps the most significant thing for the campaign was the way in which increasing Unionist extremism forced the Irish leaders to be satisfied with something less than the degree of pledge from the Liberals that they ideally (and still in some cases publicly) desired. Bryce, in particular, kept Campbell-Bannerman fairly regularly informed of Redmond's views and in marked contrast to his report only two or three days earlier wrote to him on 31 December to say that Redmond was 'quite friendly'.

> He says that unless we do *something* to indicate a change of policy in Ireland, the public opinion of his supporters in Ireland and in the H. of C. will not allow him to give us the support *he desires* to give; and in particular that he will be placed in the greatest difficulties over the Education Bill which he desires us to oppose as little as we can.[27]

On 1 January (and thereafter) Birrell, the new Secretary of State for Education, consequently defined Liberal policy on the education issue in fair and moderate terms, at Bristol, as 'strict obser-

vance of the principles of religious equality and public control',
and with the Ulstermen forcing Wyndham into the humiliating
position of denying (e.g. at Dover on 3 January) his own, earlier
policies of reform in Ireland,[28] so Bryce—and others—were
increasingly able to promise land and administrative reforms,
short of Home Rule, which clearly distinguished Liberal policy
from Unionist, whilst at the same time presenting it as a continuation of it.

This situation did not, however, diminish nonconformist
commitment to reform, and, in marked contrast to Birrell's
personal moderation, nonconformist ministers threw themselves
into the campaign with unabated vigour. In Wales, indeed, nonconformist issues came close to dominating the campaign.
Shortly before he died, in October 1905, Spencer told Campbell-
Bannerman that he regarded the renewed commitment of the
Welsh parliamentary party and the Welsh National Liberal
Council to Welsh disestablishment and educational reform as 'a
false move . . . [which worked] against the general interests and
policy of the Liberal party . . .'[29] but with the Welsh party
acting—Balfour observed—'as a more or less independent party',[30]
Sir Alfred Thomas pushed the campaign ahead with vigour. At a
meeting of the Welsh National Liberal Council on 15 December,
he expressed his conviction, in the presence of two new ministers
(McKenna and Lloyd George, the Council's newly elected
President) that 'Welsh disestablishment [was] the question which
absorbed all others in Wales', and added three days later, in the
face of a continuing absence of official statements, that Welsh
disestablishment was 'undoubtedly in the position of a great
measure . . . scheduled for legislation in the coming Parliament.
I am perfectly satisfied', he went on, 'that the honour of the
Ministry . . . is bound up with the question.' He did not have
long to wait, for whilst Campbell-Bannerman significantly said
nothing in his speech at the Albert Hall on 21 December, Lloyd
George made a speech the same evening at Caernarvon which the
Liberation Society took to be 'a proxy for the Prime Minister',
and, practically speaking, 'a call for a mandate from the British

electorate'. He emphasised that the government was absolutely pledged to religious equality in all forms, including disestablishment in Wales, and went on in another speech, a few days later, to the Welsh Campaign Committee, to underline his view that this had been part of Liberal policy since 1888, and certainly remained so in 1906. Thomas said he felt sure that Lloyd George would keep the government to its word, and within days Churchill, McKenna, and Grey came out strongly in support of his cause. The specifically Welsh campaign thereafter marched forward side by side in Wales with the other major issues of Free Trade, Chinese labour, and social reform in a way that—once again—reinforced rather than obscured them.

With the Unionist campaign failing to spark, in Wales, as in the rest of Britain, Chamberlain made two powerful speeches in West Birmingham on 2 January not only to launch his own constituency campaign but also to try to reinvigorate the flagging Tariff Reform appeal. He was (this once) in fine form, and, lashing out at Cobden's assumptions concerning the mobility of labour and capital, said that his policy was declared to secure for Britain—as it had for Germany—a larger, freer market within which production costs could be reduced, and employment increased. Scorning the Liberals as conservative and the Socialists as impractical, he urged that the £30 million worth of foreign manufactures imported each year by the colonies might just as well be made in the United Kingdom, and, appealing to working-class patriotism, he declared that if the electors wished the traditions of their country to be continued, they must 'not think that they can be continued in the Kingdom alone'. Travelling the following day to Derby, in one of his henceforth rare visitations outside Birmingham, he taunted the Liberals (in so far as hecklers would allow him in a very noisy meeting) with having no real social policy, least of all on unemployment, and he drew a series of unfavourable comparisons—with figures which Burns (and others) contested[31]—between levels of unemployment and pauperism in 'perfect' England and protectionist Germany and claimed—before interruptions forced him to sit down—that

Germany and the United States were not only growing richer but were growing happier with 'a more general distribution of this world's goods'. Back at Saltley on 6 January he said that he had 'always supported the legitimate interests of Trade Unionism' and mocked the way in which, he said, some trade unionists were more interested in disestablishment and temperance than in vital labour reforms: as a popular ITC leaflet, prominent in Birmingham, read, 'Tariff Reform . . . means more work. Free Trade . . . more workhouse . . .'

These speeches were plausible and strong and they completely outshone Balfour's more modest statements in which—as Campbell-Bannerman said of his election address (at Liverpool, on 9 January)—'Fiscal Reform fluttered like a ghost'; but to an electorate recalling some of Chamberlain's earlier words on fiscal and social issues alike, they lacked credibility. Speaking at Fulham on 3 January, Lloyd George claimed that Chamberlain's notion of imperialism was to think of the 11 million outside the United Kingdom and to forget the 41 million inside—hence protection and Chinese labour; and the following day—in Manchester—Churchill sardonically but seriously recalled Chamberlain's own warning in 1897 that 'anything in the direction of an Imperial commercial league would weaken the Empire internally . . . excite the permanent hostility of the world, [and] . . . check the free imports of the food of the people'. The Unionist Free Traders—of whom Hugh and Robert Cecil and Richard Cavendish were the most frequently reported—quoted Salisbury's opposition to 'forcing upon even a minority what they have every right to resent,—namely that the cost of an Imperial Policy should be thrown on the necessary food of the people' and—whilst honest Balfourites and trimmers alike were increasingly regarded as protectionist *malgré eux*—the great majority of them, and (as has been seen) the majority of candidates, fought shy of wholehearted acceptance of Chamberlain's programme. So far, indeed, from the Tariff Reformers mounting a campaign which could in any way compensate for the diversionary tactics surrounding the Irish and Chinese labour issues, the Liberals were able to carry the fight into the very heart of Chamberlain country.

Contesting all the seats in the city for the first time since before the Home Rule split, they enjoyed the useful (and much publicised) support of Chamberlain's own brother Arthur, who was president of the Liberal association at nearby Aston Manor; and the energetic young Australian (Outhwaite) who opposed Chamberlain in the Eastern division wrote to Carrington, early in January, that if only they could get canvassers 'to conduct a raging tearing propaganda for the last few days', anything might happen.[32] Hudson similarly wrote to plead with Burns to go, if he could, to speak in North Worcestershire, a county division right up to the boundaries of Highbury where—to Chamberlain's 'indescribable anger'[33]—one of his former protégés, J. W. Wilson, was standing as a Liberal and Free Trade candidate. Furthermore, the campaigns of the two LRC candidates in Birmingham, Glasier (Bordesley) and Holmes (East Birmingham)—who were both supported by the local Liberal associations—added a new factor which worried the Unionist sufficiently, in Holmes's case at least, to send down additional party workers. These LRC candidates gave short shrift to Chamberlain's claims—e.g. at Saltley on 6 January—to have the real interests of the trade unions at heart. Speaking on 13 January, in Keir Hardie's presence, Holmes said that Chamberlain only believed in trade unions 'as the fox believes in rabbits' and, charging him—like Glasier and the Liberals—with faithlessness to his 1895 election promises, he promised in place of Tariff Reform, real social reform, cheap bread, and the abolition of the Chinese Labour Ordinance. Shortly before polling, Balfour expressed 'profound interest' in the new Labour development, which, he felt, might carry away seats in the Midlands, still undeclared, 'which under other circumstances would have been practically safe',[34] and with Austen Chamberlain laid up for most of the campaign with sciatica, his father was reduced to fighting hard to keep his hold even on the Midlands.

Meanwhile, the Liberal leaders—who were more vigorous and

H

prominent throughout—counter-attacked persuasively against
the Unionist charges of their imperial and foreign irresponsibility.
Speaking at Sheffield and Alnwick on 4 January, Asquith and
Grey both pledged their party to uphold the Entente Cordiale
but, recalling the lack of foresight and preparation which had
contributed to the humiliations of the Boer War, equally criticised
their opponents for spending so largely whilst still leaving the
army and navy weak. Haldane, following Churchill into the
financial bastions of the City, outlined his own ideas on the small,
highly mobile army which—he said—the country needed (and
which, he said, the Unionists had failed to create) and—greatly
expanding the 'perfectly platitudinous and truistical declaration'
that Campbell-Bannerman had authorised him to make 'in
favour of an efficient army'—he gave a specific assurance that
the Prime Minister laid 'such stress . . . on efficiency that, if
necessary he [was] prepared to find more men and money'.
Asquith wrote to Campbell-Bannerman that he 'read with a cold
shudder that fantastic sentence and inferred that by what Hegel
called the small "dialectical process" the Idea had received a
good deal of expansion since he had left [him]'. But—having no
doubt read *The Times*' comment (on 5 January) that the speech
would be 'received with great satisfaction by the country'—he
added quietly 'I don't think any harm has resulted'.[35] Speaking at
Sheffield on 5 January, Carson replied that Haldane and Asquith
were but the great imperial decoys for an anti-imperialist party,
and—'sailing very near the wind in going on a platform [once]
the writs [were] out'*—Lansdowne added, in Manchester, on
8 January, that nothing the Liberals said would carry conviction
unless Campbell-Bannerman cleared his mind of certain ideas
with regard to general disarmament and the formation of a
'League of Peace'. Arnold-Forster similarly warned his Croydon
electors, on 10 January, that 'if the Government tried their
blessed experiment of reducing armaments there were other
countries eager to deprive us of our Colonies', and many Union-

---

* Carrington in a letter to Burns; adding—it 'shows how frightened they
must be in Manchester . . .'[32]

ist speakers and papers expressed doubt as to the Liberal party's willingness to support Grey and Haldane, however proper their external and defence policies might be. However, even the *Daily Mail* expressed satisfaction over Grey's promises of continuity in foreign policy, which were also well received in France, and the *Daily Telegraph* regretfully recorded on 13 January, on the eve of polling, that 'one of the biggest Unionist achievements [had thus been] turned to Liberal account'.

The influence of the Liberal Leaguers over social policy was— for the Liberals—less helpful. Exercising a fairly tight control over *specific* expenditure pledges, Asquith even remonstrated, if gently, with Campbell-Bannerman over his not unimportant pledge, to the Scottish Miners Federation on 30 December, that repeal of the coal tax was 'one of the first matters with which they might hope to deal',[36] and he publicly emphasised the need to restore sound finance before reform could proceed. Haldane similarly told his constituents on 10 January (in words remarkably reminiscent of many more recent political statements) that it was a pity that the Liberals had not been able to take office in 1895 when 'there was a huge surplus of revenue and [when] any man who had taken up the situation at the time with earnestness could have given the country better education, and could have made better provision for the old age of the poor', and added that the Liberal government 'could not make great promises because they had . . . [first] to pay off a load of debt . . .' Yet promises were nevertheless made, on the hustings, as in the election addresses. Carrington followed up Campbell-Bannerman's Albert Hall speech by outlining a programme of land reform to the Co-operative Smallholdings Association, which included the introduction of compulsory purchase power for county councils and of a permanent Smallholdings Commission, to buy up land and act as a Court of Appeal; and, denying Chamberlain's charge that the Liberals were 'blind-eyed lotus-eating optimists', even Asquith himself promised steps (in his speech at Alnwick) to provide for better technical education. Speaking at Derby on 8 January—'a great and glorious meeting, where J.C. failed

through temper . . .'[37]—John Burns again maintained that
Chamberlain was confusing the *creation* of wealth with its
distribution, and said that a country which spent £100 million a
year on war and £170 million a year on drink could well afford
the money for unemployment relief and old age pensions; and
when e.g. the Bradford Liberals met a delegation of unemployed,
the following day, they made clear pledges to greater taxation of
the rich, land value taxation, and old age pensions for those over
65. The Liberals were equally clear in their platform promises
to reform the law on trade unionism. When, speaking at Stockton
on 9 January, Asquith promised legislation which 'would put
the law of combination upon a sound and reasonable footing . . .
[and] protect trade unions against the new hazards to which by
the decisions of the courts they had recently been exposed',
Chamberlain sought to cast doubt upon his words by recalling
Asquith's opposition to Whittaker's Bill in 1905; but—as Dilke
pointed out at Gloucester two days later—Asquith had then
attacked the Bill's deficiencies and not the Bill itself (which a
majority of Liberals had supported, including the new Lord
Chancellor, Loreburn), and his platform pledge stood in clear
contrast to Walter Long's statement, at Bristol on 11 January,
that the Taff Vale judgement had been 'in the interests of the
working men themselves'.[38]

Furthermore, whenever issues arose that presented a clash
between powerful and popular interests, the Liberals were
invariably readier and quicker to respond. In London, where
Conservative acquiescence (in the Lords in 1905) in the Westminster City Council's unpopular and unreasonable refusal (on
amenity grounds) to allow the connection, across the bridges, of
the northern and southern tramlines caused much resentment,
the large number of Liberal county councillor candidates called
municipal issues into play to bolster up their national appeal.
Whilst Hayes Fisher (the Unionist candidate at Poplar) said—in
Balfour's presence at the Queen's Hall—that Burns's appointment to the Local Government Board meant that such check as
there had been on LCC extravagance had gone, his Liberal

opponents urged government action—and won evident support—
on a programme of rate equalisation and land value taxation to
garner the social increment of the city's rapidly developing fringe
areas. In Hawick and Roxburgh, similarly, the Liberal candidates
cited Conservative acceptance of prosecutions for poaching on
the privately-owned Tweed Fisheries as one more example of
the way in which the Unionists made the land a pleasure ground
for the rich rather than the treasure house of the nation that
Campbell-Bannerman said, at the Albert Hall, it should be; and
many of their Scottish colleagues came out—more strongly than
the Unionists—against the continuing encroachment (despite
the Congested District Boards) of the deer forests on to agricultural land. As the analysis of party programmes (above) suggests,
local Liberal candidates were often, perhaps, in advance of the
leadership, but Campbell-Bannerman nevertheless returned to
what was perhaps the central issue of the election when in his
last tour before polling of some of the towns of north-west
England (including Chester, Liverpool, Wrexham, and Shrews-
bury) he reiterated, with reference to bad housing, rural de-
population, and old age that the election was about the alteration
of the whole 'tone, spirit, temper, and tendency' of public policy.

In an implied comparison with the empire-building of the
nineteenth century, the *Daily News* similarly said that the work
of the twentieth century was 'the rectification of social injustice',
and in its very first number on 15 January, the *Tribune* posed the
choice in striking phrases.

> The vast resources of modern industry make the material basis
> of [the good life] easier of attainment for a great population than
> it has ever been before. It is possible to utilise these resources as
> to enrich the mining magnate or the lord of finance beyond the
> dream of avarice, to enslave more backward races, to carry fire
> and sword against smaller peoples, to paint the map of the world
> red, to swell the national consciousness with the pride of victory
> and to purchase that victory at the price of a people impoverished,
> ill-housed, ill-fed [and] half-employed. It is possible again to
> direct them so that the ever increasing gains of industry may be
> diffused among a contented and peaceful people finding their

pride in their own political and individual freedom as showing to
the world an example of self-restrained power. For ten years we,
as a nation, have worked abroad upon the first part, now we enter
upon the other.

Thus, although LRC speakers continually sniped at Featherstone
Asquith, at Morley, who cautiously warned at Montrose (on 8
January) against footling with capital, at Haldane, and at Grey,
there was as close a coincidence of Liberal-Labour campaigns as
of policies; and the harsh words bandied in three-cornered
(Liberal, Unionist, LRC) contests were marginal compared with
LRC attacks on Chamberlain (who in turn described its candidates
as mere 'appendages of the Liberal Party')[39] and on Tariff
Reform. Chamberlain's unfulfilled promises of social reform—
especially of pensions—were frequently and bitterly recalled on
Labour and Liberal platforms. Walsh, the Labour candidate at
Ince, described his new proposals as the 'claptrap of the dis-
graced politician';[40] the Liberal MacNamara similarly said in
Camberwell that in considering Chamberlain's promises the
electors should also remember who made them; and *Punch*
observed, on 10 January, that candidates who lacked jokes had
only to refer to 'Joey' for effect; when Clynes's opponent in East
Manchester, Galloway, referred to the cheers there had been for
Chamberlain only six years earlier, hecklers replied—'we have
found him out . . . He has done us', and 'we won't have any more
[of him]'.[41]

In the great majority of constituencies covered by the electoral
agreement, indeed, Liberal and Labour candidates campaigned
in close co-operation. At Gorton, St Helens, and Ince, for
example, Hodge, Walsh, and Glover enjoyed the active support
not only of the local Liberal associations but also of the local
Free Trade leagues; and MacPherson at Preston also of the
(Free Trade) Cotton Spinners Association (significantly headed
by a former chairman of the local Conservative association). In
Sunderland Liberals campaigned for Summerbell (LRC), despite
some fear of vote-splitting with the Unionist Free Trader
Pemberton, and in Barrow where Cayzer (Unionist) described

himself as 'true Labour candidate',[42] Duncan (LRC) placed Free Trade and social reform together in the forefront of his programme and publicly and specifically said that Campbell-Bannerman's Albert Hall speech would give a 'good deal of satisfaction to workers in various parts of the country'.[43] In Newcastle, Hudson visited the Liberal Club—'a pretty strong step to be taken by a Labour candidate';[44] in Wolverhampton Labour and Liberal representatives met together to discuss election campaign tactics; at York—so the *Manchester Guardian* reported on 12 January—there was 'a distinct tendency to bring the two progressive and Free Trade partners together'; at Halifax there was similarly close co-operation; and at Eccles the Textile Workers Union elected to support the Liberal, Pollard, rather than the absent Tillett. *The Times* observed, on 9 January, that 'the pioneers of trade unionism have derived such material benefit from their co-operation with [the Liberals] that their loyalty may be expected to remain unshaken', and just before polling began *Reynolds News* commented of the north of England that with one or two disastrous exceptions 'Labour is co-operating with Liberalism in every constituency for the overthrow of the common enemy'.

IRELAND

Lying outside the mainstream of British politics, and as much divided in 1906 as in 1973 between Protestantism and Catholicism, between root-and-branch and moderate reformers, and between Ulster and the south, Ireland presented a predictably different picture. With the O'Brienites and—in the end—Healy, all unopposed, there were only three inter-Nationalist party contests in the south—at East Kerry, North Galway, and Newry in County Down—and, reflecting as much personal as political factors, these were of small importance. The election thus effectively marked the end of the divisions that had plagued the Nationalists for the previous two or three decades. In these circumstances the programme put forward by the United Irish League in its

manifesto dwelt almost entirely upon the failure of Salisbury's
1886 prophecy that twenty years of resolute government would
kill the demand for Home Rule, and the appeal Redmond made
in Belfast on 13 December was for 'a party of pledge-bound men
who would give their whole time to Parliamentary work' and
ensure the success of the Home Rule cause—which he described
as '. . . a matter of life and death . . . for the Irish race . . . a
question which comprehends religion and morality, the chance
of eternal salvation almost for her race . . .' Most of the interest,
therefore, focussed on the tactics to be adopted, *vis-à-vis* the
Irish vote in the rest of the United Kingdom; and Redmond
came under attack from time to time for what some regarded as
too close alliance with the Liberal party. But he expressed confidence that he was going back to Parliament under more favourable circumstances than any that had existed for the last ten years,
and his brother William said similarly at his adoption meeting
in East Clare, on 8 January, that in his opinion the prospects for
Home Rule had never been brighter.

In Ulster, however—then, as now, and certainly more than
previously—new political movements were struggling to assert
themselves between the upper and nether millstones of intran-
sigent Unionism and unrepentant Nationalism. On 7 December,
the *Manchester Guardian* described the Ulster election as 'the
most interesting for twenty years', and although *The Times* and
Tribune commented on the 'perplexing cross currents'[45] of the
region a commentator in the *Contemporary Review* significantly
entitled his January 1906 assessment 'Stands Ulster Where it
Did?' The first and least significant of the reformist movements
was T. H. Sloan's attempt to establish an order of Independent
Orangemen of Ireland based on an ending of Ulster Protestant
and southern Catholic hostility and on joint devotion to the
programme of reform outlined in the Megharamorne manifesto,
published on 14 July 1905.

> Castle government stands self-condemned. All parties are agreed
> as to the necessity of sweeping reforms in the government and
> administration of Ireland. Bureaucratic government, it is every-

where recognised, must be superseded by the government of the people. We do not hide from ourselves the dangers that have to be faced in the further extension of the democratic principle in the Government of Ireland, but the principle having already been conceded by the Unionists, under the Local Government Act, cannot now be seriously disputed and must now proceed to its logical conclusion.[46]

In his own constituency of South Belfast, Sloan accused the Unionists of accentuating divisions for the purpose of maintaining political control and expressed himself in favour of a form of devolutionary administrative reform. *The Times* accused him of playing straight into the hands of the second major group of reformers—the Russellites—who, despite their leader's strictures on 'English and Scottish Radicals who are not interested in Irish landlords',[47] campaigned in effect as Liberals, with official Liberal support.

The Russellite movement was much more broadly based than Sloan's. It was a movement of small Ulster farmers interested primarily in the activation of the 1903 Land Act through an amendment to give local authorities the power of compulsory purchase, and its leader, T. W. Russell, summed up its aims and its inspiration in a speech at Moy (County Tyrone) on 5 January, when he said that the Land Act was being throttled by the landlords. Whilst 180,000 small farmers had been settled, he said, there remained 220,000 who still awaited land to till and to live on and —rejoicing in the thought that it would bring the great landlords to their senses—he commended compulsory purchase in every case where a landlord refused to accept the matching investments in return for his land. All six of the Russellite candidates, and T. W. Russell's 'ewe-lamb',[48] the independent Unionist Major Glendenning, in North Antrim, made the same point on various occasions. On other aspects of policy the Russellites were almost wholly in line with the Liberals; they vigorously condemned the war policies of Chamberlain and his party and maintained that the policy of retaliation, if exercised against the United States, would 'instantly be met by a retaliatory policy and Irish linens

would probably be shut out by a prohibitive duty . . . thus
seriously imperilling our great Ulster industry . . .'[49] The
movement was also characterised by an element of nonconformity
and puritanism, redolent of nonconformist attitudes in England,
Scotland, and Wales. In James Wood's constituency of East
Down 'the eternal topic of the land [i.e. Home Rule] was less
discussed than the subject of bazaars in Protestant churches
which some austere persons held to be immoral, or the opening
of public houses on the Sabbath';[50] and in West Down, Beattie
had strong support from the Irish Temperance League against a
Unionist candidate with liquor interests.

All the Russellites were vigorously opposed by old-style
Unionists, but—interestingly—Russell himself and James Wood
were both against the creation of a Roman Catholic university
in Ulster, whereas Carson and some other Unionists were in
favour, and—to survive at all in the Ulster political situation—
they all came out openly against Home Rule in the Gladstonian
sense. On 18 December—perturbed by overt Nationalist support
for Wood at North Down—Russell assured the Election Committee of the Ulster Farmers Union that none of his supporters
were Home Rulers, and he went on to say that whilst he did not
for a minute believe that the new government would attempt to
introduce a Home Rule bill, he and his supporters would be
bound to oppose it if they did.[50] His group's views were in fact
very close to those of the Irish Reform Association which at a
special election meeting in Dublin on 30 December reaffirmed
its belief that the Liberals were not planning a Home Rule bill
and passed a resolution expressing the earnest hope that the
leaders of all parties would accept the compromise they offered
and so 'remove Irish politics from the arena of party politics';
but, whilst 'composed of prominent Irish patriots', the Irish
Reform Association probably controlled few votes.[51]

The third new thread in Ulster politics was simultaneously
being woven by Walker, the LRC candidate for South Belfast, in
association—to some extent—with Devlin, the Nationalist
candidate for West Belfast—who appealed to a particular, i.e.

working-class, section of the community, rather than primarily
to either of the religious groups in society. Walker so openly
described himself as a unionist that the LRC's National Executive
Committee investigated whether he was using the word in any
party sense, and he sought to make a straight appeal to Protestant
and Catholic working men alike on a programme of Free Trade
plus social reform. Devlin of course made his appeal primarily as
a Nationalist but, holding 'the cause of Ireland and the cause of
labour to be identical', he attacked the Unionists as the enemies
equally of both interests—as 'the landlord party, the capitalist
party, the enemies of labour, the enemies of reform, and the
enemies of Ireland'.[52] He roundly condemned Chamberlain, and
Tariff Reform (both of which were supported by his Unionist
opponent, Smiley), and challenged the Unionists to point to one
good thing done by the previous member for the division—
Arnold-Forster (prudently removed to Croydon)—over the previous ten or fifteen years. And at the same time he had sought to
attract Liberal voters away from their indolent and unimpressive
candidate, Hildred Carlile, by pledging himself to the standard
Liberal reforms—pensions, land value taxation, reform of trade
union law, and so on.

   And yet whilst these new movements cut across old divisions
and lent an unusual degree of interest to the 1906 campaign in
Ireland, and in particular in Ulster, the paramount issue still
remained the union, and the major political pressures, the maintenance or ending of it. Pressure was brought to bear on Sloan
to recant his adherence to the Megharamorne manifesto, and
whilst some of his supporters made their disapproval known by
campaigning against Smiley in West Belfast (another factor in
Devlin's favour), Sloan did in the end do so; and the Irish
Reform Association's policy of administrative devolution—its
attempt to build bridges—was discredited meanwhile by the
appearance of one of its leading members, Talbot Crosbie, on a
Nationalist platform. The incident was much exploited by the
Unionists—not least by Long on his visit to Dublin on 3 January
—and led to the resignation of one of the Association's Vice-

Presidents (Sir Arthur Coote) right in the middle of the campaign. Similarly, the statement made by one of Devlin's supporters that the capture of West Belfast would be worth over £25,000 to the Nationalists (by demonstrating that the whole of Ulster was not Unionist) was widely used both against Devlin himself and against Walker by implied association. Thus whilst new circumstances brought forth new and more flexible movements, they also stiffened the hard core of Orange resistance to the 'peculiar peril of the veiled attack',[53] and at an Orange demonstration on 2 January Lord Abercorn stressed that 'it mattered little . . . whether it was by the first Parliament or the next Parliament that they might meet their fate . . . the Government would begin by putting the enemy in every commanding position', and subsequent Orange and Unionist meetings continually emphasised this theme.

In his brief, terse election address, E. J. Sanderson, the Orange Grand Master and a leader of the Ulster Unionists, gave as the one and only reason why he was seeking re-election 'the reappearance of our old enemy, Home Rule, above the horizon, under the direct protection of the present Government',[54] and in West Belfast his college colleague Smiley well summed up the strong, simple themes of the Ulster Unionist campaign in the words—'Loyalty versus . . . Disloyalty' and 'Religious . . . versus . . . Sectarian Ascendency'.[55] Whilst in England, Scotland, and Wales many Unionist speakers and papers increasingly turned to the Home Rule issue as the campaign went on, and drew forth Liberal complaints that they were deliberately playing down the *fiscal* issue, Sanderson, by contrast, accused the Liberals, at Portadown on 9 January, of seeking to 'place . . . a tariff extinguisher over the Home Rule issue'.[56] Here, precisely expressed, was the difference between the campaign in Ireland and in the rest of the country.

Notes to Chapter 4 will be found on pp 218–21

5 PLATFORM AND PRESS: THE CONDUCT OF THE ELECTION

In some measure, the difference in the campaigns in Ireland and in the rest of the United Kingdom was also reflected in the general tempo and character of the election. Centred—as it was—so much more exclusively around one issue (and with the majority of the candidates unopposed) the campaign in Ireland—excepting only Belfast—was relatively uneventful; whereas in England, Scotland, and Wales, if less boisterous than the Khaki Election of 1900, it was anything but quiet. In an age that was neither served nor distracted by radio and television, nor yet—in general —rich enough to be able to view the poor performance and unkept promises of politicians with a degree of sceptical detachment, the election presented a combination of seriousness and gaiety, of hope and entertainment, rationality and riot, which those born to calmer, more comfortable, days might find it hard to comprehend.

The fact is that the period between the granting of a wider franchise and the rise of the popular media of information—the great dailies, the radio, the cinema, and television—was above all else 'the golden age of the Political Meeting',[1] and as Joyce Carey makes Chester Nimmo say in his novel, *Prisoner of Grace*, 'no one who has not fought in one of those "revolutionary" elections at the beginning of this century . . . can ever imagine the excitement of them or how one could be carried away by enthusiasm for one's own side and scorn and hatred for the other'.[2]

Around 9,000 people heard Campbell-Bannerman make his important speech at the Albert Hall on 21 December and John Burns's diary records the large numbers that came to hear him early in January:

2 January. Left for Nottingham at 12. A prodigious meeting in Victoria Hall. 6,000 more unable to get in.

5 January. Great meetings in Battersea . . . 3,000 outside hall, 3,000 in hall.[3]

Even the smaller meetings were well attended. A. E. W. Mason, novelist and Liberal candidate, wrote in one of his novels of the 'memory of little bare raftered school rooms, hot with gas light, crowded with white faces so . . . intolerably hopeful',[4] and at both the larger and the smaller meetings, parties sought to boost this morale of the faithful and to get their messages over with all the propaganda paraphernalia then at their command.

Halls were freely decorated with symbols—big and little loaves for the Liberals, empire maps and union jacks for the Unionists—and processions were enlivened with banners, mock Chinamen, and other political clowns. Party colours, not yet standardised into the conventional red and blue (the Unionists varied from blue in Barnet, to red in South Hertfordshire, to purple and yellow in Croydon, to purple and orange in Maidstone, and the Liberals from red most generally, to orange in Hull, and blue in Maidstone and Falmouth), were widely displayed on clothing, buildings and vehicles, and party songs were sung with gusto at many gatherings and processions. In addition to their determination to 'stamp, stamp, stamp, upon protection' the Liberals adapted popular tunes to the words of 'do ye Ken Bob Peel' and 'food and fire and drink it is, and it don't seem right to me, to make us pay a pennyworth of tax, for drinking a pennyworth of tea'; whilst the Unionists used the tune of 'John Brown's Body' to declare:

> There's a country to be conquered,
> There's a battle to be won . . .
> They may say Home Rule is sleeping

> In the still and silent tomb,
> But the body snatcher's working
> In its pestilential gloom.
> He must answer Redmond's bidding
> Or go headlong to his doom
> As we go marching on . . .[5]

Thanks, furthermore, to the advent of the motor car, candidates and party workers were more mobile than previously. Horse-drawn carriages were still widely used (and indeed in greater numbers than cars) and cars were still assumed to be something for rich people only; the 1905 Royal Commission on London traffic analysed London's traffic problems without once mentioning them. But there had been a great change since 1900 when, as the *Spectator* put it, cars were still 'stared at',[6] and although it is difficult to say with any precision how many cars were used, they clearly made a sizeable impact in both rural areas (through shortening distance) and in urban areas (by their concentration of numbers). With prices that even Richard Cavendish described as 'ruinous'[7] (and, no doubt, with limited availability) it is unlikely that many were hired, but the *Daily Telegraph* estimated that about a quarter and the *Daily Mail* about half of the total of 36,000 private vehicles were called into service.[8] Balfour, Chamberlain, Redmond, Campbell-Bannerman, Asquith and many other well-known figures were pictured in cars or in motoring attire, whilst others—notably the Socialist Lady Warwick, described by the *Observer* as 'a countess in sables' in a red Mercedes,[9] and some groups of nonconformist ministers—made some of the first motorised electioneering tours. *The Motor* proclaimed that 'the General Election of 1906 will mark an epoch in the life of motorism', and the *Evening Standard*—more disinterestedly—commented that even 'if there was nothing else to distinguish this election from its predecessors there would be the introduction of the motor car as an electioneering instrument'.[10]

Quite suddenly, indeed, the contemporary political analysts became aware of the car as an integral part of the voting machinery,[11] and the *Spectator* recorded on 20 January that it was 'one of the commonplaces of electioneering that a candidate is heavily handicapped if his resources are limited to horsedrawn vehicles'. A few candidates still retained a preference for the horse, either because as in St Pancras (the headquarters of the London cabbies) they considered their constituency decidedly 'ossy' or because, like Horatio Bottomley in Hackney, they were trying to create an effect of calculated eccentricity. However, the strenuous efforts made by area organisations to put candidates in touch with sympathetic car-owners and the numerous advertisements for cars which appeared in the papers indicated the premium increasingly being placed upon them. Richard Cavendish, for instance, wrote to his uncle (the Duke of Devonshire) that he was very much handicapped in North Lonsdale for want of a motor, since he was fighting an opponent who had one, and after Devonshire had answered his call, wrote that they were 'so grateful' for it, it was 'quite invaluable'.[12]

Many other candidates left similar reports, for example, Lawson (Liberal) and Randles (Unionist) in North Cumberland, where distances were considerable and weather inclement; Baring (Unionist) at Winchester where there were a number of out-voters to be brought in; and Jane (Independent) at Portsmouth, where a car made it possible to cover more of a numerically large constituency. They all found that the car made it possible not only for them to get to more meetings but also—through the new techniques of the motorised tour—to carry the meeting to more electors, sometimes through agents or assistants armed with phonograph records of their speeches, thus anticipating the modern loudspeaker tour. The result was that candidates were generally better able than ever before to familiarise themselves with their constituencies, while many more electors similarly were able to form firsthand impressions of their candidates.

The conduct of the election was also characterised by the proliferation of pressure groups, which, as the *Daily Mirror* aptly observed on 12 January, ranged in interest over every subject 'from motor smells to Jesuit colleges'. The motor lobby itself was much in evidence. The Highways Protection League, which (like the National Cyclists Union) was hostile to the motor car, issued a manifesto in favour of reducing the speed limit (from its then level of 20 miles per hour) and of making annoyance— loosely defined to include noise, dust, and smell—an offence. The cyclists more modestly, and reasonably enough, wanted vehicles to be placed under a legal requirement to carry lights. On the other side were several motorists' organisations which sought a reasonable rationalisation of the law on vehicles and in some cases the abolition of all 'artificial' speed limits. (The AA issued a circular urging owners not to lend cars to candidates who would not pledge themselves to this.)

Whilst *The Car* prophesied—and rightly—that transport issues would in the end eclipse even Home Rule as a centre of political controversy,[13] the militant WSPU demonstrated with some success, in a number of constituencies, that the same might be said of women's suffrage and of feminist interests. Its efforts were primarily concentrated on (and against) Winston Churchill in North-West Manchester, but Campbell-Bannerman and Asquith were among the other Liberal leaders to suffer its attentions. Its individual members were active in support of Keir Hardie and several Labour candidates and it was rarely far from the news headlines throughout the campaign weeks.

Apart from the para-party organisations that sprang up around the tariff issue—particularly the Free Trade Union and the Tariff Reform League—most of the other pressure groups were much more limited in the human and financial resources which they could bring to bear, despite their modern-sounding names. The National Service League lobbied widely for compulsory military training and the Peace Society for general disarmament; the Liberty and Property Defence League asked for greater justice for property owners; the Association of Trade Protection Societies urged—*inter alia*—the adoption of the metric system; and the Marriage Law Reform Association wanted nothing more dramatic than change in the law to permit marriage to a deceased wife's sister. The Tax Payers Protection League urged taxpayers

I

to enrol as missionaries in the great Free Trade campaign against
the 'quackery and deceit' of the tariff-mongers, and Sir Gilbert
Parker established the Imperial South Africa Association specifically to refute Liberal 'misrepresentations' about the war and
about Chinese labour.

Many more pressure groups were no more than historical
curiosities. The Compulsory Character League, for example,
lobbied for compulsory employers' testimonials and—the oddest
of them all—the Anti-Vaccination League for an end (*per contram*)
of all compulsory vaccination. In Sleaford, as Snowden has
recalled, the Liberal Arnold Lupton fought almost entirely as an
anti-vaccinationist.

> For some time before the election he and his wife nursed the
> constituency. They worked it on bicyles. They would go out to a
> village, spend the afternoon in house-to-house canvassing horrify-
> ing the women with tales about the terrible consequences of
> vaccination; and then in the evening go round the villages with a
> big bell . . . collecting an audience which he and his wife addressed
> on the green.[14]

Perhaps, in the round, these weirder groups exercised some
influence on results: one or two candidates even attributed their
defeat to the persistence of 'faddists' of every kind in demanding
favourable replies to their strings of questions. But, as part of the
communication of society, their major contribution was perhaps
to add colour and character to the election and heighten the
sense of expectancy and change. As Spender later wrote, all these
factors combined to create a public atmosphere of 'thrills and
pains, exultations and depressions' which later generations would
know no more.[15]

ELECTORAL VIOLENCE AND CORRUPTION

Inevitably, perhaps, this excited, carnival-type atmosphere led—
on occasions—to violent and unruly scenes of which Balfour's
experiences at Leamington and Chamberlain's at Derby were
only the most publicised. Sir Robert Purvis (Unionist, Peter-

borough) was rolled in the mud at one of his meetings and had to be rescued by the police, and many candidates found themselves on the receiving end of missiles of various kinds—from bricks and bottles (Pollock, Unionist, Spalding), to a symbolic 'red herring' thrown at Arthur Balfour (in Manchester), and to flour bags at Silas Hocking (Liberal, mid-Buckinghamshire—to whom 'arguments with fisticuffs were all in a day's work').[16] One of Wyndham's meetings at Dover ended in a brawl with chairs flung about, and rival party meetings at Wellingborough on 10 and 11 January were broken up by gangs of partisans. In Birmingham, Tariff Reformers debannered and ducked many Free Traders taking part in a big demonstration in the city centre on 13 January, and in Oswestry organised gangs of colliers and farm labourers (a significant combination) assaulted the Unionist Committee rooms and overturned the Unionist candidate's car. The *Observer* commented wryly on 14 January that 'personal invective, vilification and vituperation are mingled as if the whole were an American game of football'; adding one week later that it had 'on the whole been a peculiarly ill-natured election'; and the *News of the World* aired a common opinion when it said (on 7 January) that 'disorderly meetings, if not the order of the day, were at any rate very frequent'.

When all but the last few votes had been counted, *Punch* published couplets laying the blame specifically on popular mass involvement.

> His hooligans are out with stones and dirt
> And in the darkness you must hide your head,
> Nor look to chivalry to salve the heart
> For Demos reigns instead.[17]

Many of the Unionists, who suffered most, wondered pessimistically whether 'argument by clap-trap' represented any advance at all on 'argument by broken pate' or whether the Derby rowdyism was any advance on Eatanswill violence. After Derby *The Times* hoped for the sake of England's reputation throughout the world as 'a nation bred above all others in the practice and habit of self government', that the discreditable scene which had taken place would not be repeated,[18] and it went on—later—to cast doubt (along with other journals) on the very practice of electioneering.

> The personal and independent solicitation of voters is in our judgment neither necessary, expedient, nor really effective. We hope the day may not be far distant when candidates will abolish it by mutual consent. When that day comes we shall all wonder why we tolerated it so long. Electioneering is no very attractive art at the best. Let us at least purge it of some of its less attractive methods.[19]

Some Liberals found a certain *schadenfreude*, in this situation, in recalling Balfour's comment in the House of Commons in 1900 that 'if Liberal principles were so unpopular as to create disorder they should not be expressed' and voiced some pleasure that Chamberlain and Balfour had been served up with their own sauce.[20] However—as one Conservative journalist admitted—his party's real trouble in 1906 lay not so much in the violence, as in the party's sheer lack of platform talent.

> Balfour would not be what he is, and . . . we would not have him either for his sake, ours, or his country's, if he had the demagogic arts which stir great public meetings to passion and the enthusiasm that wins elections. No one could say of him *numium gaudens popularibus auris*. For a Prime Minister it is the most dangerous of gifts (e.g. Gladstone). None of our former Prime Ministers had it, or having the gift, used it. Russell, Palmerston, Derby, Disraeli, and Salisbury never stumped the country. Rosebery was a little given that way but not very much; they all had understudies that did the platform work for them. Where were ours? They simply did not exist. What had we to set against Asquith, Grey, Haldane, Lloyd George, or even Winston [Churchill]? And Bonar Law, the best of our platform speakers, was kept in Glasgow, as it turned out to no good purpose . . . Ministers could not with safety stir beyond their own borderline. Stanley . . . was courageous enough. Anson, on a platform, would have been ridiculous. Our other occupants of 'safe seats' were equally ill-equipped for the electioneering campaign. I hate demagogues and tub-oratory and all the rest of it, but I recognise that we must have 'samples' of it at an election time, and we had none at all. . . . We may laugh at our tub-thumpers, such as the Ashmead-Bartletts of the past,

at our impudent gamins, such as was Randolph, and such as is Winston Churchill, but we cannot do without them.[21]

Whilst, indeed, the Unionists were at a disadvantage, and consequently complained, the conduct of the election—by parties and by the electorate—represented an improvement, by and large, over 1900 and the late Victorian years.

There was, furthermore, a marked decline in the element of petty corruption. The law on corrupt practices and election expenses (enshrined in the Corrupt Practices Act of 1883, as amended on agency in 1895) still left a number of loopholes— on the use of public buildings, carriages and cars that could be used, and on treating ('the provision directly or indirectly, before during or after the election of the expense of meat drink entertainment or provision to persuade voters to give or withhold their vote'), and these loopholes all parties sought to turn to advantage. The royal commission that investigated the Worcester election reported the existence of a class of voters 'consisting mainly of the needy and loafing class but including a considerable number of working men in regular employment who are prepared to sell their votes for drink or money';[22] and, commenting on the election petition presented at Yarmouth, Mr Justice Grantham himself said that the line between nursing and treating was extremely difficult to draw.[23] For a number of candidates this combination of need, greed, and the possibility of winning votes proved irresistible.

At South Hackney, for instance, Bottomley proved himself to be a past master in the art of treating short of bribery—which the *Edinburgh Peoples Journal* believed to be rife—and at Hoxton, Claude Hay found it possible, and no doubt politic, to distribute between £200 and £300 worth of Christmas presents in the form of 3s 6d parcels of food, and of coal (thus influencing—perhaps— 1,700 electors). At Nottingham Lord Henry Bentinck invited 1,500 guests (out of an electorate of 9,000) to a dinner; at Hastings, so Shuttleworth reported to Campbell-Bannerman on 14 January, 'Du Cros was scattering money and promises freely';[24] and at Taunton, Ponsonby complained bitterly of his opponents' 'free beer and flagrant bribery'.[25] At Yarmouth, the ex-secretary of a Conservative ward association admitted that he had given money to sixteen or seventeen voters—not, he said, to bribe them, but to enable them to buy a 'little bit of bread and cheese'—and was convicted of improperly using a horse and trap of the local Conservative committee to take voters to the poll.[26]

However, only six petitions against corrupt practices were actually filed (at Appleby, Attercliffe, Bodmin, Maidstone, Worcester and Yarmouth), only five heard (the petition against the Liberal at Appleby was withdrawn, and therefore never proceeded to a hearing), and only two (Worcester and Bodmin) allowed.[27] This represented a considerable decline compared with previous years. At Bodmin, where the Liberal agent was found guilty of 'the corrupt practice of treating', the judge went out of his way to comment that there was 'no reason to believe that corrupt or illegal practices have *extensively* prevailed'.[28] Even the licensed victuallers, who continued to push out anti-Liberal propaganda almost as a matter of form, showed that they had learned from their loss of working-class custom in 1900 (when it was often transferred from pubs to clubs) and were in general far more moderate in their behaviour than in previous elections. The kind of claim circulated by Unionist candidates (in Hull for example) that 'EVERY VOTE GIVEN TO the Liberal candidate will mean that BEER will COST . . . a halfpenny a pint MORE'[29] probably had little effect. Bribery, in 1906, was on the wane, and it is likely that as many votes were lost by it as won; and few enough in either direction.

INFORMATION AND THE PRESS

Furthermore, if less bribeable or at least less bribed than in previous elections, electors were also on balance better educated. Universal education may still have been—was—somewhat rudimentary; but the emergence of an electorate educated under the post-1870 system was already ten years or more old; and if the reduction in the proportion of illiterate votes is any guide, there had been a substantial improvement over 1886 (as the first election on the wider franchise).

Table 15

PERCENTAGE OF ILLITERATE VOTERS, 1880, 1886 AND 1906[30]

	1880	*1886*	*1906*
England and Wales	1·0	1·6	0·4
Scotland	0·07	1·3	0·3
Ireland	2·1	18·7	9·2
Total	1·0	2·6	0·6

Perhaps more important than this, however, was the evolution of a mass circulation press, able—without as yet destroying the provincial papers—to bring news and views to the breakfast table, or place of work, of millions of ordinary people. Between 1887 and 1903 six halfpenny papers were founded (of which the most famous was the *Daily Mail*) and these were joined in 1904 by two more—the Liberal *Daily News* and *Daily Chronicle*— which reduced their price from one penny to a halfpenny. The new liner trains, introduced in the 1890s, ensured that these could be distributed daily to every city and village in the land.

In the eyes of many, the results were disastrous. As the battle for circulation began so the conservative Victorian layouts were discarded in favour of bold headlines and brief paragraphs, editorials were shortened and sharpened, and, as George Gissing graphically complained in his satirical novel, *New Grub Street*, literature was reduced to a trade. Writing in *Clarion* in November and December 1905, Julia Dawson analysed the contents of the *Daily Mail* and concluded that newspapers were 'the very mischief', since 'but for them men would think and come to conclusions', and Keir Hardie complained that, so far from seeking out the truth, the 'new' journalists were hired to plead *ex parte* cases like advocates in a court. 'The daily press', he said 'is becoming more and more the representative of certain great wealthy interests . . . [by whom] newspapers are bought and sold like so much merchandise';[31] and when Harmsworth's peerage was announced in December 1905 the *Daily News* commented that it marked an unfortunate epoch in the history of both peerage and press.[32]

And yet although the provincial press increasingly became a scissors and paste epitome of the London papers and although a trend towards the commercial and sensational exploitation of the mass of lower middle and working-class readership had begun, the conventions of the taxed press—when space was at a premium—remained in evidence in Edwardian papers. In 1906 the *Daily Mail* still contained one solid page of political news, and whilst news and trivia appeared together they were not mixed up together to anything like the extent to which later generations have had to become accustomed, except in the *Daily Mirror* and the *Daily Express*. If triviality and sensationalism were increasingly used to sell newspapers, they were also still used to sell news. Furthermore, the advent of a popular press had not yet begun to drive the more serious (local as well as London) papers out of business (though the fact that it took over

Table 16

NUMBER OF DAILY PAPERS, 1850, 1880, 1906 AND 1972[33]

Morning dailies	*1851*	*1880*	*1906*	*1972*
London	7	13	26	10
England and Wales	–	59	66	14
Scotland	–	13	10	5
Ireland	–	13	7	6
Total	7	98	109	35
Evening dailies	*1850*	*1880*	*1906*	*1972*
London	5	5	8	2
England and Wales	–	41	96	72
Scotland	–	7	10	7
Ireland	–	4	8	4
Total	5	57	122	85
GRAND TOTAL	12	155	228	120

Source: *The Newspaper Press Directory*, 1850, 1880, 1906 and 1972. The figures for 1851 refer to the period before the repeal of the stamp duties; those given for Ireland for 1972 include both Northern Ireland and the Republic of Ireland; only general newspapers have throughout been included.

thirty times as much capital to found the *Tribune* in January 1906 as it had to found the *Daily Mail* in 1894 was an ominous sign);[34] and it was still possible for papers like *The Times*, the *Morning Post*, and the *Daily Telegraph* (albeit precariously) to survive on circulations of around 50,000. Indeed, the total number of daily papers went on growing right up to 1906.

THE INFLUENCE OF THE PRESS

On the face of it, the influence of the press was thrown predominantly on the Unionist side, before and during the election. Until the appearance of the *Tribune* on 15 January 1906—at the very beginning of polling—every one of the serious penny newspapers gave general support to the Unionist party both in editorial policy and in the selection of news; and, of the 'popular' halfpenny press, the *Daily Mail* alone had a greater circulation—numerically and geographically—than the three leading Liberal papers—the *Daily News*, the *Daily Chronicle*, and the *Morning Leader*—which had only small circulations outside the metropolis and the southern part of England.

The imbalance was similar among the national evening papers. In the *Westminster Gazette*—which Curzon described as 'in the lead of thoughtful Liberal opinion'[35]—the Liberals probably had the best of the bunch. It inclined to the Liberal Imperialist side but, with Spender as editor and Carruthers Gould as cartoonist, it was a paper of character and some force. Arrayed against it, however—among the evening penny papers—were the *Pall Mall Gazette*, the *Globe*, and the *Evening Standard and St James's Gazette*; and among the halfpenny evening papers, the *Evening News* outsold the *Star* and the *Echo* combined. Following the defection of *Lloyds*, only *Reynolds News* and the *Sunday Sun* remained openly and actively Liberal among those Sunday papers which showed any interest at all in politics.

The only section of the London press, indeed, where the Liberals enjoyed equal or perhaps even greater support was among the weekly magazines: in the *Speaker*, the *Independent*

Table 17

CIRCULATION OF LONDON DAILIES, 1906

Unionist papers	Price	Circulation
The Times	3d	30,000
Morning Post	1d	60,000
Standard	1d	80,000
Daily Telegraph	1d	285,000
Daily Graphic	½d	100,000
Daily Express	½d	300,000
Daily Mail	½d	750,000
Total Unionist		1,605,000
Liberal papers		
Tribune	1d	[new]
Morning Leader	½d	150,000
Daily News	½d	200,000
Daily Chronicle	½d	200,000
Total Liberal		550,000
Independent		
Daily Mirror	½d	350,000

Review, and—to a lesser extent—the *Fortnightly Review* and *Nineteenth Century* they had a quartet of thoughtful and progressive journals served by a number of journalists of high repute —Massingham and Masterman, Herbert Paul, McNamara, Samuel, Scott Palmer, and others; and they were wholly supported by the two economic journals—*The Economist* and the *Economic Journal*—and by St Loe Strachey's *Spectator* which the *National Review* described as 'holding a weekly brief for the Liberals'.[36] On the other side were the *Empire Review*—notable for Kinloch Cooke's articles on Chinese labour—Leo Maxse's *National Review*, the *Saturday Review* and Garvin's small but militant magazine *Outlook*. The only papers to put a Labour point of view were the weeklies—*Labour Leader*, *Clarion*, the Social Democratic *Justice*, and a handful of locals like the *Croydon Citizen*, the *Barrow Citizen*, and the *Woolwich Pioneer*—all of which were propaganda sheets rather than newspapers and often contained much the same material as each other.

During the course of the campaign, Liberal and Labour commentators more than once gave vent to their frustration at this situation. Speaking at Culross on 12 January, Campbell-Bannerman deplored the fact that—as he put it—'the newspaper press has largely. . . got into the hands of combinations of capitalists . . . and that [in consequence] they could not have their former confidence in individual newspapers giving personally disinterested advice'.[37] A few days later, in Northamptonshire, Birrell complained that, increasingly controlled by 'a narrow clique of persons', the press 'was becoming powerless . . . to play the great part a free press might be expected to play with educated people'.[38] 'The great thing we suffer from', wrote Campbell-Bannerman to Herbert Gladstone in the planning days of the *Tribune*, 'is that we have no organ in the press and the public never hears the truth'.[39] Following an animated debate in 1904, the TUC similarly instructed its parliamentary committee to see what steps could be taken to form a co-operative press to speak for unions' interests, and at its 1905 annual conference the LRC appointed a committee to sound out the trade unions for the money for the establishment of a daily paper—if possible—before the general election.

However, although the Unionists enjoyed infinitely stronger support in the London press than their opponents, from 1886 to 1903, there were signs from 1902 and 1903 onwards of a tilting of the balance back towards the Liberals—if not to Labour. Whilst the circulation of the *Daily Mail* declined from its wartime peak of 1,000,000 to about 750,000 in 1906, the expression of Liberal (or at least anti-Unionist) opinion was significantly enhanced by the popularisation of the *Daily Chronicle* and *Daily News*, after 1904, as halfpenny (instead of penny) papers, and—even more, perhaps—by the rapid growth of the new, independent, but radically minded *Daily Mirror*, which finally came out strongly against any renewal of the Conservative and Unionist mandate. Furthermore, whilst so many of the major provincial papers were Unionist—e.g. the *Birmingham Daily Post*, the *Yorkshire Post* (in Leeds) and the *Scotsman* (in Edinburgh)—that W. J. Fisher (an ex-editor of the *Daily Chronicle*) complained in *Nineteenth Century* in July 1904 that there was 'no representative Liberal daily between Bradford and Glasgow', the balance between Liberal and Conservative papers in the provinces was very much more even than it was in London. With the fiscal issue, indeed, there was a steady trickle of provincial papers (like the *Liverpool Daily Post* and the *Aberdeen Free Press*)—largely lost as a result of the Home Rule issue—back to support of the Liberal party, and this affected not only many of the so-called independents but also a few important papers like the *Glasgow Herald*, which—although remaining nominally Unionist—came out as strongly against Tariff Reform (and incidentally in favour of land and tax reforms) as any avowedly Liberal journal.

Just, therefore, as the Liberals undoubtedly suffered in the 1890s from the coincidence with the rise of the new journalism of the unpopularity of their policies, so—equally—they bene- fitted, in the press as on the platform, in the years immediately before the election, from increasingly catholic support on the major issues on which their victory was won. As one contempor- ary Unionist wrote:

> From all Lancashire and from most parts of the country outside the environs of Leeds and Birmingham came the unanimous cry that thousands upon thousands of working men's votes [had been] lost for the lack of a halfpenny evening paper. In Manches- ter ... the disappearance of the *Evening Mail* was most severely felt. And as it was in Manchester, so it was in different degrees elsewhere.[40]

Even more important, perhaps, than a relative revival of the Liberal press in London, and a relative Conservative and Unionist weakness in the provincial presses, was the publicity which Conservative and Unionist papers consistently gave to the party's divisions over fiscal policy. Only the *Daily Telegraph*— described by Leo Maxse as 'long the mouthpiece of the Balfour clique'[41]—and *The Times*—after some equivocation between 1903 and 1905—finally came out in clear support of Balfour. Owned by Pearson (of the *Daily Express*) and edited by Gwynne (one of Leo Maxse's compatriots) the *Standard* was consistently Tariff Reform, the *Morning Post*—edited by Fabian Ware—was 'in some respects more "Joeite" than Joe [Chamberlain] himself',[42] and in one degree or another the Conservative evening and popular daily papers were all anti-Balfourite and in favour of reformist fiscal policies (whether Tariff Reform—or, as with the *Globe*—outright Protectionist). Following the 1905 NUCA conference, Wyndham consequently complained to Balfour, on 19 November—in words strangely reminiscent of Campbell-Bannerman's and Birrell's—that they were 'suffering from the "press" not speeches'. 'The ordinary man reads the leading articles in a newspaper', he continued, and 'these tell him that retaliation means nothing ... boycott your policy ... and undermine your authority ... What we need is newspaper support.'[43] In the event, what the *Standard* called the 'press created crisis'[44] of 22–24 November 1905 ensued (see pp 32–3), almost before the ink was dry on Wyndham's letter, and although Unionist papers thereafter sought, like the Unionist party leaders, to paper over the cracks, they signally failed to present any common platform save opposition to the new Liberal government. With the *Standard* and the *Morning Post*, the 'popular' *Daily Mail* and *Daily Express* continued—fairly clearly—to support Tariff Reform (whilst devoting 75 per cent of their editorials between 1 and 15 January to Home Rule and Chinese labour); but *The Times* and, up to a point, the *Pall Mall Gazette*, advocated a more cautious approach; and the Free Trade Unionist papers—like the *Glasgow Herald*—equated all fiscal reform with protection and consequently with a threat to living standards. As the *Observer*—a Unionist paper—said, 'Protection has risen for the rich and socialism [meaning social reform rather than social ownership] for the poor.'[45]

The Liberal press, for its part, was not uniformly helpful to the leadership. Its full-news treatment of Rosebery's Bodmin speech led Campbell-Bannerman to complain to Grey on 1 December that '. . . as usual the press, not purely of malice, but as a mere matter of paper-selling has fanned the flames',[46] and Morley expressed disgust at the attempts of the *Westminster Gazette* and *Spectator* to influence Campbell-Bannerman against acceptance of office. 'When the election comes', he wrote to Campbell-Bannerman on 25 November, 'Liberal Leaguers, Whigs, Roseberyites . . . [want to] be able to trot out Lord R[osebery] or Asquith, or Grey as the man they would choose and respect. If you read the first article in the *Spectator* today you will see more than one sentence in which this ugly cat comes out of the bag.'[47] Furthermore, the Labour papers throughout sought to emphasise that—as the *Labour Leader* said—the election issue was 'not peace, retrenchment, and reform; not protection and free trade . . . [but] the right to work', and scorned the last-minute appeals for Liberal-Labour unity in the *Daily Chronicle*—ridiculed by *Clarion* as 'the Daily Crocodile'[48]—and the *Daily News*.

But the message that came over clearly from the combination of independent, Liberal, and Labour papers was nevertheless first and foremost one of condemnation of the Unionist government and its policies—past and proposed—just as the divided state of the Unionist party came over more clearly than anything else in the Conservative and Unionist press. Muller's judgement, as a confirmed supporter of Balfour, was no doubt *ex parte*, but his comment nevertheless makes interesting reading.

When the fiscal problem was raised our [former] strength [in the press] was turned into weakness. There are only two daily papers in London which . . . can *afford* to take an independent line in politics—the *Times* and the *Telegraph*—the *Times* because it has a sort of recognised privilege of upholding the government of the day whatever its politics . . . the *Daily Telegraph* because its popularity and circulation depend much more on the variety and completeness of its general contents than upon its political articles . . . The *Telegraph* was loyal to the Chief [ie Balfour] throughout, the *Times* wobbled a good deal . . . until the elections were in sight was definitely Chamberlainite . . . rallied splendidly at the last . . . The policy of the others was dictated largely by business conditions of rivalry; while the *Standard* and *Express* were expressly secured as organs of the Tariff Reform League. The

Pall Mall Gazette and *Evening Standard* were Chamberlainite, and the *Globe* (Orange and sheer jingoism) was anti-government. The *Pall Mall Gazette* (for reasons not known to me) always 'crabbed' the Chief. *The result was that while no daily paper rallied to the official opposition the strength of the Chamberlainite faction in the London press exaggerated and magnified beyond all reason the importance and depth of our internal divisions.* And except in a few cases—not more than two or three—the London press exercised a great, perhaps unconscious, influence over journalism in the provinces. The weekly papers count for very little in the development of popular opinion; but they do influence the smaller country houses, vicarages, etc. where the leaders of local opinion should be found, and the ratting of the *Spectator* . . ., the rise of the avowedly Chamberlainite *Outlook*, and the Laodicean attitude of the not very influential *Saturday Review* all helped to deepen the impression that we were a hopelessly divided party. All these things tended to damp party ardour at the very moment it required fanning and stoking.[49]

The plain fact was that whatever imbalance in numbers there was in the press, in 1906, was largely offset by the publicity that was given in Unionist, as in Liberal, papers to Unionist party divisions and to unpopular policies. As numerous commentators from Brougham to Ostogorski, to Milne and Mackenzie, have observed,[50] newspapers do not so much influence public opinion as on the one hand indicate, and on the other hand 'expose' readers to, their particular views. But, if they exposed them to views, they also exposed them to news; and in a period when newspapers succeeded in combining greater partisanship with less selectivity of political news than in more recent times, it is very probable that, even leaving their divisions on one side, Conservative and Unionist papers influenced voters as much against their party, in 1906, as for it. The *Observer* commented on 28 January that the belief that newspapers had any particular effect in moulding public opinions in the direction of their editorial policy had 'suffered considerable damage' in the election, and when they were home and dry the Liberals rejoiced that their fears about the adverse influence of the press had been exaggerated: as one of them wrote to Bryce on 30 January 1906, it was 'a magnificent thing' to see the common sense of most when a vital question was 'brought fully before the country'.[51]

Conclusion

Thus whilst the election contained an element of nineteenth-century carnival, it also gave signs of a growing political sophistication. There was a decrease in both violence and corruption, and through well-packed meetings and widely distributed propaganda (both assisted by the appearance of the car) a more educated electorate was presented with its choices in a clear, convincing way. Of course—as Lowell observed (in 1908)—hecklers' questions were not always 'propounded by honest seekers after truth',[52] but the conservatively-inclined *Scotsman* pointed out that, although repetitive, hecklers often dealt with 'the minutest details of fact and the abstrusest of principles'.[53] The extraordinary feature of the often noisy questioning of Chamberlain, commented the *Daily News*, was the hecklers' real intelligence, and the evident respect with which they were treated by the rest of the audience,[54] and it is clear that, with and through the theatricalities and noise, the electorate was trying—arguably more than before—to confront its would-be representatives with its own queries. As a Kentish newspaper—by no means Liberal— observed, in an age that was 'better educated . . . more critical, [and] far less credulous . . . old fashioned oratory of the courtly magnificent school has given way to urgent insistence upon plainer speaking and less of it'.[55] Demos was a child no more.

Notes to Chapter 5 will be found on pp 221–3

6 THE POLL AND THE RESULTS

As the first day of polling approached on 13 January 1906, there
was little doubt in anyone's mind that the Liberals would win.
As early as October 1904, Henry Lucy wrote that there was a
'rare consensus of opinion' that the next general election would
place a Liberal ministry in power,[1] and the 1905 edition of the
Annual Register recorded that this was 'on all hands' felt to be
'certain'; in October 1905 Balfour confessed to Devonshire that
'every school among the political prophets seems to agree that
the Unionists are to be defeated';[2] and, as the *Manchester
Guardian* observed (on 16 October 1905), even ministers were
falling into the habit of talking as if a Liberal victory was inevitable. In November 1905—with the *Daily Mail* speculating
on a Liberal majority of 136—the *National Review* foresaw a
Unionist débacle, and Hicks-Beach wrote to his son on 21 December to say that he thought the Unionists would suffer 'the very
greatest smash . . . that any party has had in my time'.[3] On the
Liberal side, expectation grew steadily from a majority of 1892
proportions to one of 1885 proportions. Herbert Gladstone, who
in February 1904 had anticipated not more than 100 gains, was
hoping for about 130 fifteen months later, and Henry Lucy
produced a more scientific survey late in 1904 that substantially
supported this.

> . . . by-elections are not to be accepted as infallibly indicating the
> drift of public opinion, but it is a simple mathematical proposition
> that if the proportion of Unionist disasters at the poll, indicated

K   145

throughout the last twenty months, is spread throughout a General
Election, Liberal candidates will be returned by a majority
recalling the triumphs of 1880 and 1885.[4]

Surprisingly, sophisticated statistical analyses that appeared
in the press shortly before polling began, rammed the point
home. Writing in the December *Review of Reviews*, Stead
demonstrated that in sixty by-elections between 1895 and 1905
the Liberal poll had gone up, overall, by 37 per cent (Liberals
plus 30 per cent, Unionists minus 7 per cent) and the *Daily News*
showed, on 13 January, not only that this had increased to 39
per cent in the period between the Khaki election and 1905, but
also that (as Table 18 makes clear) the trend had gathered even
more momentum between the year of the Education Act and of
the Corn Tax (1902) and the dissolution.

Table 18

THE RISE OF THE LIBERAL AND DECLINE OF THE UNIONIST POLLS
IN BY-ELECTIONS, 1902–5 (PERCENTAGE)

Area	*Liberals*	*Unionists*	*Difference in Liberal favour*
London	+90	+ 5	+85
English boroughs	+39	— 1	+40
English counties	+30	— 5	+35
Scotland	+48	—18	+66

On 22 January, when the Liberals were home and dry, the
paper confessed that, these figures notwithstanding, many
Liberals had contemplated the election 'with some anxiety',
wondering if the Home Rule scare, the 'specious promises of
Protection' or the fact of a Liberal government in power would
(as Balfour hoped) reverse the verdict of the by-elections and
leave their victory incomplete; but on the basis of its by-election
analysis its public forecast was of a Liberal total of nearly 360;
and most of the Liberal speakers who chanced their arm in this
uncertain field—Tweedmouth and Morley among them—similarly declared their confidence that the party would win just
about the 150 (or so) seats that it needed for an overall majority.

Despite their relatively ineffective campaign, Unionist commentators affected a renewed confidence (or at least a diminished pessimism) in the period between resignation and polling. Whistling, no doubt, to keep his courage up, Wyndham said at Dover on 4 January that he thought that Campbell-Bannerman would do no more than scrape a majority, and in a review of prospects published on 12 January *The Times* observed that 'since the jubilant days of December there has been evidence of a more chastened spirit in the Liberal party . . . Anticipations of reducing the Unionist party to absolute insignificance have become markedly less confident.' A broad consensus developed among Unionist speakers, including Balfour and Chamberlain, that the assumed Liberal majority over the Unionists would be sufficiently small to leave the party dependent on the Irish, the LRC, or both, and even the (Liberal) *Liverpool Daily Post* wondered on 13 January whether the Liberals might not find themselves dependent on Labour for the majority over Unionists and Irish Nationalists that they sought. The *Review of Reviews* presciently forecast the Labour total at thirty to forty seats, and several LRC speakers and sympathisers—including Keir Hardie and Joe Devlin—went along with it.

Although the expectation of a Liberal victory thus remained common to all, interest in the poll was keen, and when Ipswich opened, on 12 January, with what the *National Review* described (in February) as 'suggestive [Liberal] majorities', interest turned to the order in which the constituency declarations were due.

Luck, here again, favoured the Liberals, for with Manchester rather than Birmingham (as more usually) the first to poll, Liberal expectations—and Unionist fears—of an early Lancashire swing were keen. Joynson-Hicks, opposing Churchill in North-West Manchester, sought to warn his supporters that 'if the Conservatives lost . . . Churchill would go flying over like a comet crying "Gentlemen of England, the Conservative stronghold of Lancashire has fallen" ',[5] and a Liberal optimist similarly observed that 'if [Balfour] goes out as I hear very probable and if

Winston [Churchill] wins as is almost certain, it will mean blue ruin for Toryism everywhere . . .'.[6]

Table 19

THE ORDER OF POLLING*

Date of declaration of poll result	No of seats (incl unopposed returns) per day	cumula- tive	Major constituencies polling
Friday 12 January	6	6	Ispwich†
Saturday 13 January	48	54	Manchester, Bradford, and Halifax
Monday 15 January	96	150	Liverpool, Leeds, Sheffield
Tuesday 16 January	80	230	Most of London
Wednesday 17 January	75	305	Birmingham
Thursday 18 January	63	368	Edinburgh and Glasgow
Friday 19 January	56	424	First county results
Saturday 20 January	55	479	East Anglia, Home Counties
Monday 22 January to Monday 29 January	187	666	Remaining county seats
Monday 5 February to Thursday 8 February	4	670	Last seats, concluding with Orkney and Shetland

* Figures compiled from *The Times* reports
† 1 double constituency, plus 4 unopposed returns

POLLING

In the event, Balfour did go out, and Winston did win, in a day of polling (on 13 January) that was as remarkable as any in British electoral history. In Manchester and Salford, the Unionists lost not merely the four or five seats expected by the *Manchester Guardian* but every one of the eight they held—six to the Liberals and two to the Labour candidates, Kellcy and Clynes. In not one of the total of nine seats was the swing less than 12·5 per cent, and several of the turnovers of votes were, by any standards, remarkable.

Table 20

FOUR MANCHESTER RESULTS

Division	Winning candidate	Unionist majority, 1900	Liberal/ LRC majority, 1906	Turnover	Swing, per- centage
South	Haworth—L	1,272	4,232	5,504	25
East	Horridge—L	2,453	1,980	4,433	22
North-East	Clynes—LRC	706	2,432	3,138	19
South-West	Kelley—LRC	1,619	1,226	2,845	22

Furthermore, with Ashton, Burnley, Bury, Oldham, Preston, and all the Lancashire boroughs that polled, except Wigan, electing Liberal and Labour candidates, the victories were 'so decisive and so numerous' as to surprise even the Liberals themselves.[7] Cotton, said Mr Chamberlain, will soon go. 'On Saturday', commented the *Manchester Guardian* with satisfaction on the Monday, 'it left him violently, ironically.' So also did wool, across the border in the West Riding, where Leeds and Bradford followed Manchester in giving the Liberals and LRC a clean sweep. No majority was smaller than 800, and no swing against the Unionists less than 7 per cent, and several distinguished Unionists, including the Tariff Commissioner Sir Vincent Caillard (East Bradford) lost their seats.

Even more significantly, in the longer run, there were plenty of signs that Liberal success would not be confined to the industrial north. The Liberal capture of Newington-Walworth, the first of the London boroughs to poll (15 per cent swing); their unexpected double victory at Portsmouth; the fact that they came within fifty votes of capturing so Conservative a town as Kidderminster close to the Black Country (where Stanley Baldwin lost by 271 votes); their capture of Boston in Lincolnshire (11 per cent swing) and their greatly increased majority at Perth in Scotland (14 per cent swing)—all these results indicated that the trend was likely to be nationwide and that the northern results were not, as the *Evening Standard* hoped, a mere flash in the pan. *The Times* and the *Morning Post* found small rays of consolation in the victories of Pike Pease at Darlington (over Isaac Mitchell, LRC, General Secretary of the GFTU), Parker at Gravesend (over Liberal and Labour) and Wyndham at Dover, but these were insignificant compared with a net gain by Liberal and Labour of 23 (or nearly half of the seats declared) on the first day of polling. 'Can the oldest of you remember anything like it?' asked Campbell-Bannerman at Glasgow. 'Not a single seat lost to the Government and more than a score of seats won, and this not by small chance haphazard majorities, but by resounding numbers. Everywhere, East, North, South, West, the same story is told.'[8]

The excitement was tremendous, not only in the north, but in Kingsway and Fleet Street, and the Bull Ring in Birmingham, where the results were flashed on to giant indicator boards and rockets were fired to inform the outlying districts; and not only in the streets but in the West End clubs. In the National Liberal Club normally sedate members danced on the tables, whilst the grave little groups in the Carlton and Constitutional Clubs might have wished to see their ticker-tapes break down, as they did in the Reform Club, under the strain. Channing, who spent the evening in the Liberal clubs at Wellingborough and Kettering recorded that nobody who was in them would ever forget the scene on that Saturday night, when telegrams came in one by one announcing 'almost unbelievable defeats'[9] and Silvester Horne who was at a meeting at Whitfields, in the Tottenham Court Road, has left a vivid impression of the scene in London.

> We began at Whitfields at 8.30, the place being densely crowded. At 10 o'clock the editor of the *Daily Chronicle* (Robert Donald) was on his feet when he heard a roar in the street and up came a man. . . . Churchill was in. Then followed the various Manchester divisions one after another. Any attempt to continue our meeting properly was ridiculous. Bradford came next, the same verdict. Still we waited for the big Manchester verdict. Then at last (about 10 o'clock) there was a sound of the multitude outside as the screen told the fatal news and in ran W—— to us breathless and almost hysterical. The whole meeting was on its feet. Everybody fought

everything. 'Balfour's out' they yelled. Connell was on his feet, trying to speak and bellowing at the top of his voice '2,000 majority'. I was standing on a chair waving a handkerchief and it is a literal fact that until we were physically exhausted there was no cessation. In came the telegrams. Everywhere the Tories swept out of existence. London was the culmination . . . the wild hurrahs of the multitude were incessant. Wallace's triumph at Perth stirred up the enthusiasm afresh. Then York, Plymouth, Morpeth and the rest. . . . Nobody will ever forget it.[10]

Liberals, like Kay-Shuttleworth, first rejoiced that Free Trade had been saved—for at least the coming parliament and perhaps for a generation;[11] but they also affected to find, in these early results, a deeper revolt against tactics that Herbert Gladstone generously described in a letter to his chief as 'a splendid vindication of your policy . . .'[12] Campbell-Bannerman himself caught the mood of many platform speeches exactly when he saw something beyond the attachment to Free Trade that lay beneath 'these splendid and inspiring results'.

Is there not something in the earnestness, in the fury, with which the voters were going to the polls which suggests a deeper significance? Is it the mind only of the people that is moved? Is it not also the heart and the conscience? . . . The springs of action which the late government avowed seemed to take no account of [these] . . .[13]

This, as much as Free Trade, was the message the exuberant successful Liberal and Labour candidates now carried into the counties and remaining boroughs and, commented the *Pall Mall Gazette* gloomily on 15 January, '. . . since success and failure at the polls are highly infectious, Saturday may very likely prove to have been, as the *Daily News* calls it this morning, the First day of the Deluge'.

Meanwhile Balfour, in defeat, behaved with his accustomed phlegm; he had 'suffered the common lot', he said, and would suffer it again when he had to go back to office to correct Liberal blunders 'as far as possible'; and Chamberlain—who magnanimously described him, in a speech at Nuneaton, as now, more than ever, Unionist leader—hazarded that the Unionists would in the

end have won nearly 50 per cent of the votes. He described
Manchester as a fickle city, that had sent Bright to Birmingham,
scorned the suggestion that the election would put paid to the
Tariff Reform, and speaking in Nottingham later that same day
(15 January) appealed to Unionists for a fight to the death. He
expressed confidence that Birmingham at least 'would be true
to its old friends'. But into Unionist comment at large there crept
an element of near-hysteria. Whilst the *Yorkshire Post* warned
of the new danger of educational extremism, the *Globe*, not
untypically, spoke of a 'fierce cry to transfer property from the
pockets of those who have to those who have not'; and whilst in
Edinburgh the mild-mannered Leonard Courtney 'figured on
the placards as a Socialist',[14] the Lancashire Liberals were vigorously attacked (e.g. in Blackburn) for 'splitting the vote with
Socialism'.[15] Thus whether the keynote was empire or union,
Unionists up and down the country sought to make virtue of
necessity and turn to account the alarm of cautious men. 'Is
Balfour out, then all the more reason for putting Smith in',
proclaimed F. E. Smith in Liverpool; whilst in Chelsea, Whit-
more (Unionist) besought the electorate to 'vote . . . Unionist
and dam the flowing tide'.

The results of the second full day of polling, however, brought
the Unionists no relief. Of the Lancashire boroughs only rain-
drenched Liverpool provided a centre of resistance; J. E. B.
Seely won the Abercrombie division, and R. R. Cherry (the new
Attorney-General for Ireland) the Exchange division, if narrowly;
but, contrary to Liberal hopes, F. E. Smith just held Walton,
and the Unionists were still left with six out of nine seats in the
city. Apart from these, however, the Unionists held only Wigan,
which the veteran Sir James Powell won on a minority vote, and
one of the two seats at Blackburn which they shared with Labour.
Making nine gains, on its most successful single day, Labour
also captured Stockport and Barrow. In the Yorkshire boroughs
a similar tale was told. Leeds followed Manchester and Bradford
with a clean sweep in which the Liberals retained the Eastern
division with a narrow majority over Unionist and Labour

combined, and Gerald Balfour shared his brother's fate; and at the end of the day the only Yorkshire boroughs that the Unionists held outside Sheffield were York (one seat), Central Hull, and—narrowly on a split vote—Wakefield. In Sheffield the Unionists held three out of the five seats, including the Central division where Sir Howard Vincent disappointed Liberal hopes that Stanley Udale, Secretary of the FTU, would win; but, the Liberals won back the Brightside division—lost in a by-election in 1897—and in Hallam, Unionist since its creation in 1885, came within 81 votes of victory. Outside Lancashire and Yorkshire they did equally well. In Bristol, they captured three out of four seats, including the Southern division which as late as 14 January Herbert Gladstone had expected Walter Long to hold, and several smaller towns like Cambridge, Bath, and Dudley. In the whole of the country, only Maidstone—and later Hastings—went against the swing, even as they had in 1900, and on 16 January *The Times* admitted that Saturday's results appeared to have been 'more or less accurately typical of what was going on all over the country'.

Next day, Tuesday 16 January, London drove the point home when the Unionists *lost* fifteen out of the twenty-two seats that polled, and when—surpassing even their own expectations—the Liberals won St Pancras South and—for the first time ever—Brixton, Kennington, and North Lambeth. When evening fell the Liberals had won 75, or just half, of the 150 needed for a majority free from Irish (or Labour) pressures, and Balfour privately confessed that if the trend continued the Unionists might not win more than 50 seats. When on the next two days (17 and 18 January) seventeen of the nineteen 'well-to-do . . . residential and flourishing London constituencies',[16] on which *The Times* had pinned its hopes, fell into the Liberal maw, and the swing to the Liberals and to Labour continued with near-monotonous regularity, it seemed that he could well be right. In a political upset that 'surprised everyone by its thoroughness'[17] and seemed to the *Tribune* even more remarkable than the results in Lancashire, the Liberals won 90 per cent of Gladstone's category 'A' seats, 100 per cent of category 'B' and 30 per cent (even) of category 'C' (Table 8 refers); whilst the Unionists lost 64 per cent (34) of the 53 London seats they won in 1900. Elsewhere Nottingham went the way of Manchester, Lyttleton was rejected at Leamington, and such divers boroughs as Whitehaven, Salisbury, Tynemouth, Chester, and Exeter voted the Unionists down. Liberal successes in West Bromwich, Wednesbury, Dudley, and Handsworth indicated that even 'Chamberlain country' was not safe, and when J. W. Wilson, the Unionist seceder, held North Worcestershire, thus capturing it for the Liberals, the tide of Liberalism rolled to the very doors of Highbury, Chamberlain's Birmingham home. The city of Birmingham, which polled on 17 January, alone remained solidly Unionist—a triumph, claimed Chamberlain, for conscientious political education in the principles of Tariff Reform—but it was hardly true to claim, as the *Morning Post* did, that 'reconstruction has begun'.

Certainly the last great urban centres of Edinburgh and Glasgow showed little sign of it when they went to the polls on Thursday 18 January. Leonard Courtney failed to capture West Edinburgh—because, said his wife, some Unionist Free Traders were 'frightened at the great flood of Liberals and Radicals'[18]— and the Unionists recaptured Ayr Burghs and St Andrews, both of which they had lost in by-elections. But these were the only checks to the swing. In Edinburgh the Liberals held all the other three seats and in Glasgow (where all the Unionist *members* were standing) they captured four out of the seven seats and the LRC captured one more. The Liberals gained not only St Rollox— as was felt likely—but also the Central, College, and Bridgetown divisions (defeating Scott-Dickson in the latter), whilst Barnes won Blackfriars for the LRC against Unionist and Liberal opposition. As the *Tribune* observed, toward the end of the borough polls, the Liberals had gained all but the 'inaccessible Tory heights' of Orange Liverpool, Chamberlain's Birmingham, the City of London, a few residential suburbs, and some of the small stranded boroughs where the ale was good.

As a result, the party leaders' shadow boxing became more

shadowy than ever. With Balfour tired, Chamberlain dispirited, and the Liberal leaders sated with success, only the Labour victories breathed freshness into the stale proceedings. Four seats won on 13 January, nine on the 15th, six on the 16th, one on the 17th, three more on the 18th not only made an impressive beginning for the new party, but provided fuel for the assiduous warnings of Wyndham, Arnold Forster, Long, and other Unionists of the dangers of the nascent Radical-Socialist alliance. These became so loud in the midst of the borough polls that the *Tribune* aptly commented (on 17 January) that 'for the vision of Mr. Redmond leading the Irish members to College Green, was substituted the picture of Keir Hardie setting up the guillotine in Palace Yard'. The Liberal leaders made light of such dire visions. Herbert Gladstone at Harrogate and Grey at Berwick said that the LRC leaders were not revolutionaries but practical, cautious men of sound judgement, and speaking at Montrose on 17 January Morley commented that their opponents 'talked as if the skies were about to fall because 20 or 30 Labour members had got into the House of Commons' and asked, amid laughter, whether the electors of Montrose 'were frightened of that'; and two days later Asquith said (at St Andrews) that 'no student of political development could have supposed that they could always go along in the same groove, with one party on the one side and another party on the other side, without the intermediate ground being occupied by groups and factions having special ideas and interests...' As *The Times* commented in a prescient editorial on 20 January, what they were seeing was 'the logical result of successive reform bills', the assertion of power by those who had hitherto 'been content not to put forward their full strength'.

In any event the county voters, who began their polling on 19 January, showed themselves disinclined to pay much heed to the Unionist alarms. If it was hardly surprising when suburban Middlesex followed the lead of London, Nuneaton that of Wolverhampton and the Yorkshire and Lancashire villages the examples of the big northern towns, the defeat of Ailwyn Fellowes in North Huntingdonshire, of Captain Pretyman in South-West

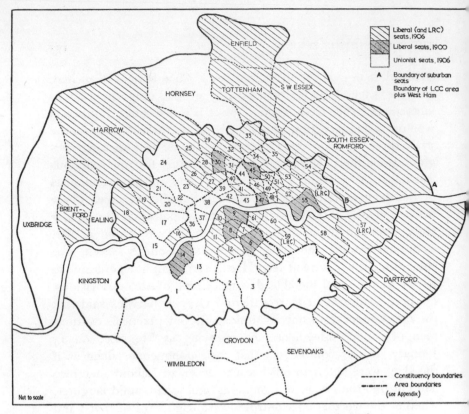

Map 1   The London results, 1900 and 1906

KEY TO CONSTITUENCIES

Western and southern suburbs

1 Wandsworth
2 Norwood
3 Dulwich
4 Lewisham
5 Peckham
6 Camberwell North
7 Walworth
8 West Newington
9 Southwark
10 North Lambeth
11 Kennington
12 Brixton
13 Clapham
14 Battersea
15 Hammersmith
16 Chelsea
17 South Kensington
18 Fulham
19 North Kensington
20 South Paddington
21 North Paddington
22 West Marylebone
23 East Marylebone

24 Hampstead
25 North St Pancras
26 West St Pancras
27 South St Pancras
28 East St Pancras
29 North Islington
30 West Islington
31 South Islington
32 East Islington
33 North Hackney
34 Central Hackney
35 South Hackney

Business area

36 St George's
37 Westminster
38 Strand
39 Holborn/Finsbury
40 Central Holborn
41 East Holborn
42 City
43 City

East End

44 Hoxton
45 Haggerston
46 South-West Bethnal Gre
47 Whitechapel
48 St George's-in-the-East
49 Stepney
50 North-East Bethnal Gree
51 Mile End
52 Limehouse
53 Bow and Bromley
54 West Ham North
55 Poplar
56 West Ham South
57 Woolwich
58 Greenwich
50 Deptford
60 Rotherhithe
61 Bermondsey

Suffolk, and of Henry Chaplin in North Kesteven (in what the Liberal agent could only describe as 'an act of God'),[19] and the Unionist loss of small rural constituencies like South Dorset, Guildford, Kendal, and South Herefordshire, and many more in the Home Counties and elsewhere, made it abundantly clear that the Unionists had little left to hope for. Commenting on the downfall of so many great county families,* the *Speaker* (27 January) said that the county results confirmed what it had said earlier, namely that the 'tragedy' of the disappearing villages was 'at last impressing itself on the mind of the community'; and, as the *Daily Telegraph* admitted on 19 January, these results meant that the last hope of a change in Unionist fortunes had gone. 'The lost County divisions', it declared, 'are thoroughly typical of rural England, the old-fashioned England of small agricultural townships, as distinguished from the industrial villages of York-

Table 21

LIBERAL/LABOUR GAINS AND RESULTS DECLARED

Date		(a) seats decided	(b) Liberal and Labour gains	(c) (b) as percentage of (a)	
	Jan				
Boroughs	12	6	1	17	
	13	48	23	48	
	15	96	43	45	av
	16	80	24	30	40
	17	75	34	45	
	18	63	28	45	
Counties	19	56	23	41	
	20	55	13	24	
	22	24	7	30	av
	23	29	8	20	34
	24	49	16	33	
	25	28	15	54	

* Chaplin at Sleaford (after 38 years); the Hon Tatton-Egerton at Knutsford (after 23 years); Ailwyn Fellowes, North Hunts; a Bathurst at Cirencester; a Brymer in Dorset; a Strutt at Maldon in Essex; a Kenyon in Derbyshire; and a Lowther in Eskdale.

shire and Lancashire, or the great mining constituencies where Radicalism had long been in the ascendant.' As Table 21 shows, the tide rolled almost as remorselessly over the counties as it had over the boroughs before.

Everywhere the scale of the victory exceeded the most optimistic Liberal hopes. In Cheshire, where the *Manchester Guardian* (22 December) expected a gain of two, the Liberals in fact gained six and made a clean sweep of all eight constituencies. In East Anglia, where only Great Yarmouth and Bury St Edmunds remained Unionist, the Liberals gained five more seats than an anticipated eight. In the Home Counties the by-elections had augured well for the Liberals, and the Unionists were known to be worried about the possible extent of their losses, but even the *Daily News* (22 January) confessed its surprise at their actual extent. Kent, Surrey, Sussex, and Hampshire, which had returned only two Liberals in 1885 and had presented a solid Unionist front from 1886 to 1906, returned ten Liberals in 1906, including several who, Mrs Corbett told Bryce, had 'hardly dared hope for success'.[20] The West Country had a more Liberal tradition, but even there there was surprise at some of the results —especially at the defeat of Durning-Lawrence at Truro and Bateman Hope's conversion of a Unionist majority of 500 in North Somerset into a Liberal majority of nearly 2,500.

Meanwhile Wales and Scotland were filling in the margins. On 19 January, the Liberals captured the only three Unionist boroughs in Wales—Denbigh, Haverfordwest, and Montgomery (by 83 votes only)—and when in the next two days their two county seats also fell, the Liberal hope and prediction of a clean (Liberal/Labour) sweep was fulfilled. At Gower, where the *Cambria Daily Leader* had feared that the Liberal/Labour split might let the Unionist in, the Unionist came, in fact, well bottom. In Scotland in the North-Western and Govan divisions of Glasgow (as well as in Glasgow Camlachie), Liberal/Labour splits proved more damaging to both parties involved, with the Unionists holding two seats on minority votes; and Campbell-Bannerman described the Liberal loss of St Andrews (won in a by-election) as 'provoking'.[21] However, despite these setbacks, the Liberals won 58 seats in the country as a whole—ten more than Tweedmouth had anticipated.

In Ireland the story (again) was somewhat different. The ex-Liberal Unionist, Major Glendenning, gained North Antrim, and T. W. Russell retained North Tyrone; but the *Tribune* was less perceptive than *The Times* when, on 20 January, it interpreted Sloan's victory at South Belfast as evidence of a change in Ulster. The defeat of all the Russellites save Russell himself indicated that even if a reformer had some chance inside the Unionist party, he had very little chance outside it. The *Irish Times* was gratified and consoled by these results, and also by Walter Long's capture of South Dublin from the Nationalists on 19 January; but by winning Galway City and West Belfast (Joe Devlin, by the narrow margin of sixteen votes) the Nationalists nevertheless increased their total by one, to 83.

Apart from the solidarity of Ulster and the gain of South Dublin, and a handful of seats in Britain, there was little consolation for the Unionists except, as Wyndham observed, the recapture of some of the seats lost in by-elections, and the retention of the University of London seat, in the face of Sir Michael Forster's secession to the Liberals. Speaking at Barnstaple, Brodrick felt that these results showed that the Liberals would not for long keep many of their gains, but they hardly amounted to what *The Times*—as late as 20 January—could bravely call 'a counter trend'. On 19 January, indeed (with over 40 per cent of seats yet to be declared), the Liberals gained an overall majority, and by 20 January, interest in the election as a whole was flagging fast. At Romford Alderman J. H. Bethell converted a Unionist majority of 3,062 into a Liberal majority of 8,885 to provide one of the election's most dramatic turnovers (22 per cent), but no new trends emerged and the note of boredom grew. 'At the end of a week of unexampled electoral excitement', said the *Manchester Guardian* on 20 January, 'the interest of particular results, wonderful as they are, is pretty well exhausted', and the same day Asquith wrote to Campbell-Bannerman from Fifeshire that he was kept there until his polling day the following Friday (26 January) 'trying to play the game in a farcical contest'.[22]

Nevertheless, as Campbell-Bannerman declared in his last speech at Larbert, the results 'encompassed a tremendous disproportion of power', which—if not 'wholly undeserved', as Curzon said[23]—appeared to Ponsonby to be almost 'alarming in extent'.[24] They may have become monotonous; they may have installed what *The Times* sourly (27 January) called 'the worst conceivable . . . but still British . . . Government'; but they brought forward the shadow of new political forms and problems, and left the participants as well as the spectators to seek, again and again, for the explanation of it all.

Distribution of Seats

The final results of the election indeed confounded all Unionist hopes of a recovery and exceeded the most optimistic Liberal hopes by totally reversing the extreme and war-exaggerated count of 1900. Whilst the Liberal ranks were swollen from 186 to 400, the Unionists were reduced to a mere 157, interestingly smaller than the Liberals in 1900 by just about the total (30) of successful Labour candidates. Only the number of Nationalists stayed more or less the same, at 83. The Liberals gained 224 seats (against a loss of 8); topped the *Daily News* forecast by 34 (chiefly by making unexpected gains in London, the south-east, and the boroughs); won a clear majority of 130 over all parties; and won the enormous majority of 356, with Labour and Nationalist members, over the Unionists alone.

The only seats which the Unionists won against the trend were Hastings and Maidstone, in straight fights with the Liberals, Govan and Lanark in three-sided contests against Liberal and Labour, and seven of the seats which they had lost in by-elections between 1900 and 1905 (Rye, St Albans, St Andrews, Ayr Burghs, Oswestry, Whitby, and Barkston Ash). Thus despite the general expectation of a Liberal victory, the President of the Royal Statistical Society felt able to describe the result as 'the

Table 22

THE NATIONAL RESULTS

(i) NET GAINS AND LOSSES OF SEATS

Area	Year	Unionist no of seats	loss	Liberal no of seats	gain	Labour no of seats	gain	Nationalist no of seats	gain
United Kingdom (including Ireland)	1900	402		184		2		82	
	1906	157*	245	400	216	30	28	83	1
England Scotland and Wales	1900	374		183		2		1	
	1906	132	242	397	214	30	28	1	−

(ii) GROSS GAINS AND LOSSES OF SEATS
(incl Ireland)

Party	Gains from U	Lib	Nat	Lab	Losses to U	Lib	Nat	Lab	Total Gain	Loss
Liberal	223		1		4			4	224	8
Unionist		4	1		223	2		25	5	250
Nationalist	2					1			2	1
Labour	25	4					1		29	1

* Incl 24 Liberal Unionists out of 94 who stood

most surprising of any that has taken place since 1832'.[25] Spender, who had been expecting a good result, confessed that it 'took all parties by surprise and not least the Liberal leaders';[26] Chamberlain honestly confessed (to Margot Asquith) that he had 'for once . . . been quite out in his estimates'.[27]

It was, in effect, the victory for which Gladstone had hoped but which he had failed to achieve in 1885. It not only restored most of the seats which the Liberals lost in 1886, 1892, and 1900 in their main traditional areas—in Wales, Scotland, the West Riding, Tyneside, and the central midland counties—and effected substantial gains in the rural areas of the west, east and north in which the party had not done well since 1885, but also brought the success in London, urban Lancashire, and in many of the smaller boroughs of the south-east, which had eluded the party in 1885 and so disappointed its leader. These areas (A1 & 2, B3 and G14 in Table 23) provided the Liberals with 41 per cent

L

Table 23

THE GEOGRAPHY OF LIBERALISM, 1885, 1900 and 1906

| Reference/ Area* | Number of seats | | | Increase in seats | | Labour increase |
	Total no	Won 1885	Won 1900	Won 1906	over 1885	over 1900	over 1885/1900
England:							
A1 London	61	25	8	39	14	31	3
2 The Suburbs	14	2	—	7	5	7	—
B3 South-East	61	10	5	32	22	27	1
South-West:							
C4 Devon and Cornwall	20	13	10	17	4	7	—
5 The rest	31	21	8	26	5	18	—
D6 West Midlands	11	6	—	3	−3	3	—
East Midlands:							
E7 Norfolk and Suffolk	18	12	6	15	3	9	1
8 The rest	21	13	6	17	4	11	—
F9 The Black Country	22	18	3	9	−9	6	1
10 The Potteries	3	3	—	3	—	3	—
11 Derby and Notts	16	13	10	14	1	4	—
12 Leicestershire etc	18	14	9	17	3	8	1
13 Staffordshire etc	14	11	4	13	2	9	—
G14 Lancashire	62	19	11	33	14	22	13
15 The West Riding	38	28	22	30	2	8	3
16 Durham and Tyneside	24	22	13	16	−6	3	4
17 The North and East Ridings	12	5	3	6	1	3	—
18 Northumberland etc	10	5	4	9	4	5	—
Wales:							
H19 Industrial	14	13	10	13	—	3	—†
20 The rest	20	17	17	20	3	3	—
Scotland:							
I21 The Lowlands	19	16	8	15	−1	7	—
22 Clyde and Lanark	18	14	5	13	−1	8	1
23 Firth of Forth	9	9	6	8	−1	2	—
24 The North-East	12	12	10	11	−1	1	1
25 The Highlands	12	11	5	11	—	6	—

* See Appendix for detailed breakdown of areas
† One seat (Merthyr) won in 1900

(87) of their gains over 1900 and 63 per cent (57) of their gains over 1885, from a mere 27 per cent of the seats contested by the party in the election; and, together with the statistically less important area of Cumberland, Westmorland, and rural Northumberland (G18 in Table 23), effected a conspicuous change in the political geography of Liberalism, both in absolute and regional terms and in proportional and national terms. Against them, the

continuing 'loss' of much of Birmingham and its surrounding areas was of small significance in the overall result.

Table 24

MAJOR CHANGES IN THE POLITICAL GEOGRAPHY OF LIBERALISM, 1885/1906 (INCREASE/DECREASE)

	Liberal seats as percentage of all seats within the area	Regional holding as percentage of national total
Northumberland etc	+40	+1·0
South-East	+36	+5·0
London	+24	+3·4
Lancashire	+22	+2·5
East Anglia	+18	+0·5
West Country	+17	+0·5
Midlands	+11	—0·6
Wales	+ 9	—6·7
Yorkshire	+ 5	—0·7
Scotland	— 6	—4·1
Durham and Tyneside	—25	—2·7
West Midlands	—28	—1·1
Black Country	—41	—3·2

The most striking feature of the poll, however, was not this shift in British political geography *per se*, but the sheer uniformity and ubiquity of the Liberal successes, to which of course this shift made its own notable if temporary contribution. Map 2 shows that the Unionists retained a majority of seats only in the Black Country and the west midlands, and that—as the *Pall Mall Gazette* observed in its election supplement—the rest of their seats were 'curiously scattered'. The Liberals won not only their traditional rural areas but also much of the south and east; not only what Morley once called the 'middling towns', but also much of Conservative Lancashire and London; and not just predominately rural *or* urban seats, but both in good numbers. Manchester and Salford, London, Bradford, and Leeds may have dramatised the results by virtue of their urban concentration, but the pattern of Liberal gains reflected with unusual precision the proportion of rural and urban seats. It is not even possible to define these gains in terms of the size of the electorate. Urban or rural, large or small, the proportion of Liberal gains was similar; and whilst the Unionists won a noticeable 8 per cent more of their seats in constituencies with electorates of less than

Table 25

LIBERAL GAINS IN URBAN AND RURAL AREAS

Type of seat	No of seats	Per-centage of all seats	No of Liberal gains	Percentage of all Liberal gains	No of Liberal and LRC gains	Percentage of all Liberal and LRC gains
Urban areas	308	56	113	54	140	58
Rural areas	245	44	99	46	102	42

10,000, the average size of all Liberal seats (12,400) was only marginally larger than the average size of Unionist seats (11,800) and there was a conspicuous similarity between the profile of Liberal and Unionist seats, with only the LRC polling chiefly in constituencies of larger than average size. As the following analysis of the voting patterns shows, this was a factor of very considerable importance.

DISTRIBUTION OF VOTES

The most obvious features of the voting—of which Chamberlain quickly made the most—were that it took a swing of only 10·5 per cent to effect a net transference of 38 per cent of seats, and that the Liberals won 71 per cent of the seats with barely half the votes cast in the high 83·7 per cent poll. Taking Liberal and LRC together, the effect was that 3 million votes (55·5 per cent) were represented by 427 MPs (76·5 per cent), whilst 2·3 million votes (43 per cent) were represented by a mere 130 MPs (23·5 per cent)—a result which—together with the advent of a second 'progressive' party—gave considerable stimulus to the movement for proportional representation, or at least for a second preferen-

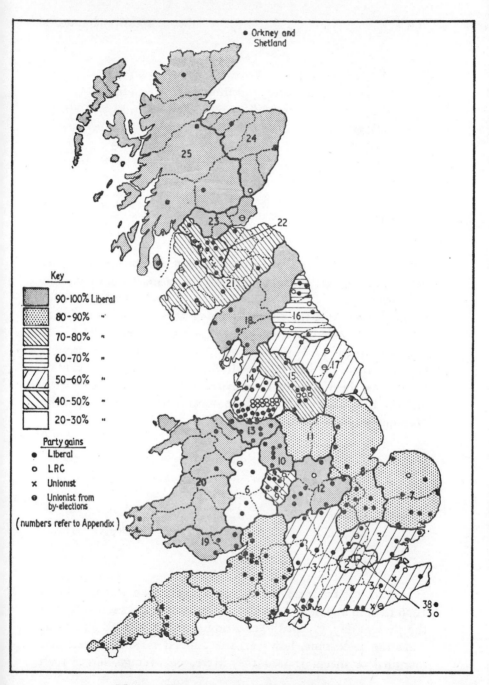

Map 2   The geography of Liberalism, 1906

Table 26

TOTAL NUMBER OF VOTES CAST FOR EACH PARTY

(votes cast in double constituencies are counted as
one vote for each seat)

Party	Total vote	Percentage
Liberal	2,699,217	49·5
Unionist	2,345,694	43·0
LRC	326,664	5·9
Independent Socialist	47,521	0·9
Others	39,495	0·7
Total	5,458,591	100·0

tial vote. 'What a travesty of representation it is', wrote one critic, 'when . . . the official leader of a party with more than 2 million supporters finds himself without a seat in Parliament . . . under which 3 per cent of the voters changing sides can turn a majority of 40 for one side into a majority of 100 for the other.'[28]

Had there been a fairly exact system of proportional representation in 1906, the Liberals would have lost about 30 per cent of their seats, the Unionists would practically have doubled theirs, and the Liberals would have been dependent on Labour and the Nationalists for a majority.

Table 27

ACTUAL AND WOULD-BE PROPORTIONAL REPRESENTATION IN 1906
(England, Scotland and Wales)

Party	Seats won	Proportional
Liberals	397	285
Unionists	130	236
LRC	30	36

Indeed, as Table 28 shows, the exaggeration was greater in 1906 than in any other major electoral victory between 1885 and the present day, except the coalition victories of 1918 and 1931.

At the same time, however, the Liberal majorities were not marginal or mean. Indeed they were, on average, larger than

Unionist majorities in the seats which the Unionists held. Whereas the Liberals would have held about 80 per cent of their seats if there had been a 5 per cent swing away from their 1906 results, and about 60 per cent if there had been a 10 per cent swing, the Unionists, had there been a further 5 per cent or 10 per cent swing against them would have held only 65 per cent or 40 per cent (approximate figures).

Table 28

PERCENTAGE VOTES AND SEATS SECURED BY THE WINNING PARTY
OR COALITION, IN SEVEN ELECTIONS BETWEEN 1885 AND 1970
(England, Scotland and Wales, rounded to nearest 1 per cent)

Party	Year	Percentage votes received	Percentage seats won	Percentage distortion*
Liberal	1885	54	59	8
Unionist	1900	52	67	23
Liberal (only)	1906	50	60	29
Coalition	1918	50	77	35
National	1931	68	90	32
Labour	1945	49	62	21
Conservative	1959	49	57	14
Labour	1964	44	50	13
Labour	1966	47	58	18
Conservative	1970	46	53	12

* ie number of seats over and above exact proportional representation, expressed as a percentage of the actual number of seats won

Table 29

THE SIZE OF PARTY MAJORITIES IN CONSTITUENCIES

Party	Size of majority as percentage of vote in each constituency					
	0–5%	5–10%	10–15%	15–20%	20–30%	over 30%
Liberal seats (%)	20	17	20	13	17	13
Unionist seats (%)	33	23	18	8	10	8

There was thus something of a paradox, with the Liberals winning an 'unrepresentatively' large number of seats but winning them with large majorities. The explanation of this paradox

—which is the *statistical* explanation of the size of the Liberal victory—is that the Liberals won many of their votes in just those places where they were most needed, areas with large Unionist majorities or long Unionist records. In short, their vote was distributed to the best possible advantage, and not simply piled up and 'wasted' in the large urban constituencies.

A glance at the statistics of the swing illustrates the point, for whilst the swing against the Unionists *averaged* 10·5 per cent, throughout England, Scotland, and Wales (and the swing to the Liberals 7·1 per cent and to Labour 2·0 per cent), it was significantly higher in hitherto Unionist Lancashire (13·1 per cent) and London (15·0—or 21·3 per cent including the suburbs), and also in the West Riding (11·8 per cent) where, again, many important urban gains were made. In the same way, the swing in south-east England (8·8 per cent) was, with certain Scottish exceptions, larger, albeit marginally, than that in any other chiefly agricultural area, not excluding those which had been Liberal in 1885 and were in 1906 returning to a traditional allegiance. In other words, the Unionists lost most support, whether through conversion, abstention, or failure to attract new voters, in just those areas where they might normally have expected to have done best.

Table 30

LIBERAL AND LABOUR GAINS IN RELATION TO THE SIZE OF THE
SWING AGAINST THE UNIONISTS (PERCENTAGE)

Seats	Swing against the Unionists				
	0–4%	5–9%	10–14%	15–19%	20% and over
Held by Liberal/Labour	61	44	28	22	19
Gained ,,	26	44	64	72	66
Total won by ,,	87	88	92	94	87
Held by Unionists	13	11	8	6	15
Gained by Unionists	—	1 seat*	1 seat†	—	—

* Gain of North-West Lanark on a minority vote, with the Unionist vote falling by 8·1 per cent and the Liberal vote by 15·8 per cent, with a Socialist polling 23·9 per cent.

† Gain of a second seat—Govan—on a minority vote, with the Unionist vote 13·4 per cent down, the Liberal vote 15·6 per cent down, whilst the Socialist polled 29 per cent.

An analysis of the swing in relation to the electoral record of constituencies in the five elections preceding 1906 (1885, 1886, 1892, 1895, and 1900) serves to emphasise the point. There is no exact correlation, but, as Figure 5 shows, the swing certainly *tended* to be larger in those constituencies which had consistently voted Unionist and, taking a 10 per cent swing against the Unionists as an approximation to the average, it can be seen that the percentage of above-average swings rose appreciably with the number of Unionist victories between 1885 and 1900 (both dates inclusive). Indeed, as Table 30 shows, the swings in individual constituencies 'complemented' the 1900 Unionist majorities in a remarkable way, bringing not only increased Liberal polls, but, in so many cases, gains of seats. The table clearly demon-

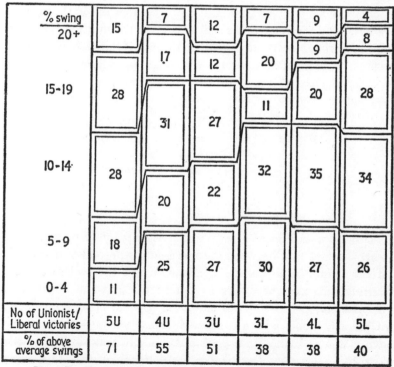

Figure 5   The Swing and Political Tradition, 1885–1900

strates the way in which the swing increased as the number of
Liberal-held seats declined, bringing the total number of Liberal
and Labour seats, gained and held, to roughly the same level in
each group.

A number of Unionist commentators—following Stead's
comments on the by-elections—attributed the large swing in the
general election to the increase in the poll. They were prepared
to admit that the Liberals had succeeded, if not in converting
voters, at least in calling out a number of voters who had ab-
stained in 1900, and in attracting many of the half- to three-
quarters of a million young, new voters who had registered since
then. Indeed, there was some correlation between swing and poll
increase, particularly in the English country areas (the south-east,
for instance, where the swing was 8·8 per cent against a poll
increase of 8·9 per cent), and the very large increase in the average
Liberal, and the relatively small decline in the average Unionist,
poll in borough seats suggests that Liberal victories may to some
extent have been due to their success in attracting—and in
organising—new voters or former abstainers.

Table 31
THE AVERAGE SIZE OF THE LIBERAL AND UNIONIST
POLLS IN THE BOROUGHS, 1885, 1900 AND 1906

	Average borough poll	
	Liberal	Unionist
1885	3,363	3,123
1900	3,602	3,980
1906	4,836	3,803

However, as Figure 6 suggests, it is impossible to make any
general correlation between the increase in the poll and the size
of the swing. In Glamorgan, indeed, where the poll rose more
sharply than anywhere else except in the Firth of Forth area
of Scotland, the swing was as low as 3·3 per cent; conversely,
in the Highlands where the poll increase was 3·3 per cent the
swing was as high as 11·5 per cent. There was similarly little
correlation between the *size of the poll* (which was to a large
extent uniform throughout the country) and the size of the swing,

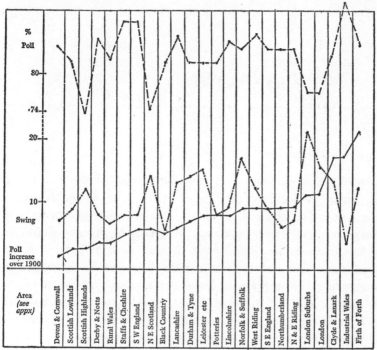

Figure 6   Swing, Poll, and Poll Increase

which was highest in four areas where the total turnout was lowest, namely, the Highlands, the north-east of Scotland, East Anglia, and London. Whilst, therefore, the conversion of Unionist voters probably took place on a *larger* scale in certain areas— in London, urban and industrial England, and rural Scotland and Wales—it is *prima facie likely that it took place on a considerable scale all over the country*, especially in view of the correlation between voting record and swing. The truth was that the Liberals won seats because they won votes and that they won not only new votes, or floating votes, or abstainer votes, but the votes of a large number of Unionists as well; and they won them where they needed them. The question is—why?

Notes to Chapter 6 will be found on pp 223–4

7 ANALYSIS

THE FISCAL ISSUE

Liberal commentators—and candidates—hailed the final results as primarily a decisive Free Trade victory; and there is little doubt that—in the length and breadth of the country—the majority of voters opted for the fiscal *status quo*. Many of them no doubt did so less from enthusiasm for the principles of political economy than from a determination to ensure that other reforming issues should take prior place to fiscal change; and many more—no doubt—as part and parcel of the general disgust with the Unionist record; but there is equally little doubt that in two of the areas of major Liberal gains—Lancashire and the south-east—it was— *mutatis mutandis*—an issue of central importance.

In Lancashire, Liberal *and* Labour candidates certainly *believed* that this was so. Harold Cox, who wrote to Bryce that the Preston Liberals were 'beside themselves with joy at winning the seat after being 40 years or more in the wilderness', claimed that their victory had 'of course' been won on Free Trade,[1] and most of the other Liberals in the county—including Churchill in Manchester and Maddison in Burnley—credited their successes to it. Even Clynes and Snowden, for Labour, agreed— after a genuflexion in the direction of 'specifically' Labour issues, that fiscal policy had been an important factor in victory in Manchester and Blackburn respectively, and when the election was over, Duncan (Labour, Barrow) went out of his way to thank the *Barrow News*—which had described his victory as 'Barrow's great victory for Free Trade'[2]—for all the help that it had given them during the campaign. The smooth operation in the county of the Liberal/Labour electoral agreement was also a most important factor, but the *Manchester Guardian*'s considered comment on the election in Lancashire was not, nevertheless, so inept:

> A candidate had only to be a Free Trader to get in, whether he was known or unknown, semi-Unionist or thorough Home Ruler, Protestant or Roman Catholic, entertaining or dull. He had only to be a Protectionist to lose all chance of getting in though he spoke with the tongues of men and angels, though he was a good employer to many electors, or had led the House of Commons or fought in the Crimea.[3]

Despite his reasoned arguments—and his courage in contesting North-East Manchester when he could, as late as November 1905, have had a safe City seat—Balfour quite failed to dispel the fears of the cotton manufacturers that any kind of fiscal reform would deprive Manchester's principal export of the 'invincible cheapness' which forced its way all over the world;[4] and whilst C. A. Macara, President of the Master Cotton Spinners Association, issued an effective little pamphlet condemning all Tariff Reform as bad for the cotton industry and for the consumer alike, Horridge, the Liberal candidate (and numerous questioners at Balfour's own meetings), repeatedly asked how retaliation could be carried out against the United States without endangering Lancashire's supply of raw cotton. Whether, as the Liberal paper *Tribune* said on 15 January, Balfour 'enraged his constituents by his over-refinement and subtlety' or whether, as the more sympathetic *Daily Graphic* commented, these constituents were 'unable to pronounce on subtle distinctions born of too scrupulous an honesty', Balfour clearly failed to allay prevalent fears in the city about either cheap raw materials or cheap food; and with trade reviving well in 1905 both sides of the cotton industry (and—less unanimously—of the worsted industry across the county line) rallied to the Liberal cause.

The Manchester Free Trade League, established as 'a purely ad hoc non-party organisation',[5] was both active and influential, and—through it—Winston Churchill (and other Liberals) re-

ceived the public and active support of some of the city's best
known Conservatives. Aided, indeed, by the opposition of the
city's influential Jewish population to the Aliens Act it became
so common for Unionists to appear and speak on Liberal—and
occasionally even on Labour—platforms—that Coningsby Disraeli, standing on a moderate fiscal platform at Altrincham,
complained in a letter to *The Times* on 13 February that the
Unionist Free Traders had notoriously exhorted their fellows
throughout the country to vote against their party. The *Liverpool
Catholic Herald* said on 19 January that no one who knew the
constituencies could doubt for a moment that 'a large number of
Conservatives' had left their party on the question of Free Trade
and voted with the Liberals. Indeed, as Table 32 shows, there
was a unique combination in Lancashire of relatively low poll
increase, a high swing against the Unionists, and a low negative
correlation between the number of ownership (and predominantly
Unionist) votes and the swing. It thus seems probable that a
greater proportion of the propertied middle and upper-middle
classes voted Liberal in Lancashire than in most other parts of
the country, and that, coupled with the Irish and working-class
votes, this accounts for the region's extraordinary swing.

Table 32

POLL, SWING AND OWNERSHIP VOTES, LANCASHIRE AND OTHER
MAJOR DISTRICTS[6]

District	Percentage poll	Poll increase	Swing	Correlation coefficient between ownership votes and swing
Lancashire	86·4	6	13·1	—016
South-East	83·6	9	8·8	—171
South-West	86·1	6	7·8	—191
East	81·8	9	8·4	—183
North-East	85·2	9	10·1	+033
North-West	84·2	9	12·5	—392
Scotland	77·1	10	11·3	—267
Wales	86·2	12	5·6	—911

Something of the same effect also occurred in the rural areas, where—as one commentator forecast in August 1905—'free food' and 'land for the people' played 'a most prominent part'[7] in the largely unexpected Liberal victories. The farmers cared little for policies which offered *industrial* protection but *agricultural* preference, and which—as Sir Gilbert Parker put it at Rochester —sought to regain in colonies the 'lost balance between agriculture and industry in England';[8] and the labourers, existing on 15s a week, were solidly against any new taxation of their food or clothing. Sir E. Vincent warned Balfour in November 1905 that 'any idea of food taxation would be fatal in the counties'.[9] A correspondent of Balfour's wrote of Tariff Reform in Scotland that 'the lairds like it, the farmers fear it and the working men hate it', and Edward Porritt wrote of England that Chamberlain's only firm supporters were landowners, *some* farmers, and the clergy.[10] Both Joseph Arch, the founder of the Agricultural Labourers Union, and G. J. Holyoake, the veteran Chartist, issued appeals to the rural electorate to vote against Tariff Reform, and references to the 'bad old times of Protection', sometimes in the circulation of facsimile copies of Anti-Corn Law League propaganda, were legion throughout the campaign period. The plain fact is that as the agricultural depression of the 1880s and 90s moved into its secondary phase, so the Tariff Reform proposals helped to weaken further the social— and often direct—pressures on the agricultural labourers to vote for their squires.

However, this rural swing was not *simply* a revolt of the oppressed against the oppressors, the poor against the rich. As Table 32 again suggests (in the low negative correlation of ownership votes and swing), Liberal candidates in the south-east once again received unprecedented support from well-known Unionists in the localities (despite, it may be added, the studious fiscal moderation of many Unionist candidates). In the Colchester division of Essex, the son of a well-known local Conservative family worked for Sir Weetman Pearson on the grounds that the Tories had tarnished their country's honour in the Khaki election, with Chinese labour, their failure to fulfil earlier election promises, and their Tariff Reform proposals, and Andrew Johnston, the Conservative chairman of Essex County Council, actively campaigned for the Liberals, in more than one constituency in the county, against what he called Chamberlain's spurious imperialism. Augustine Williams, the Liberal candidate for the Mid-Kent division, similarly received a good deal of support from influential Conservatives who may—as county men—have shared his evident antipathy for Chamberlain and all his works. Associations of Unionist Free Traders sprang up in counties and towns as conservative as Surrey, Brighton, and Bath, and— no doubt influenced by 'the defection of the Duke of Devonshire . . . [whose] influence was *always* . . . enormous with . . . their well-to-do middle and upper middle classes . . .'[11]—even the more cautious of them, like the Surrey Unionist Free Trade League, finally issued specific advice to their members to vote for the Free Trade candidates, 'where the Unionist candidate does not express himself as willing to oppose the Chamberlain and any kindred policy and where the Liberal and Free Trade candidate declares that no Home Rule Bill must be passed in the next Parliament'.[12] The element of leadership which they provided was a further solvent in loosening the traditional ties of social and occupational loyalty, in these county areas.

In both town and country, moreover, women played a more than usually significant role. They were out in force in 1906 canvassing, campaigning, and 'prevailing'—as Lowell has it— 'upon men who were lukewarm to go to the polls . . .';[13] and, influenced by a combination of the cheap food and suffrage issues, they unquestionably threw their influence more heavily on to the Liberal and Labour side than at any time before. Although the WSPU canvassed vigorously against Churchill and some other leading Liberals, its influence was not substantial except perhaps at Wigan where, financed by female cotton operatives, Thorley Smith stood as Women's Suffrage candidate; and on the more generally adopted NUWSS test of support for the 1904 (suffrage) bill, the Liberals came out well (6:1) compared

with their Unionist opponents. But 'fears about prices' undoubtedly had the greatest weight with what the *Daily Telegraph*
unflatteringly called 'the ignorant female mind, unable to look
beyond the limitations of the . . . weekly wage', and—referring to
Tariff Reform—the Secretary of the WNLF said halfway through
the poll that 'there has never been an election that has come home
to women as this has done'.[14] 'When they told me our food would
cost more', wrote a widow to Chamberlain in 1909, 'I would not
let [my husband] vote Conservative as he had always done',[15]
and there were many like her, working directly or openly to make
the election a 'women's election' (as *Women's Weekly* called it)
in a double sense, with the Liberals (and Labour) doubly the
beneficiaries. Whether or not Channing (Liberal, Eastern
Northamptonshire) was right in saying that Tariff Reform was
never a national demand and had never commanded the brains
and hearts of the people, it was certainly tried and found wanting
by all those commercial and consumer groups interested first
and foremost in cheap food and raw materials.[16]

Speaking, predictably, for all Tariff Reformers (on 22 January),
the *Morning Post* entered a most emphatic protest against St Loe
Strachey's assumption that the election had been fought on
Chamberlain's proposals for fiscal reform.

> Nobody was more anxious that this should be the single issue
> than . . . Chamberlain himself. But the Liberals, for reasons best
> known to themselves, have made Chinese Labour their first
> weapon of attack [and] from all parts of the country comes
> information that the 'slavery' cry has accounted for the defeat of
> the Unionist candidates.

Arnold Forster added, with characteristic assurance, that the
Unionists had *not* lost votes on Tariff Reform and with other
convinced Tariff Reformers argued that where—unlike what
Outlook (20 January) called 'the Lancashire hairsplitters'—
Unionists had explained Chamberlain's policies patiently and
consistently, they had met with better success. Chamberlain
himself attributed the Birmingham results to the conscientious
education of his electorate on the tariff issue, and to good

M

Unionist organisation and preparation, and *The Times* agreed on 18 January that they 'show what can be done by a clear thinking, painstaking and well-informed man, dealing with an electorate which has been taught very largely by himself to appreciate sound arguments and serious treatment of political questions'. Commenting earlier (16 January) on Hoxton, the *Pall Mall Gazette* said that Claude Hay's increased majority had been 'produced partly by patient and skilful attention to the constituency in season and out of season . . . but chiefly . . . by handling Tariff Reform in the reverse fashion from that followed by many Unionist candidates.' Mr Hay, it continued, did not apologise for his fiscal opinions or try to 'sugar them over with temporising explanations', but laid the grounds of his policy 'clearly and confidently before the electors and rubbed it into their minds until it became the strongest article of their belief and safest plank on his platform'. If the party had 'evinced more courage in this connection, from top to bottom', the history of the election 'might have borne a different complexion'. In the same way the *Sheffield Daily Telegraph* described the victories of Vincent, Wortley, and Roberts in the Central, Hallam, and Eccleshall divisions of Sheffield as triumphs of political education in the principles of Tariff Reform, and the *Standard* and the *National Review* weighed into the argument by citing—*inter alia*—the results at Grimsby and Central Hull, Pike Pease's defeat of Isaac Mitchell at Darlington, Sir Gilbert Parker's 'ridiculously easy' victory over both Liberal and Labour at Gravesend, Travis Clegg's increased poll at Stalybridge, T. H. Benn's eclipse of Hugh Cecil at Greenwich, and the success of the only three cabinet ministers to hold their seats, Austen Chamberlain, Akers-Douglas, and Arnold-Forster.

These apologists were, however, selective in their examples, for—as Table 33 shows—Birmingham was by no means immune to the tide of opinion. The *Speaker*—rightly—said (on 27 January) that Chamberlain would have held it 'if he had suggested the abolition of the Monarchy'; but—as Grey pointed out at Berwick on 19 January—it was still reduced 'from a continent to an island'. (Herbert Maxwell likewise wrote in the February edition of *Nineteenth Century* that the Birmingham results 'were no more a vote for Tariff Reform than . . . for the improved cultivation of orchids'.)

Table 33

SIX BIRMINGHAM CONSTITUENCIES—THE SWING
FROM THE PREVIOUS CONTEST

Division	Previous contest	Swing per cent
East	1900	—11·2
North	1895	—1·3
West	1895	—4·2
Bordesley	1895	—7·4
South	1895	—11·7
Central	1892	—4·6

The same was true of Central Hull where there was a 10·3 per cent swing, Sheffield Eccleshall where there was a 10 per cent swing, Sheffield Hallam where there was a 3·8 per cent swing that left Stewart Wortley with a majority of only 81, and to a greater or lesser degree in most of the other cases cited. In both Gravesend and Grimsby the Unionists were materially assisted by poor Liberal candidates and by Liberal/Labour divisions, and of the ministers Akers-Douglas was the only one to hold his own in terms of votes; Austen Chamberlain's poll was 3 per cent lower than it had been in 1892, and Arnold-Forster won in Croydon only because of the bitter divisions between his Liberal and Labour opponents.

Even more telling was the defeat of numerous well-known Tariff Reformers—including six members of the Tariff Commission itself—who devoted every bit as much care to the education of their constituents as Chamberlain or Hay. Leverton Harris was defeated at Teignmouth, which had never before returned a Liberal, and Sir Alfred Hickman and Sir Alex Henderson lost at West Wolverhampton, which had last returned a Liberal in 1885, and at West Staffordshire which had last returned one in 1886. Henry Chaplin was defeated at Sleaford, which he had represented for twenty years, by the unknown and eccentric Liberal 'anti-vaccinationist', and in Bradford Caillard and Gibbs saw their polls fall below their 1900 levels despite considerable increases in the number of voters. Walter Long was drummed out of Bristol by over 2,500 votes, and whilst D. Shackleton (Labour) beat one of Lancashire's few Tariff Reformers (B. J. Belton) by over 8,000 votes, his more famous namesake lost in Dundee, 'drowned', he said (in a reference to the 1903 Sugar Bounty), 'in marmalade'. Other extreme Tariff Reformers lost at Plymouth, at Halifax, Kidderminster, Rochdale, Stafford, Falkirk and—like Balfourites indeed—all over the country. The final irony for Chamberlain, as the *Spectator* quickly pointed out (on 20 January), was that with the exception of Liverpool, all the cities where he made his major speeches between 1903 and 1905 voted almost solidly against Tariff Reform, and Liverpool hardly for it.

Table 34

LIBERAL GAINS IN TWELVE TOWNS AND CITIES

Town or city	Victories in 1900*	Liberal gains 1906	LRC gains 1906	Unionist Free Trade 1906
Liverpool	8 (U) 1 (N)	2	–	1
Glasgow	7 (U)	4	1	2
Leeds	2 (U) 3 (L)	4	–	–
Cardiff and Newport	4 (U)	2	–	–
Newcastle	2 (U)	1	1	–
Preston	2 (U)	1	1	–
Gainsborough	1 (U)	1	–	–
Greenock	1 (U)	1	–	–
Limehouse	1 (U)	1	–	–
Luton	1 (L)	–	–	–
Teignmouth	1 (U)	1	–	–

* Unionists (U), Liberal (L), Nationalist (N); for fuller details, see Appendix

Chamberlain could hardly argue that these cities had not heard of his policies; yet in 1906 they returned only eight Unionists

compared with twenty-nine in 1900; and of the eight, three were
unmistakably Free Traders. The long and short of the argument
about the relative success of a 'strong' and 'weak' Unionist fiscal
policy is that in some places the one paid off, and in other places
the other. If in Hoxton and Gravesend Tariff Reformers did
better, in Lancashire almost all the successful Unionists were
Balfourites; Richard Cavendish's agent wrote of Haddock, who
won at North Lonsdale, that although 'nominally . . . a follower
of Mr. Balfour . . . even in this adhesion to the retaliation idea he
avoided committing himself in any definite manner to antagonism
to Free Trade'.[17] If, similarly, Birmingham was solidly for Tariff
Reform so—equally—was Glasgow (Unionist, Liberal and
Labour) solid for Free Trade. Whilst many would-be Tariff
Reform Unionists might have been better advised to have come
out in their true colours before, rather than after, the election,
the honours were even in the eleven constituencies in which
Unionist Free Traders and Tariff Reformers directly opposed
each other, and there is no evidence, either statistical or historical,
to demonstrate that either one or the other set of fiscal views
might, if adopted by all the party, have been more successful.
(The Unionist Free Traders did better in Birkenhead, Islington
South, Kings Lynn, Lincoln and Glasgow Tradeston; the Tariff
Reformers in Greenwich, Durham, Cambridge and the Scottish
university seats. The eleventh seat was North Lonsdale, where
Haddock hedged so on Tariff Reform that this victory was certainly not a victory for Tariff Reform policies.) A strong lead
from Chamberlain, and a wholehearted committal of the party
to his policy, might have saved more seats than it lost, but so
equally would the slower, less crusading, but united evolution of
the idea of fiscal reform under Balfour's leadership: as Sir
Edward Clarke wrote on 20 January—'but for . . . [Chamberlain]
we might have been defeated, but we [w]ould not have been
destroyed'.[18] In the event the Unionists had the worst of both
worlds, and, as one of them said, the Liberals 'had only to watch
their antics and direct the voters to watch them too'[19] in order to
ensure success.

The element of truth in the arguments paraded by both sides was that a hesitant and above all a divided party can neither attract support nor organise itself effectively for action: as T. P. O'Connor observed, it 'is never as sure to fall as when it reaches a pitched battle either in the field or at the polling booths'.[20] Acland-Hood may have been right in his judgement that the effect of Unionist divisions was 'insignificant compared to the apathy and neglect of organisation' displayed by his party generally,[21] and it would be difficult to disagree with *The Times*' verdict that 'sheer bad management . . . neglect of the constituencies by their representatives . . . slackness of organisation and resulting apathy among the rank and file'[22] were responsible for defeat in many constituencies in—especially—the south-east. But the fiscal divisions undoubtedly established a multiplier effect which led first to apathy, and then to abstention, and then to apathy again. There is *prima facie* evidence to suggest that the Unionists not only lost votes but failed to mobilise support; and that their fiscal divisions, as well as their policies, quite clearly were a major cause of this.

RELIGIOUS AND NATIONAL ISSUES AND GROUPS

If Tariff Reform was the most important single issue to bring over to the Liberals the organised support of erstwhile opponents and uncertain friends, it was closely followed by the careful and *successful* balancing act effected by the Liberals between the mobilisation of their traditional nonconformist support and the wooing and winning of those Catholic Irish votes which had, in 1886, been cast against the party with such disastrous results for it.

Having suffered from social disabilities of various kinds for decades, if not centuries, the nonconformists began to fight back increasingly during the 1880s and 90s by organising themselves first into sectional groups, and finally, in 1899, into the National Free Church Council, to promote greater unity and understanding and to articulate the voice—in 1906—of the Presbyterians,

Methodists, Congregationalists, and Baptists who made up its 4 million souls (and approximately 600,000 voters). The NFCC saw fit to reaffirm in 1906 as well as in 1905 that its mission was spiritual rather than political, but the combined pressures of political circumstances and increasing belief in social rather than individual redemption ('man cannot be saved alone', wrote Horne, 'he must be saved in society')[23] drove it inexorably towards political action. It established a special department for electoral work, and circulated millions of leaflets attacking many aspects of Unionist policy—including Chinese labour as well as education and licensing reform—and issued a manifesto which in effect made the Liberal cause in the election its own.

The manifesto declared that by making Free Churchmen legally responsible for the management and maintenance of schools 'from the religious teaching and influence of which in many cases they profoundly dissented', the Education Act had done nonconformity a 'grievous wrong'; maintained that by endowing the brewers the 1904 Licensing Act placed private profit before public good; called for the 'courageous and sympathetic treatment of social problems'; proclaimed that Campbell-Bannerman's government 'represented the people as no other has before';[24] and led the (Anglican) *Church Times* to comment on 5 January—sardonically—that whilst 'professedly non-party', it made no secret of the belief that the new government was 'about to inaugurate the reign of national righteousness'. Whilst in November 1905 Keir Hardie rejected NFCC feelers for a conference between the LRC and those whom he derisively described as 'the stucco saints' of dissent,[25] the manifesto nevertheless contained many common points with the Labour as well as the Liberal programme, and with 66 per cent of LRC candidates themselves dissenters, much informal co-operation ensued, between nonconformists and Labour as well as Liberal candidates. There can be no doubt that, as D. W. Brogan has recorded, 'nonconformity reached the height of political power [and] was most representative of the English people' around the beginning of the century before the Liberal landslide of 1906.[26]

Nonconformist opinion was not monolithic; differences of emphasis inevitably remained, reflecting the different interests—national and sectional—of various groups; but the NFCC manifesto provided an effective basis for a largely common campaign, within which a broad condemnation of Unionist policies and philosophies was comprised. And all groups were—if nothing else—*active* in their protests. Many regional free church councils —like the Metropolitan Free Church Council and the Liverpool and District Welsh Free Church Council—participated to the full in the work of canvassing and persuasion; and whilst many temperance groups badgered candidates with their questions, a sizeable number of the more prominent nonconformist ministers energetically followed the exhortation of the activist *Connexional Magazine* to do their utmost to gain supporters for the Liberal and Labour candidates.[27] Under the specific auspices of the NFCC, Clifford and Campbell-Morgan embarked on a motorised canvass of East Anglia and Lincolnshire, and whilst Silvester Horne and T. D. Jones covered the Midlands, F. B. Morgan and Thomas Yates circled round from the West Country to London and to Kent; and in the north, similarly, many of their colleagues took an active part in the campaigns of both the Northern Education League and the National Reform Union. The *Daily News*, which applauded their efforts as magnificent, said on 6 January that the 'motor-cars which are hurrying through the constituencies carrying free church speakers are spreading a new and deeper civic sense', and the *Church Times*, which naturally disapproved, said six days later that they had 'automobilised their pulpits in order to preach those doctrines of party politics which have become to so great an extent the religion of dissent'.

Furthermore, from Kent to Dorset, to Sheffield, to Stirling, came accounts of local ministers taking the chair at Liberal and Labour meetings, or otherwise actively participating in the election. The *Croydon Guardian* reported of Croydon that 'the manner in which the Nonconformist Ministers and their satellites threw themselves into the fray imparted something of religious

fanaticism',[28] and from West Derbyshire Victor Cavendish wrote
to Devonshire that 'the Nonconformist Ministers have worked
very hard . . . Leading members of the different Nonconformist
bodies [stood] outside the polling booths [at Bakewell] and every
elector had to run the gauntlet of this cross-fire of ecclesiastical
influence.'[29] Brooke-Taylor, Cavendish's agent, added that they
'brought to bear every argument which could affect the con-
sciences, pockets, or stomachs of the electors and were very
unscrupulous in their statements. Nonconformists were told
that it was their "solemn duty" to drive Mr. Cavendish from
West Derbyshire for ever and other arguments were on similar
lines.'[30] In London the Metropolitan Free Church Council
allowed itself to become virtually a caucus in the Liberal interest,
that looked benignly on Silvester Horne's use of Whitfields
Tabernacle in Tottenham Court Road as a kind of Liberal
Committee Room in South St Pancras.

> We may think, we may say [Horne openly proclaimed in his
> paper the *London Signal*] that few London candidates will have
> more powerful or united Free Church support [than P. W.
> Wilson, the Liberal candidate]. At one end of the constituency
> is the Reverend Ensor Walters and his formidable artillery of the
> West London Mission, concentrated on the entrenchments of
> vice and injustice. At the other end is the Reverend Alexander
> Connell, one of the ablest and manliest leaders of English
> Presbyterianism. On the Oxford street side the Reverend Thomas
> Phillips is a host in himself. No effort will be spared, to win the
> greatest victory in London for social and educational and
> political reform.[31]

Conservatives, not surprisingly (and not unreasonably), stigmatised the extreme level of commitment as 'disgraceful',[32] and
to some extent sought to mobilise established opinion against it.
A special conference of Anglican clergy held in December 1905
to discuss the education issue rejected the proposal that—by
analogy presumably with the NFCC—the Church of England
should form a special committee to defend the principles of
religious education and—to the admitted regret of the *Church
Times*—Archbishop Davidson merely enjoined voters to 'make

thoughtful and deliberate choice of men for the legislature' after
ascertaining on what lines they would 'endeavour to construct
and reconstruct' their laws.[33] But some of his bishops were a
shade more partisan; the Bishop of Birmingham warned that 'any
fresh departure in legislation which would ignore and traverse'
the fixed principles of religious education during school hours
and of parental choice would mean trouble, and the Bishop of
Bath and Wells stated quite clearly in his January diocesan letter
that the Birrell plan of sectarian education outside school hours
would never work.[34] Similarly, the Church Defence League and
the United Parishes Organisation—which, being mixed lay and
clerical organisations, were less inhibited than most of the church
leaders—questioned candidates about education and disestablishment in most English constituencies and invariably advised voters
to support the Conservatives—at Islington, for example, where
Lough, the new Secretary of the Board of Education was standing.

These voices in favour of the existing system of religious education in schools were—broadly speaking—supported by leading
English Catholics, as the other major interest involved. Archbishop Bourne of Westminster issued a manifesto—which Michael
Davitt privately described as being 'as equivocally mischievous
as if it had been drafted by Arthur Balfour in the interests of the
Unionist candidates'—in which he urged all Catholics to 'resist
any interference with the right of Catholic parents . . . to have
their children educated . . . in conformity with their conscientious
religious convictions';[35] and the Duke of Norfolk declared in one
of his open letters to Conservative candidates that they were not
only fighting for a cause which represented 'the unity of the
Empire and its commercial prosperity' but also for one on which
they could rely 'to safeguard the religious upbringing of their
children'.[36] His warning was reiterated by a number of Conservatives standing where Catholics were numerous (e.g. in Southwark, Hull, Barkston Ash, York); and Ripon (the only Catholic
in the cabinet) privately feared that his influence, at least among
English Catholics, would be large.

For two main reasons, however, neither the Church of England nor the Catholic hierarchy was in any position, in 1906, to lead any movement of opinion likely to be significant in electoral terms. The first reason—as Booth reported in his study of London—was that the Church of England had long since lost the active adherence of the majority of the population and— under Archbishop Davidson's easy-going leadership—had little specific contribution to make either in religious or in political terms. Indeed the Archbishop's condonation of Chinese labour— sardonically foreseen by Snowden at the ILP's 1904 conference[37] —made it easy for dissenters to caricature it, like the *Morning Leader* (30 December), as the 'moneybags Church'. As the Archdeacon of Lancaster frankly told the 1905 conference on education, it had far less in reality to fear from radicalism than from the evident combination of public hostility and apathy. In the second place, the majority—perhaps three-quarters—of the million or so Catholics in England, Scotland, and Wales were of Irish ancestry and the important question throughout was whether, as Catholic Irish, they would heed their English (Catholic) bishops or whether as Irish Catholics they would take note of the instructions of the official nationalist organisation, the United Irish League.

The League declared, in its manifesto, that the best way in which Catholics could protect their schools was by strengthening 'the power and prestige of the Irish Party',[38] and, assisted alike by Birrell's moderation and by the very breadth of issues on which the nonconformists were campaigning, the campaign tides of compromise were always running strongly. Abbot Gasquet, an influential member of the Irish hierarchy, said publicly that he did not believe that a Liberal government which included Ripon would disregard Catholic interests, and on 6 January even *The Tablet*—the staid organ of the Catholic establishment—came close to saying that the whole education dispute had been due to a misunderstanding; it suggested that the Liberals had misunderstood the meaning of the word 'managers' who, it said, were more like 'visitors' leaving the 'real' management of the schools to local authorities. Liberals, for their part, responded wherever possible by meeting the Catholics halfway; at Bradford they agreed to an arrangement involving the recognition of rate aid for the important local Catholic college of St Joseph's, and in South Caernarvon Lloyd George secured the withdrawal of a Catholic circular in favour of the Unionists by promising that neither he nor his party wished to interfere with the rights of any sect. In a review of the situation on 17 January, the *Standard* consequently complained that the Liberals were apparently prepared to offer 'special terms' to Catholics (and also Jews) whilst continuing to 'browbeat' the Church of England.

In actual fact it was one of the minor ironies of the election that the only Anglican pressure groups that were really active—the Church Association (which had seven agents and 371 electoral councils), the Imperial Protestant Federation, and various local Protestant leagues—were all concerned to oppose redistribution, ritualism, and Rome rather than to promote religious education or freedom, and thus eased, rather than hindered, the tendencies towards Liberal-Irish (Catholic) compromise. They were most active in Birkenhead, where Kensit was standing as an Independent Protestant candidate, and in Liverpool where—commented the *Liverpool Catholic Herald* (on 12 January)—'George Wise and his no-Popery gang ruled the Tories . . . as Colonel Sandys and the Orangemen ruled . . . [them] in Ireland'; but the movement was in evidence in all of the big northern towns—Hull, Barrow, Bradford, Manchester, etc—where the Irish element was large, and it undoubtedly militated against the efforts of Unionist candidates to develop a bond of common support over the education issue. When A. A. Tobin, the Unionist candidate for the Scotland division of Liverpool, sought to appeal to Catholic sentiment over schooling at the same time as he was appealing to Protestant anti-Catholicism, T. P. O'Connor aptly observed that it was 'surely an extraordinary thing to see the Catholic organ and the Protestant drum playing together the Adeste Fideles' for him;[39] and the *Daily Telegraph* commented sadly on 15 January that the Protestant extremists 'seem prepared to ignore the risk to their co-religionists in Ireland so long as they can make hay of High Churchmen . . .'

In the closing months of 1905, therefore, as Redmond struggled to make a bargain with the Liberal leaders that he could sell to his supporters, the United Irish League, operating from Liverpool with T. P. O'Connor and its General Secretary Crilby, pressed on with its electoral preparations in all those constituencies in England, Scotland, and Wales in which the Irish vote was of significance. In a memorandum entitled *Seats held by the Unionists in 1886 and 1892 which may be won by an appeal to the Irish vote*, Herbert Gladstone estimated the number of such constituencies at 110, of which he reckoned the Liberals ought to win back 97;[40] Devlin more modestly put the total for England, Scotland and Wales at 80; and the *Scotsman* numbered 36 in Scotland alone.[41] But with a coverage of 192 constituencies, and paid agents and branches in all major centres, the League's position, in either event, was one of power. It was thus a factor of great significance that, in 1906, this power was exercised almost entirely in the Liberal interest. In Midlothian, where the memory still rankled of Sir J. Gibson Carmichael's defection after the 1895 election, the League went so far as to order the Irish to vote against Lord Dalmeny; it was responsible for circulars in Leith opposing Munro-Ferguson because his attitude to Home Rule had for so long been equivocal (although his immediate electoral policy of administrative reform was not very different from that of many other Liberals); and it (not unreasonably) distinguished between the Liberal candidate for the North-Eastern division of Lanark, who was a straight Home-Ruler, and Douglas in the North-Western division, a Liberal Leaguer who, said the *Scotsman* on 11 January, should have been a Unionist. Doubts about the wisdom of supporting some other Liberal candidates were entertained until the last minute—e.g. in Paisley and in the College division of Glasgow. But the League was clearly often satisfied with something far short of a pledge to immediate, or even partial Home Rule, since West Ridgeway was included among the satisfactory London candidates, Haldane was endorsed at Haddington, and Leonard Courtney was supported—if with little enthusiasm—at Edinburgh.

Cox, the Liberal candidate for Preston, recorded—typically, perhaps—that the Irish were 'most reasonable' and moderate. 'I told them quite frankly that there could not be a Home Rule Bill in the [coming] Parliament', he wrote to Bryce, 'and they quite understood'.[42] Indeed, as the Socialist James MacDonald and the Labour press were quick to note, Liberal candidates were often preferred—in deference to Redmond's understanding with Campbell-Bannerman—to Labour and Socialist candidates who were much more forthright about Home Rule for Ireland than they were. Palmer, for instance, received UIL endorsement at Jarrow in preference to Curran, Runciman to Turner at Dewsbury, Snape to Coit at Wakefield, and Harvey (Rochdale) and Murray (Govan) to their Socialist opponents. A typical case was Dundee where—in direct response to a telegram from the Standing Committee of the UIL, dated 7 January 1906—the Michael Davitt Branch of the League issued a statement that any vote for Wilkie (LRC) would be a vote against Ireland; and although LRC candidates invariably received the League's endorsement where they were standing against Unionists only, only seven Labour or Socialist candidates, standing in three-sided contests, were actively preferred to Liberals (in Glasgow Blackfriars, Glasgow Camlachie, Burnley, East Bradford, East Leeds, Croydon, and Paisley). In the event, therefore, Liberals received official League support in 95 per cent (168) of the seats in which it gave candidates its official endorsement, and were opposed in only ten.

To the very last, cautious English—and extreme Irish— prelates continued to question the wisdom of such a close alliance between the Irish Catholics and the Liberals. Dr O'Dwyer, the Bishop of Limerick, said on 13 January that in the light of statements made by Asquith, Grey and others, not to mention the 'platitudes and generalities' of the Stirling speech, it seemed to him to be 'suicidal . . . to ask the Irish in England to throw in all their votes solidly for the Liberals and swell their majority into such a magnitude that the Government may snap its fingers at the Irish Party';[43] and on the same day *The Times*—which had been assiduously emphasising the importance of the Irish issue—expressed renewed confidence that 'a large number of Irish voters—now firmly convinced that no legislation in the direction of Home Rule was to be expected from a Cabinet controlled by men whose opinions Mr. Morley has characterised as "Unionism and water" will sulk in their tents [on polling day] with the secret approval of their chiefs'. They were both right and wrong: right in that the Liberal majority did finally prove to be uncomfortably large for the Nationalist interest, but wrong in so far as it was by no means clear to Irish voters going to poll in the big cities between 13 and 16 January that—to paraphrase the first of Howarth's letters to *The Times*—there was anything to be gained by sending Mr Long back to Dublin Castle, rather than the party 'with devolution on its banner'. And whatever private misgivings they may have had, Redmond and his colleagues remained true to their agreement and undoubtedly did everything they could to bring their supporters on to the Liberal side.

Table 35

UNITED IRISH LEAGUE ENDORSEMENT OF CANDIDATES

Country	Liberal	LRC *	†	Social- ist	National- ist	Anti- Liberal	Total
England and Wales	114	13	3	1	1	—	132
Scotland	54	—	2	1	—	3	60
Total Great Britain	168	13	5	2	1	3	192

* LRC candidates with straight fights
† LRC candidates also fighting Liberals

The Liberals thus obtained the support of the majority not only of the 600,000 or so nonconformist voters but also of the approximately 200,000 Irish Catholic men of voting age. Particularly against the background of the fiscal issue and all that involved, it was a formidable combination, which produced remarkably little friction between its potentially conflicting interests. The

nonconformist vote was probably less concentrated than the Irish
—but it was of evident importance in those constituencies in
which middle-class and upper working-class electorates often
included relatively large numbers of dissenters: the inner and
outer suburbs of London, where the Unionists lost twenty-six
seats and suffered a swing of between 16 and 21 per cent;
Birmingham, where a swing of 11·2 per cent came perilously close
to loosening even Chamberlain's personal sway over dissenting
opinion; and many of the smaller country towns—like Dover,
Southport, Ipswich, and Guildford—where, according to *The
Times*, Broderick's defeat (at the hands, it would seem, of a
mixture of nonconformists and women) caused something like
stupefaction. Its overriding significance, however, lay in the
manner in which it carried a whole community into support of
not just one item, but in effect all items of Liberal policy. In
campaign speeches and rallies the education question figured
far less prominently than the fiscal issue or Chinese labour, but
it fell not far short of these in the enthusiasm and confidence
that it engendered in the Liberal faithful and in the number of
active committee workers and opinion leaders whom it called into
the Liberal service. It was, furthermore, just because the dissenting commitment to the Liberals was so strong that the Liberals
were able to modify their language on the education issue, here
and there, and so minimise Anglican and Catholic opposition.

In the event, the Unionists held only one seat (York) of the
eight singled out by various Unionist papers as seats where
Catholic opinion (English and Irish) was likely to be pro-
Conservative, and lost four (Bermondsey, Rotherhithe, York
and Finsbury) to the Liberals—who also held the other three
(Walsall, West Southwark, and West Nottingham). Edward
Porritt observed in his survey of the election that Catholic
opinion (as such) had been far less obviously Conservative in
1906 than it had been in 1895 (or 1900), and the majority, indeed,
of the newly-elected Catholic members were Liberal or Labour.
The *Liverpool Catholic Herald* expressed pleasure on 19 January
that the 'handful of Catholic wire-pullers and autocrats' who were

identified with Toryism had not dragged Catholicism down with it, and its companion paper in Dundee expressed confidence that the Catholic masses—by which it meant in fact the Irish Catholics —were not in future likely to be found on the same platforms as the 'Norfolks and Denbighs'.

The Irish vote was, in fact, almost solidly Liberal in 1906, and Hudson was quick to pay tribute to the important part that it had played in the sweeping gains made by the Liberals in the cities of Lancashire and Yorkshire, Tyneside, and the Clyde. All but five of the ninety-seven constituencies, on Herbert Gladstone's list, that had been Liberal in 1886 and/or 1892 were regained, and in only five seats did the Irish vote contribute to Liberal defeats (although these would probably have happened anyway)—i.e. at West Leeds, Deptford and Glasgow Blackfriars, where it helped LRC candidates to victory, and Glasgow Camlachie and North-West Lanark where, by going to Socialist candidates, it contributed towards minority Unionist victories. It would be reasonable to suppose that the Irish vote therefore made a contribution towards the twenty-two seats gained by Liberal and Labour candidates in the big cities of the English north—in Liverpool, Manchester, Sheffield, Leeds, Nottingham, Bradford, Hull, and Newcastle—and towards two-thirds or more of the party's twenty-four gains in Scotland. 'Unionist electioneers' said the *Scotsman*, had been compelled by experience to regard the Irish vote as a 'lever controlled from Dublin';[44] and, commenting on the major borough results, the *Daily Telegraph* said (on 17 January) that the polling had made it clear that some kind of secret agreement had been reached with the Irish Catholics at least, concerning a waiver for Catholic education.

Moreover—and this was one of the ways in which the 1906 election differed most significantly from 1885—the Liberals succeeded in obtaining the Irish vote without forfeiting the potential support of a great many Unionists who were sympathetic over other issues (in 1906 chiefly Free Trade). Cox reported from Preston that he believed that he had had the whole of the

N

Irish vote as well as a very large Unionist vote'[45] and in Manchester Churchill obviously obtained a combination of Irish and Unionist Free Trade support. Even more curiously, perhaps—at Jarrow—Palmer received support from Irish on the one side and from Orangemen on the other, who evidently regarded him as a lesser evil than his Labour opponent. As one Unionist observer wrote after the election, 'Home Rule was still a real issue in 1895 and was so believed to be; it was also an issue in 1906 but it was not believed to be except by the Irish, and consequently the Radicals had the support of both Irish Nationalists and Radical anti-Home Rulers.'[46] In brief, the election proved Howarth, and not Balfour, to be right, and there can be no doubt that in assuming that there were votes to be won in 1906 by beating the Home Rule drum, the Unionists committed a serious strategic mistake.

One final factor—minor but interesting—in steering some erstwhile Unionist opinion towards the Liberals was the question of Jews, of the Russian pogroms and of the new Aliens Act. Despite the considerable element of anti-Semitism in Edwardian England, which some Liberals (e.g. Belloc in *Emmanuel Burdon*) directed against 'Josef Schamberlain' as the tool of the South African Jewish plutocracy,[47] frequent and harrowing press reports of poor Jewish refugees being turned away from British ports when the Act came into force on 1 January 1906 created a wave of sympathy for its victims. The result was that, even as Balfour had his historic meeting with Weizmann—the prelude to his declaration of 1917—the Jewish community in general was being confirmed in its opposition to the outgoing government. In London in the first week of January 1906 the Reverend Goldstein of the Federation of Synagogues told a meeting of Jewish electors at the King's Hall that the return of the Tories would be the 'death blow to Jewish freedom in England', and exhorted all present to vote against the Unionist candidates in their constituencies (meaning in London chiefly St George's in the East, Whitechapel, and Mile End);[48] and—taking a look at the neighbouring constituency of Stepney—the *Pall Mall*

Gazette commented on 16 January that despite a certain dislike of Jewish competition in the clothing and furniture trades, the Jews there would almost certainly vote Liberal in the hope of securing an amendment to the Aliens Act. Given his leading part in opposing the Aliens Act and his promise to consider the creation of an autonomous Jewish state within the empire, Winston Churchill's appointment to the Liberal ministry was warmly welcomed: to the *Jewish Chronicle* it provided an 'additional guarantee, if any were needed, of the friendliness of the new ministry' in its relations with the Jews, whether the question was the treatment of aliens or 'the provision of asylum to the refugees of darkest Europe'.[49] Unionist speakers who tried to defend the Aliens Act before Jewish audiences in Leeds received short shrift indeed, and their votes almost certainly played as significant a part in Gerald Balfour's unexpected defeat there as they did of Winston Churchill's victory in North-West Manchester.

CHINESE LABOUR; SOCIAL ISSUES; AND THE LABOUR VOTE

By themselves, the fiscal issue and the division that it caused, the nonconformist crusade, and the solidarity of the Irish vote would have been enough to secure the Unionists' defeat, but it is in the unexpectedly complete organisation of the Labour vote that the explanation for their total rout must be sought; for this not only bit deeply into many traditionally Conservative areas but helped to create a national solidarity of view, which—however transitorily—transcended other divisions. The reform of trade union law—following the Taff Vale case—was of course a sectional interest, just like the reform of the Education and Licensing Acts; but—as has been seen—in the reaction to Chamberlain personally and to the Tariff Reform campaign, orthodox fiscal and radical social policies were easily combined and, however protectionist many working people may, at heart, have been (and not least the Irish), they were not inclined—in 1906—to vote for the man who promised them welfare but gave them a war. Liberal—and even more so Labour—candidates pledged not some speculative and possibly spurious fiscal rearrangement, but trade union reform, poor law reform, land reform and many other measures that—with different emphases —seemed to promise, and more immediately, better things. And if these factors were not enough, the Unionists ensured—by their insensitive handling of the Chinese labour issue—that the Labour alliance in the Liberal and Labour interest would be firm.

After Free Trade, indeed, Chinese labour was probably the most important single *issue* of the election which many Unionists later seized on as a convenient explanation of defeat. Many bitterly complained that by calling Chinese labour 'slavery' the Liberals had grossly distorted the term for party ends and the *Sunday Times* said on 21 January that the Liberals had *only* won because of 'luck, the swing and the Chinese Labour misrepresentations'. Summarising the comments of many Tariff Reformers who refused to accept the election result as final, Garvin in *Outlook* epitomised the election on 20 January as 'the triumph of yellow politics'. But—like Balfour in Manchester—these Unionists totally underestimated the powerful emotive effect the issue had on working men faced with the threat to what they conceived as their union rights at home, and in so doing created a political symbol which not only outshone the original Taff Vale issue (which Ramsay MacDonald felt was over-estimated except in a few Lancashire constituencies),[50] but created another powerful link between trade union interests and the reaction against imperial adventures. As Kinloch Cooke wrote, in an honest and comprehensive account published in the *Empire Review* in April 1906:

> When speaking to Labour audiences on the question, and explaining that the Kaffir got his 2s a day besides his food and lodging, the Chinaman on an average [the same, he] was met with laughter. Food and lodging they did not or would not count, but 2s a day as a wage they looked at askance. They insisted on regarding all labour white or coloured from the white man's

standard in this country. Of course they understood nothing about
black labour. Nor did they want to. All they saw was that it was
'cheap' . . . labour and cheap labour in any form and in any
country was opposed to the teaching of the trade unions and
indirectly affected the whole question of labour throughout the
world.

And yet, having put his finger on the very heart and soul of
working-class opposition, he casually—and typically—dismissed
it as 'this very narrow view'; for, as the best historian of the
indentures has said, 'it was sufficient proof for the working men
of Great Britain that the policy of employing Chinese coolies was
the policy of employing cheap and docile labour, and that it
struck at the very foundations of Trade Unionism'.[51] The very
attempt—wrote a correspondent to *The Times* on the eighth day
of polling—stirred the British working man to the depths in
defence of his rights at home against 'the first attempt made since
modern capitalism began, to move labour from place to place
upon a scheme arranged by capital for the interests of capital
alone'. Furthermore, the working man—and indeed the soldiers
who had fought in South Africa—felt not only threatened but
cheated. They had been promised South Africa as a new field
for increased British employment, but saw—with the introduction of foreign workers—the percentage of British employed in
the mines actually decrease; and knew—as Selborne, none better
—that whatever hyperbole was used, the conditions under which
they were employed were harsh and far from free. The result—
as T. P. O'Connor said—was that the question 'was . . . elevated
into almost as great an issue . . . as Free Trade . . . by the hereditary hatred of Englishmen for anything approaching slavery, by
the vindictive dislike of the mining magnates, who had amassed
huge fortunes and were credited with having dragged the country
into [the] gigantic expense . . . by many humiliations, and the
futile issue of the war, [and] by many other facts, including
brilliant speeches and writings, inspired cartoons. . . .'[52] As
Graham Wallas observed in his pioneering study, *Human Nature
in Politics*, hatred of slavery became a hatred of Chinamen, and

the hatred of Chinamen a hatred of the Conservative party. 'More picturesque, and more lurid', if less important than Free Trade, it made 'a direct appeal to the popular heart and passion', and in the General Election of 1906 'a picture of a Chinaman suddenly thrown on a lantern screen before a working class audience . . . aroused an instantaneous howl of indignation against Mr. Balfour'.[53]

The impact of the issue, particularly in London, was great. Masterman, himself a London candidate, wrote that 'whatever may be the case in the North and the rural districts, I doubt if Protection is in any degree responsible for the winning of [the Metropolis] . . . The fear of the food tax helped in the poorest streets, but the majority of the skilled artisans and all the inhabitants of the suburbs are by nature Protectionists',[54] and it was among these above all that he felt that the Chinese labour issue had been most influential. 'What the percentage of votes affected by this "poisoned chalice" was', commented Muller, similarly, 'there will never be a means of knowing; but since I myself who moved but little about during the campaign saw at least a dozen bills of "manacled and flogged Chinese" in the windows of people of high standing and position in the single Borough of Chelsea, I imagine it to be high.'[55] And he was probably right.

However, as Campbell-Bannerman told Chamberlain—in answer to his complaint that the election had not been clearly fought on the Tariff issue—an election is not a referendum but is rather the political expression of a national mood or instinct which influences the issues as it develops, quite as much as it in turn is influenced by them; and the importance of the Chinese labour issue lay quite as much in the edge which it gave to the general indictment against the Unionists as it did in the influencing of particular votes in particular regions. Gooch wrote of Bath that although he doubted if the cry had altered many votes there 'it has helped sicken the country of the record of the Government'[56] and fortified the movement of opinion which had its roots in the fundamental but frustrated interest of the 'new democracy' in social reform in the interest of the working classes. As *The Times* said on 16 January after the first two days of polling, the results had been 'only to a limited extent a verdict on the issues which politicians have imagined themselves prescribing for the electors' and rather the culmination of another issue which had been shaping itself 'quietly and silently, and without observation', namely whether the working classes who formed the bulk of the electorate were to dictate the policy they desired. The verdict was not only—as Spender diagnosed—the final and full reaction against the wasteful, inefficient and noxious imperialism of the Boer War—although it certainly was, in large measure,[57] this—but also, as *The Times* perceptively pointed out a few days later, on 24 January, 'a protest against dilettantism in politics'. After twenty years of disappointment and diversion, the mass of the electorate, it said, was weary of the late government's method of treating politics as a game in which the business of the nation got attended to only incidentally; and just as Chamberlain's name became the symbol of unfulfilled promises and false gods, so Balfour's languid dilettantism—so significantly displayed to the unemployed in November 1905—became the symbol of a government apparently unable to act decisively save in the interests of wealth and monopoly. 'Utter disgust with the late Government's maddening methods' (Leo Maxse in February's *National Review*); disgusted with its 'inefficiency . . . nepotism . . . shuffling . . . and . . . dishonesty . . .' (the Liberal *Independent Review*); 'utter disgust and weariness' with it and its methods (Masterman in the *Daily Mail*, on 19 January)—these were the judgements freely passed by contemporary commentators of all shades of political opinion and—more sensitive than most Unionists to the importance of the Chinese labour issue—it was, indeed, the Conservatively-inclined *Quarterly Review* which summarised them most convincingly and ably, in its April issue:

> It is true that many grievances co-operated to make the Unionist Party unpopular [but] it is also true that most of these different grievances had some common elements so that they appeared to the electorate like the various counts at a single indictment rather

than a number of distinct charges. Thus the attack on Chinese Labour, on Protection, and on the Taff Vale judgement, all formed part of an accusation of plutocratic conspiracy. Even the Education Act was represented as a victory for privilege, and so fell in with the general charge that the Unionists were the party of the rich and selfish who were ready to degrade the British Empire in South Africa by gathering gold through the labour of slaves, to build up a system of monopoly by taxing the food of the poor, to keep the public schools of the nation as a preserve for their own friends and to put the workmen under the heel of the Capitalist by overthrowing the trade unions. The issue thus seemed to be Rich versus Poor . . . [and] it was to no purpose that the Unionist candidates argued one point or another. There was no escaping the general impression . . . the Unionist Party was branded as the plutocratic party; and if the particular candidate were not himself one of their conspirators, he was their dupe.

For all these reasons, and for precisely this combination of reasons, the working-class vote was more solidly cast against the Conservatives and Unionists in 1906 than at any previous election, and although the ILP's Executive Committee sought to distinguish between what it called Liberal victories won on 'Free Trade, Chinese Labour and the Education Act' and 'Labour victories . . . given to express a determination to have politics devoted to large measures of reform',[58] all the evidence suggests that working-class voters did not necessarily make any very clear distinction between the two parties. The LRC won most of its seats in what had hither-to been the most Conservative areas, and in the country as a whole it achieved an average swing of 16·8 per cent from the Unionists, which was nearly twice the average of the (9·4 per cent) swing from Unionist to Liberal (see Appendix). But in the double constituencies where Liberal and Labour candidates were standing, jointly, against Unionists, there was a fairly even divide between those (Blackburn, Preston, Newcastle, Stockport and Norwich) where Labour candidates topped the poll and those (Bolton, Halifax, Leicester, Sunderland and York) where the Liberals did best. Whilst at Dundee 2,500 'plumpers' helped Wilkie to an unexpected victory over the second Liberal candidate, Henry Robson, Clynes reported at Manchester—where

Table 36

ESTIMATED ORIGIN OF THE LABOUR AND SOCIALIST VOTE IN TRIANGULAR CONTESTS

Constituency	Victor 1900	1906	Nature of third candidacy	Percentage Lab or Soc vote	Estimated percentage Lab or Soc vote from Liberals*
A 19 seats where vote drawn chiefly from Liberals					
Deptford	L	LRC	LRC	52	⎤ ostensibly 100%
Grimsby	U	U	LRC	18	⎫ since Unionists
Gravesend	U	U	LRC	16	⎭ did not contest seats in 1900
Wigan	U	U	Soc	29	96
North-West Lanark	L	U	Soc	24	95
Northampton (2)	L	L	Soc	23	94
North-East Lanark	L	L	Soc	29	78
Govan	L	U	LRC	29	78
Wakefield	U	U	LRC	37	75
North Ayrshire	U	U	Soc	21	75
West Bradford	U	LRC	LRC	39	73
Chester-le-Street	L	[LRC]†	LRC	46	71
Eccles	U	L	LRC	26	65
Glasgow Blackfriars	U	LRC	LRC	40	64
Huddersfield	L	L	LRC	35	63
Burnley	U	L	Soc	33	61
Dewsbury	L	L	LRC	21	59
Stockton	U	U	LRC	23	58
B 7 seats where vote drawn more or less equally between Lib and Con					
Keighley	L	L	Soc	27	54
Middlesbrough	U	L	Soc	8	52
Portsmouth (1)	U	L	LRC	40	52
Croydon	U	U	LRC	21	50
Glasgow Camlachie	U	U	LRC	30	50
Monmouth	U	L	LRC	17	49
Paisley	U	L	LRC	31	48
C 7 seats where vote drawn more from Unionists					
North Aberdeen	L	L	Soc	25	40
East Bradford	U	L	Soc	22	39
Rochdale	U	L	Soc	20	36
Southampton (1)	U	L	Soc	15	32
Falkirk	U	L	Soc	17	27
Leeds South	L	L	LRC	33	25
Hammersmith	U	U	Soc	8	ostensibly 100% since Liberals did not contest the seat in 1900

* Assuming an average swing to the Liberals in these seats of 7·1 per cent: see Appendix

† J. W. Taylor who joined the LRC immediately after the selection

the largest swing (25 per cent) was to a Liberal candidate in the South-Western division—that 'the "sturdy independence" attitude has choked [Conservative working men] off'.[59] In Birmingham and Wolverhampton, every bit as Conservative before 1906 as Lancashire—not one of the three LRC candidates approached the party national average for the swing and only one —in West Wolverhampton (on, interestingly, the lowest swing)— was successful. And, as is shown by the analysis in Table 36, in the thirty-three seats where there was a triangular contest between Unionist, Liberal, and Labour (or Socialist) there is little to suggest that Labour (and Socialist) candidates generally drew more heavily for their votes on the Unionists than on the Liberals; rather—indeed—the reverse.

In these circumstances Herbert Gladstone interpreted the results as a victory—for Labour as well as Liberal candidates— on *Liberal* policies. 'Coming to the LRC,' he wrote to Campbell-Bannerman on 21 January, 'I wish to point out the general accuracy of selecting the men for whom "clear runs" against Tories were secured'. He gave the following figures for England and Wales:

Number returned to date	27
Support of Liberals given to	25
LRC men rejected	21
Supported by Liberals	3

'This tells its own tale. The Liberal party had brought these men in.'[60] And commenting on the results the following day, the *Daily Chronicle* said that it was 'news indeed to the commercial men, the bankers and the captains of industry, to the steady-going professional classes, to the prosperous body of noncon-formists and the vast body of skilled artisans' that—as many Unionists were then saying—the Liberal victories had, *per contram*, been due to socialist influences. 'It would be truer to say', it continued, 'that the LRC candidates benefited by the nation's disgust at the barren and wasteful years of Toryism, by the intense hatred of Protection, and by the people's desire to giving Liberalism a chance to show what it [could] do'. Socialists,

indeed, like Bernard Shaw complained that 'on the war, education, Free Trade (etc) Labour candidates rushed to the heels of
Mr Lloyd George and shouted for peace, retrenchment and
reform, passive resistance and the historic delusion of the Big
versus the Little loaf',[61] and MacDonald himself confessed that
many men had voted for LRC candidates 'for the sole reason that
they were determined to demonstrate against Protection or
Chinese Labour or the Education Act'.[62] There was certainly a
striking contrast between the 58 per cent poll of the LRC in its
thirty-one straight fights with Unionists (of which it won 24, or
77 per cent) and the 29 per cent poll achieved in its eighteen
triangular contests (of which it won only 4, or 24 per cent).

However, if Labour candidates were elected on Liberal issues,
with Liberal votes, the reverse was equally true. Cecil said of
Greenwich, where no LRC candidate was standing, that it too 'felt
the impact of the Labour movement',[63] and that this prevented
the Unionists from getting the support of the working men,
which went to his Liberal opponent instead; and—his other
views notwithstanding—Herbert Gladstone admitted on hearing
of the Lancashire results that Liberal and Labour co-operation
had 'produced a solidarity of voting especially in the big towns,
which I have scarcely dared hoped for'.[64] If Labour candidates
largely fought on Liberal issues, Liberal candidates equally
profited from what Masterman described as a united and determined uprising of the working classes; and whilst Joseph
Burgess—typically among socialists—complained that only
Burns' promotion had deterred working men *en masse* from
deserting the Liberal party for the Labour party,[65] all the signs
are that working-class voters—Liberal as well as Labour—made
their decisions as much on an assessment of the relative Liberal
and Labour chances as on ideology or the operation of a new
working-class political loyalty. George Lansbury—who was an
LRC candidate in all but name—recorded of Middlesbrough that
the iron and steel workers were in the main strongly opposed to
his candidature because they were afraid that he would let the
Tory in,[66] and at Eccles the textile workers went even further in

the direction of supporting the Liberal, Pollard, against Ben
Tillett; similarly at West Bradford—where Herbert Gladstone
commented that Jowett's victory justified their official attitude[67]
—and at Deptford it is clear that many Liberal voters consciously
switched their votes from the Liberal to the Labour candidate.
The Times commented on 16 January that working men had
clearly voted Labour wherever possible but had elsewhere done
the next best thing and, sinking their own political differences,
had concentrated on the Liberal candidate; and many Liberals—
equally—voted Labour where Labour had the best, or only,
chance of winning.

In the circumstances, the electoral agreement between the
Liberal and Labour parties was of profound importance. It
minimised the 'wasted vote' bogy, with the result that only three
out of the seventeen seats in which Liberal and LRC candidates
opposed each other were 'lost' to the Unionists, and 'enabled
both parties to evade for a time the logic of the British electoral
system at the expense of the Conservatives'.[68] But even this—
important as it was—could not, in the nature of things, have
worked as smoothly as it did without the undoubted parallelism
of Liberal and Labour policies, and—as MacDonald knew well—
the LRC would probably have lost more in 1906 without this than
would the Liberals. Through its psychological—as much as its
psephological—effect it thus enabled Liberal and Labour together to maximise the effect of the swing against the Unionists;
but the effect of the issues and emotions underlying it would in
any event have been profound; and in 1906 the Unionists just
did not have the leadership, the influence, or the support to
overcome them.

CONCLUSIONS

It can be seen, in retrospect, that between them Balfour and
Chamberlain committed almost every conceivable tactical error
open to them. Balfour underestimated Chamberlain's challenge
to him and mistakenly believed that it would be possible to hold

the party together on the basis of a middle-of-the-road fiscal policy, which lacked either commitment or inspiration; but Chamberlain on the other hand—by his own confession—under-estimated the feeling roused by the threat of increased prices inherent in his proposals. Somewhat remote from rank-and-file opinion, Balfour completely failed to give due attention to the maintenance of communication within the party through its representative and official organisations, whilst Chamberlain, unsuccessful in his attempts to capture them, failed to recognise the widening gap between the party caucuses—which increasingly came under his influence—and the opinion of the party rank-and-file. And whilst Balfour was primarily responsible for almost certainly holding on too long to office, both he and Chamberlain misjudged the effect that the Home Rule issue, the manoeuvring of the Liberals into office, and exploitation of the Chinese labour issue would have on opinion up and down the country. And yet, when all these things are said—and they were influential and important—the Liberals won, with Labour, because of the intimate way in which, aided by better leadership and organisation, the various issues knit themselves together.

Free Trade brought together not only the Liberals themselves but Liberals, Unionist Free Traders and Conservative working men, textile manufacturers and the mill hands they employed, miners in Yorkshire, dockers in London, and agricultural labourers in Sussex. Chinese labour joined the self-interest of the worker to the self-righteousness of the nonconformists. Taff Vale provided a vital bridge of interest between the trade unionist and the socialist, and realisation that imperial adventure had obviated social reform at home linked both with the increasing number of socially-conscious radicals, and indeed citizens at large. And last, but by no means least, the Ulster revolt, the adroitness of Campbell-Bannerman's handling of the Home Rule issue, and the organisation and discipline of the United Irish League swung to the Liberals a whole brigade of Irishmen whose votes were a factor of great importance in securing many of the industrial seats of Scotland and the north of England. Middle and working-class,

employer and employee, nonconformist and Irish Catholic (and
also Jew), Unionist and Liberal Free Trader—these were the
forces that, abetted by Unionist maladroitness, joined hands to
provide the Liberals with their greatest—and last great—victory.

Together they created a *leadership of opinion* which in 1906
worked for once against the interests of the Conservatives. Those
Unionist Free Traders and Socialists, those Irish and Jews, who
spoke out against this or that facet of Unionist rule or policy, may
not always have won converts directly, but they created a climate
of opinion which made it easier for the floating voter and even
the committed Conservative to vote against the Unionists in
1906. This, indeed, was the particular importance of the nonconformists. Massingham and Porritt probably exaggerated the
direct effect of the religious education issue on voting decisions,
but it would be impossible to exaggerate the effect that the 'wrath
of dissent' had upon Liberal morale and enthusiasm; and the
same was true, in varying degree, of the support of the many
other groups. At the same time, the Liberals were greatly helped
by their superior organisation and propaganda. The Unionists
had nothing to match the Liberal symbols—the loaves and
sausages and Chinamen—nor for that matter the Liberal election
songs, for, as Graham Wallas wrote, 'the truth embodied in a tale
has more emotional power than the unembodied truth'.[69] The
Liberals therefore won for a whole series of reasons which, like
hailstones, melt into each other and become hard to distinguish
one from another. But, put at their simplest, they amounted to
the coincidence of four developments—the climax of the movement of opinion against imperialism, the development of the
movement for social reform, the Ulster revolt against Irish
reformism, and the emergence of a number of issues which re-
united the Liberal party and quickened its reforming as well as its
traditional heart. This fourfold coincidence made it possible
for the conservative and progressive wings of the party to act in
harmony and for the Liberal party to attract support from both
Conservative and Radical, as well as more traditional groups. As
Sandars said, attributing the debacle to a double-swing of the

pendulum (after 1895 and 1900), to Chinese labour and the Labour vote, and to nonconformity, 'any one of these might have injured [the Unionist party] seriously, but their combination, operating on a stale party, overwhelmed [it]'.[70]

Even so, the Liberal victory would not have been so far-reaching had not the party responded to the opportunities presented to it in the form of improved organisation, energetic campaigning, and an election platform which had a greater social content than ever before. The question which remained interestingly open after the end of polling on 8 February 1906 was whether it could similarly respond to the further and far greater opportunities offered by its own phenomenal success and above all contain within its own political future the formidable challenge implicit in the emergence of the Labour party.

Notes to Chapter 7 will be found on pp 224-6

8 EPILOGUE: THE ELECTION AND AFTER

Unionist and Labour commentators were naturally quick to argue that the Liberal triumph would prove to be short-lived. It had been won on a unique combination of radical and conservative issues and appeals which—they suggested—time would not sustain.

Typifying many of his colleagues, Wyndham commented that if the election had been a blizzard, blizzards never lasted long, and more than one *Times* correspondent suggested that since it had been one of the most conservative ever fought—'except from the party point of view'[1]—support for the Liberals would soon evaporate, to right as well as left. 'For the moment they have profited' the paper itself said, on 16 January, but 'judging from the records of the two parties in social legislation, it is not the Unionists who are least-fitted to the new order of things . . .' Despite continuing recriminations over the fiscal issue—culminating in 'a tremendous outburst of discontent with Balfour'[2] —Unionists of both and all shades of opinion agreed that there was no *party* cause for alarm. Garvin forecast in the February *Outlook* that the Liberals would be 'ground between the upper and nether millstones of Tariff Reform and Socialism', and Hugh Cecil—whose vision of a strong and conservative party of the centre could hardly have been more different—nevertheless told Devonshire as early as 19 January that he thought the Liberals 'likely enough to split in a year or two's time'.[3] Two days earlier, in the midst of his party's worst defeats, Balfour wrote calmly to Austen Chamberlain to forecast that the 'new development' (of the LRC) would end 'in the breaking up of the Liberal party'.[4]

Labour speakers were only too happy to take the same line. When the new parliament met, the LRC group not only decided to adopt the title of the Labour Party, but also—as a point of principle as well as of practicality—to sit on the opposition benches; and Keir Hardie told an exuberant party meeting (held in February) that it was 'obvious to everyone who took the slightest interest in public affairs that the old two-party system [was] breaking up'.[5] Writing simultaneously in the Conservative *National Review*, he added that Labour's real fight at the next election would be 'against the Liberals', when—Snowden forecast—the result could not be doubted. 'We shall see the Labour Party strengthened to the extent of dominating if not directing the Government of the country'.[6] *Clarion* similarly declared (on 19 January) that the workers had crossed the rubicon of independent political power, and the Social Democratic paper *Justice* proclaimed the following day that whilst the Tory Party, as 'the party of frank reaction', would remain—reaction always did—the Liberal Party, as 'the party of sham progress', would be eliminated.

In retrospect these contemporary opinions—and there were many more of the same kind—can only seem to have been more than usually vindicated by the passage of both time and events. But it is important not to confuse effect with cause or political reality with its games. The facts are that the Liberal party that emerged from the election was certainly more collectivist than at any previous time, that many Liberals were themselves aware of the risks and challenges they faced, and that the infant Labour party was by no means itself a homogeneous or united force. Contemporary sources can give clues in these important areas also.

The balance of forces within the Liberal party was certainly a delicate one. 'Your coach has about twelve horses', Chamberlain wrote to Margot Asquith, 'and will require skilful driving.'[7] There were some grounds for doubting whether this skill was

o

sufficiently at hand. As the campaign showed, Asquith was an
influence for caution, and Campbell-Bannerman's first thought on
the preparation of his government's programme for inclusion in
the 1906 King's Speech epitomised his difficulty. 'If we have
two sops for Labour', he wrote to Asquith on 17 January, 'we
ought to have some other Bills of general interest to balance them.
Otherwise the enemy . . . might . . . blaspheme and colour will be
given to the assertion which seems to be their main weapon just
now that we are in the hands of Labour . . .'[8] The party had,
however, always been a coalition and it seemed—to Herbert
Gladstone—to be not less but 'more homogeneous than in 1885
and 1892'.[9] If there was 'no sign of any *violent* forward movement
of opinion',[9] the more active elements—Beatrice Webb approv-
ingly observed—were socially constructive and collectivist, and
at its thirty-ninth annual conference, held in September 1906,
the TUC expressed satisfaction that a Government had been
returned numbering among its ranks many friends of Labour.[10]
Between 1885 and 1906 the broad economic and social composition of the party did not alter much, except away from the land;
but its representation of professional and working, as opposed to
industrial, commercial, and financial interests, became more
marked, and—as was seen in the candidates put forward—there
was an undoubted shift in emphasis. As an early historian of the
period has so aptly observed, 'throughout the election the reliance
of Liberals was placed even if sometimes unconsciously upon a
wider basis than the old middle class support'.[11]

The more thoughtful Liberals were well aware of this. Spender
reflected their view when he wrote in the April edition of the
Contemporary Review that 'in the last resort the party has to be a
success with the working classes . . .' and—enjoining it to
'Remember 1880'—Graham Wallas realistically warned that if it
failed to bring forward the social legislation now expected of it
it might not get another chance.[12] The pressures on the leadership thus were there. Furthermore, there was a wide-spread
appreciation among the party's organisations and officials that
without a flood-tide to carry it over, three-cornered contests

might not be so innocuous next time round. Soon after the election, for example, the Scottish Liberal Association passed a significant resolution requiring its secretary 'to prepare a Report on the number of triangular elections which occurred in Scotland . . . how many seats [had been] lost . . . in consequence, . . . and what action . . . [was] desirable to prevent a recurrence of them in future, by way of pressing for a second ballot or otherwise . . .'[13] It would take a bold—or a foolish—man to say that, given adequate policies of social and franchise reform, the demise of the Liberal party had, in 1906, become inevitable or even likely.

If—furthermore—the Liberal party was a coalition, at once progressive and imprecise, so too was the Labour party. As the *Standard* pointed out on 17 January, there were 'Labour Whigs and Labour revolutionaries', and committed Socialists presciently forecast difficulties and disagreements between the party's trade union and reformist, and its revolutionary, wings. 'If the LRC were already socialist' commented the *Social Democrat* in February 1906, 'much trouble which is likely to arise in the future might have been avoided'.

The Labour party had its own choice to make between complete independence and ultimate revolution and what Henderson described at its 1906 Conference as its 'responsibility for keeping the Government up to scratch . . . and of shaping their [i.e. Liberal] policy in harmony with public necessity'.[14] Amid the immediate post-election euphoria the *Labour Leader* admitted that it was possible (if, it thought, not likely) that the Liberals might dish the foundling party by carrying out the very—reformist—measures that it sought, and the *Daily News* reasonably commented, on 26 January, that if Liberalism and Labour 'accomplish sound and steady reforms for the benefit of the people, the progress of bringing the masses to understand and adopt socialism' was unlikely to be rapid. Moderate papers like the *Observer* and the *Statist* expressed the belief that if Liberals— and Unionists—behaved sensibly the consummation of the Labour party's wilder hopes was unlikely for many a long day, and Lloyd George confidently claimed quite soon after the election that if

the Liberal government tackled the landlords and peers as they
had tackled the parsons Labour would call in vain on the working-
men of the country to desert it.[15]

It was at least as good a possibility as the alternative. There
was nothing to suggest—pre-Osborne—that the TUC would be
willing to underwrite the number of Labour candidates that would
be required to give the Labour party at least the opportunity of
winning a majority, and although the (1906) advent of the miners
nearly doubled its Parliamentary size, this increase also served
to deepen tension between its reformist and revolutionary wings.
By 1911 Joseph Burgess was complaining, as a socialist, that in
its legislative capacity it was too like the left wing of the Radical
party, and indeed that 'with some half dozen exceptions one
could select from among the Radicals 40 men more advanced
than the rank of the Labour Party'.[16] Was Asquith so wrong to
suggest, in retirement, that the disintegration of the Liberal
party began not between 1906 and 1911 but with the coupon
election of 1918?[17]

This study of the 1906 election cannot—and does not seek—
to provide answers to this and to the similarly speculative questions posed many times then and more times since. It does,
however, suggest that the election left the political future full of
interesting political possibilities, about which contemporary
opinion was itself at variance. Chastened by a salutory defeat, the
decimated Unionists remained divided (if now with a more
evident Chamberlainite majority); yet to Chamberlain and his
supporters the verdict was less a condemnation than a trial by
fire, and Tariff Reform remained a policy that would have a very
real chance if—Masterman suggested—trade declined or unemployment rose.[18] Equally, a renewed Liberal party faced not
only the opportunity of guiding into new and more fruitful
channels the aspirations of new democracy and of nation alike,
but also the challenge of an ebullient, but as yet uncertain, and
certainly young, Labour party: the problem, in short, of con-
solidating its enlarged working-class base without prejudicing
its middle-class moral and intellectual inheritance. The election

created opportunities for both—and for all—parties; but it did not foreclose the options or possibilities for any of them. Their resolution was another, longer, and equally fascinating story.

Notes to Chapter 8 will be found on pp 226–7

REFERENCES

Chapter 1 BACKGROUND: THE FRANCHISE AND ITS EFFECTS (pages 15–35)

1 Blewett, N. 'The Franchise in the United Kingdom,' *1885–1918. Past and Present*, 32 (December 1965), especially 29 and 39
2 Priestley, J. B. *The Edwardians*, p 105
3 Booth, Charles. *Life and Labour of the People of London*, first series (1902), i, 26–7
4 Lowell, A. Lawrence. *The Government of England*, i, 213
5 Figures based on Money, L.G.C., *Riches and Poverty*, 28–43, and on the *Financial Reform Almanac* 1905
6 McDowell, R. B. *British Conservatism 1832–1914*, 135 and 143
7 Hutchinson, T. W. *A Review of Economic Doctrines 1870–1929*, 11
8 Hammond, J. L. C. P. *Scott of the Manchester Guardian*, 72
9 Kennedy, A. L. *Salisbury 1830–1903. Portrait of a Statesman*, 253–4
10 Based on Tables 1 and 2 in Chapter 3 of Peacock, Alan J., and Wiseman, Frank. *The Growth of Public Expenditure in the United Kingdom*
11 *Parliamentary Debates*, Fourth Series, cxxviii, 4
12 Masterman, C. F. G., and others. *The Heart of the Empire*, 26
13 Money, L. G. C. op cit, 318
14 Cecil, Robert, *Life in Edwardian England*, 7–8
15 Balfour, Lady Frances. *Ne Obliviscaris. Dinna Forget*, ii, 404
16 Jesse Herbert to Herbert Gladstone, 6 March 1903. *Viscount Gladstone Papers*, Add MS 46025, ff 126–36
17 Douglas, Roy. *History of the Liberal Party 1895–1970*, 90
18 Bealey, F., and Pelling, H. *Labour and Politics*, 141
19 Balfour to Devonshire, 27 August 1903, *Devonshire Papers*, 340, f 2943
20 Austen Chamberlain to Balfour. Petrie, Sir Charles, Bt. *The Life and Letters of Sir Austen Chamberlain, K.G., P.C., M.P.*, i, 141–7. See also, *The Times*, 16 May 1903, and the *Empire Review*, June 1903
21 Balfour to Devonshire, 27 October 1905. *Devonshire Papers* 340, f 3155. Although written in 1905, this letter summarises Balfour's consistent view from 1903 onwards
22 Amery, Julian. *The Life of Joseph Chamberlain*, 6, 210
23 Petrie, Sir Charles, Bt, op cit; see also *Balfour Papers* Add MS 49774, ff 69–74

24 MacDonald to Stewart, of the Australian Labour party, 16 November 1904. *Pease Collection*, i, 276–8
25 *Report of the Fifth Annual Conference of the Labour Representation Committee*, 38
26 Hardie, J. Keir, 'A Government of Scavengers', *The Speaker*, 7 October 1905; and see Hook, A., 'Labour and Politics', *Independent Review*, June 1905
27 Bealey, F., and Pelling, H. op cit, 209 ff; *Pease Collection*, i, 299–302
28 *The Times*, 7 November 1905; the *Labour Leader*, 14 November 1905; and McDowell, R. B., op cit, 137
29 Lansdowne to Balfour, 27 October 1905, *Balfour Papers* 49729, ff 202–5
30 *Balfour Papers*, Add MS 49764, ff 63–5, 98, 109–14, and 130–2
31 *Balfour Papers*, Add MS 49771, ff 53–6
32 Balfour to Devonshire, 27 October 1905, *Devonshire Papers*, 340, f 3155
33 Bell, G. K. A. *Randall Davidson, Archbishop of Canterbury*, 495
34 Crewe to Campbell-Bannerman, 14 November 1905. *Campbell-Bannerman Papers*, Add MS 41213, ff 337–8
35 O'Connor, T. P. *Sir Henry Campbell-Bannerman*, 73–5
36 Labouchere to Campbell-Bannerman, 30 November 1905, and Morley to Campbell-Bannerman, 22 November 1905. *Campbell-Bannerman Papers*, Add MS 41222, ff 121–2 and 41223, ff 160–1
37 *The Times*, 25 November 1905
38 Crewe. *Rosebery*, ii, 593–5
39 *Balfour Papers*, Add MS 49858, f 65
40 Campbell-Bannerman to Asquith, 1 December 1905. *Asquith Papers*
41 Trevelyan, G. M. *Grey of Falloden*, 101; see also Stead, W. T. *The Liberal Ministry of 1910*, 10; and for Asquith's view—the *Spender Papers*, Add MS 46388, ff 111
42 Askwith. *Lord James of Hereford*, 291
43 Letter to Burns, *Burns Papers*, Add MS 46298, ff 214–15

Chapter 2 PARTY ORGANISATIONS AND CANDIDATES (pages 36–63)

1 Corder, Percy. *The Life of Robert Spence Watson*, 27; and Douglas, Roy, op cit, 18
2 *Viscount Gladstone Papers*, Add MS 46105, ff 1–50; 46105, ff 215–36; and 46022, ff 34–5
3 Mallet, Sir Charles. *Herbert Gladstone, a Memoir*, 190–9
4 *Viscount Gladstone Papers*, Add MS 46023, ff 221
5 *Proceedings in connection with the Twenty-Seventh meeting of the National Liberal Federation*, 27
6 R. J. Wells to Crook, 1 May 1905. *Viscount Gladstone Papers*, Add MS 46024, f 203

7   *Viscount Gladstone Papers*, Add MS 46042, ff 141–2, and 46024, f 203

8   *Minutes of the Scottish Liberal Association 1903–1906*, 10

9   Acland-Hood to Balfour, 25 September 1905. *Balfour Papers*, Add MS 49771, ff 49–52

10 Campbell-Bannerman to Asquith, 26 December 1903. *Asquith Papers*

11 Dickson-Poynder to Asquith, 18 December 1903. *Asquith Papers*

12 *Balfour Papers*, Add MS 49764, ff 52–7

13 Lady Aberdeen to Balfour, 25 September 1905

14 *Proceedings in connection with the Twenty Seventh Annual Meeting of the National Liberal Federation*, 48

15 Bealey, F. and Pelling, H., op cit, 143

16 As he wrote of Croydon. *Viscount Gladstone Papers*, Add MS 46106, f 35

17 *Independent Review*, August 1905

18 Bealey, F. and Pelling, H., op cit, 240 and 259

19 *Pease Collection*, vol 1, 216

20 Bealey, F. and Pelling, H., op cit, 255. *Pease Collection*, vol 1, 180–1, 226, 234–5 and 229 ff

21 Bealey, F. and Pelling, H., op cit, 261 ff. *Clarion*, 10 November and 8 December 1905; and the *Labour Leader*, 1 December 1905

22 Speech on 9 January 1906. *The Times*, 10 January 1906

23 *Proceedings in connection with the Twenty Seventh Annual Meeting of the National Liberal Federation*, 17

24 Expression of opinion by Croydon Women's Liberal Association, *Croydon Times*, 18 April 1904

25 *Croydon Advertiser*, 11 January, and *Croydon Citizen*, 13 January 1903

26 *Croydon Times*, 18 February 1903

27 *Croydon Times*, 11 March 1903. Provided also, the Liberals added, that his name was submitted to them first for approval

28 *Hammersmith Folio*

29 Bealey, F. and Pelling, H., op cit, 260

30 *National Review*, October 1905

31 Sandars to Balfour, 10 October 1906

32 *The Times*, 14 November 1905 and 3 January 1906

33 Acland-Hood to Balfour, 16 October 1905. *Balfour Papers*, Add MS 49764, ff 52–7

34 Memorandum by Iwan-Muller (a Unionist journalist). *Balfour Papers*, Add MS 49797, ff 115–59

35 Powell Williams to Devonshire, 22 October 1903

36 Memorandum by Lord James, 9 November 1905. *Balfour Papers*, Add MS 49858, ff 12–18

37 Sandars to Balfour, 13 December 1905. *Balfour Papers*, Add MS 49764, ff 123

38 *Balfour Papers*, Add MS 49797, ff 115–59

39 *Report of the Second Annual Conference of the Tariff Reform League*, 3–5
40 See *Balfour Papers*, Add MS 49858, ff 12–18
41 Acland-Hood to Sandars, 22 December 1905. *Balfour Papers*, Add MS 49771, ff 131–2
42 Sandars to Balfour, 25 October 1905. *Balfour Papers*, Add MS 49764, ff 85–6
43 *The Times*, 15 November 1905
44 *Balfour Papers*, Add MS 49771, pp 144–7
45 Acland-Hood, undated memorandum (? December 1905). *Balfour Papers*, Add MS 49771, pp 144–7
46 *Devonshire Papers*, 340, f 3178
47 Wyndham to Sandars, 18 November 1905. *Balfour Papers*, Add MS 49805, ff 96–9
48 *Balfour Papers*, Add MS 49764, ff 85–6
49 *Balfour Papers*, Add MS 49771, ff 53–8
50 *Proceedings in connection with the Twenty-Seventh Annual Meeting of the National Liberal Federation*, 40
51 Sources: Thomas, J. A., *The British House of Commons, 1906–1911*; *Dods Parliamentary Companion*; *The Constitutional Yearbook 1895–1910*; *Pall Mall Gazette 1906 Election Supplement*

Chapter 3 PARTY PROGRAMMES (pages 64–94)

(NB All quotations from candidates' election addresses taken from the Folios in the National Liberal Club)
1 Bryce to Campbell-Bannerman, 2 November 1905. *Campbell-Bannerman Papers*, Add MS 41211, f 304
2 *The Autobiography of Margot Asquith*, ii, 78
3 'A Word to the Women', LPD Leaflet No 2027. *Pamphlets and Leaflets*, 1905
4 Cited in the *Daily Mirror*, 22 December 1905
5 Cf Campbell-Bannerman's comment to Bryce on 26 January 1906: 'The truth is, we cannot provide for a fighting Empire and nothing will give us the power. A peaceful Empire of the old type we are quite fit for.' A. P. Thornton, *The Imperial Idea and its Enemies*, 106. See also Asquith's *50 Years of Parliament*, ii, 3 for a modern-sounding statement of the Liberal view of the empire as a 'corporate union of free and self-governing communities'.
6 *Campbell-Bannerman Papers*, Add MS 41213, ff 39–43
7 LPD Leaflet No 1938, *Pamphlets and Leaflets*, 1903; LPD Leaflet No 2054, *Pamphlets and Leaflets*, 1905
8 LPD Leaflet No 2072, *Pamphlets and Leaflets*, 1906
9 *Report of the Fifth Annual Conference of the Labour Representation Committee*, 52
10 Cf the comment made to Ramsay MacDonald by J. C. Watson (of

the Australian Federal Labour Party). 'As to your remark about the Protection and "chains for the wage-earner" I confess to knowing little of its effect in Europe, but to our far-off ears the clank of the chains sounds as insistent from Free Trade as from Protectionist countries.'

11 *Report of the Fifth Annual Conference of the Labour Representation Committee,* 52

12 *Report of the Proceedings of the 39th Annual Trades Union Congress,* 50

13 F. Bealey and H. Pelling, op cit, 264–5

14 Unlike the LRC manifesto, the ILP manifesto directly attacked the Unionists and Liberals. 'The main reason for the existence of Liberals and Conservatives', it said, 'is to protect the interests of the rich and keep you divided. This they accomplish by keeping you wrangling over matters which concern you slightly, if at all. They appeal to your religious prejudices, your racial animosities, your patriotism and your pride and whilst you quarrel among yourselves, they quietly fill their pockets and empty yours.' *Reformers Yearbook, 1907,* 53

15 *National Union Leaflet No. 492,* Conservative Research Department Collection

16 *The Times,* November 1905

17 *Edinburgh People's Journal,* 20 January 1906

18 *T.R.L. Leaflet No. 24,* LSE Collection (LSEC)

19 *Tariff Reform League Short Handbook for Speakers,* 48

20 *I.T.C. Leaflet No. 63,* LSEC

21 *Balfour Papers,* Add MS 49764, ff 130–2

22 *Balfour Papers,* Add MS 49764, ff 123–7

23 Memorandum by Sandars, ? December 1905. *Balfour Papers,* Add MS 49764, ff 130–2

24 *T.R.L. Leaflet No. 36,* LSEC

25 Resolutions were passed at both conferences. The 1905 resolution, which was the more critical, trusted that the Volunteers would 'receive every encouragement from H.M. Government in the future'. National Union Gleanings, XIII, 383, and XXV, 465

26 *Edinburgh People's Journal,* 20 January 1906

27 'Nothing will generate Party enthusiasm more than the prospect of an election at an early date, an election moreover in which we shall be the attacking party.' Sandars to Balfour, 22 November 1905. *Balfour Papers,* Add MS 49764, ff 109–14

28 *Balfour Papers,* Add MS 49858, ff 92–5

Chapter 4 THE ELECTION CAMPAIGN (pages 95–124)

1 *The Freeman's Journal,* 14 December 1905

2 'Was there ever', he asked, 'such an impotent force?' Channing, Francis Allston. *Memories of Midland Politics 1885–1910,* 317

3 Hewins, W. A. S. *The Apologia of an Imperialist*, i, 153

4 Asquith drew Campbell-Bannerman's attention to it. *Campbell-Bannerman Papers*, Add MS 41260, ff 254–5

5 *Daily News*, 14 and 16 December 1905

6 Sandars to Balfour, 13 December 1905, reporting Lyttleton's views. *Balfour Papers*, Add MS 49764, ff 123–7. Devonshire wrote again, a few days earlier: 'Some of our friends of *sanguine* disposition are of opinion that there might be some possible advantage to the future of the Unionist Party if in the present changed circumstances there could be some further communication between us . . . [If you could make any declaration of differentiation from Chamberlain] it could not relieve me or other Unionists whom you may deem irreconcilable Cobdenites but [it] might certainly modify the character of such criticism.' *Devonshire Papers*, 340, f 3165

7 Hyde, H. Montgomery. *Carson*, 213

8 *Daily Mail*, 19 December 1905, and *Outlook*, 23 December 1905

9 Hewins, W. A. S. *The Apologia of an Imperialist*, ii, 157

10 M. S. Stewart to Balfour. *Balfour Papers*, Add MS 49858, ff 36–7

11 Telegram from Goschen to Devonshire. *Devonshire Papers*, 340, f 3169

12 'I had hoped very much that the Leeds speech would have met with your approval, and even now do not despair of seeing you and Balfour fighting side by side . . . The Leeds speech seems to me exactly to carry out the view of Adam Smith on the subject of vital duties as expressed in a passage occurring in the 2nd Chapter of Book IV (p 201–2 of the 3rd edition, 1784) on the Wealth of Nations, from which I quoted when speaking at Inverness.' Finley to Devonshire, *Devonshire Papers*, 340, f 3172

13 The words were carefully chosen to indicate an immediate change of policy without suspension of all existing licences which, said Asquith to Campbell-Bannerman on 27 December, would have been difficult to justify to the taxpayer

14 Dillon to Bryce, 19 December 1905, and Bryce to Campbell-Bannerman, 20 December 1905. *Campbell-Bannerman Papers*, Add MS 41211, ff 331–3

15 *The Times* and other papers, 22 December 1905

16 *Daily News*, 22 December 1905

17 O'Connor, T. P. *Sir Henry Campbell-Bannerman*, 88

18 Morley to Campbell-Bannerman, 22 December 1905. *Campbell-Bannerman Papers*, Add MS 41223, ff 182–3

19 *Birmingham Daily Post*, 1 January 1906

20 Seely, J. E. B. *Adventure*, 113

21 Labouchere to Campbell-Bannerman, 28 December 1905. *Campbell-Bannerman Papers*, Add MS 41222, f 123

22 'Your speech at the Queens Hall is claimed by Mr. Benn's supporters as being on his side, and some of us who have been disposed to

support Lord Hugh Cecil were taunted that you are against his candidature and that if we desire to remain loyal to your lead we ought not to remain loyal to Lord Hugh . . .' B. G. Stillman to Balfour, 1 January 1906. *Balfour Papers*, Add MS 49858, f 117

23 Balfour to Lansdowne, 6 January 1906. *Balfour Papers*, Add MS 49729, ff 206–7

24 Elgin to Campbell-Bannerman, 28 December 1905. *Campbell-Bannerman Papers*, Add MS 41214, ff 35–8. *Annual Register*, 1906, 40

25 Askwith, Lord. *Lord James of Hereford*, 29

26 Wyndham to Balfour, 27 December 1905, saying that he had been approached by a journalist 'to discover whether you would depute someone to meet someone deputed by "Joe" to arrange terms'. *Balfour Papers*, Add MS 49805, ff 111–13

27 *Campbell-Bannerman Papers*, Add MS 41211, f 334

28 Wyndham said at Dover, on 3 January, that his policies had had to be shelved because the constitutional issue had been raised; Long, however, said in Dublin that they had been reversed with full Unionist approval because they were wrong. *The Times* and the *Birmingham Daily Post*, 4 January, and the *Speaker*, 6 January 1906

29 Spencer to Campbell-Bannerman, 11 September 1905. *Campbell-Bannerman Papers*, Add MS 41229, ff 318–19

30 Balfour to Devonshire 27 October. *Devonshire Papers*, 340, f 3155

31 Chamberlain said that the number of able-bodied paupers had risen to one million, whereas—as Burns pointed out on 8 January—it was 747,000. Hewins recorded that 'Chamberlain's speeches . . . contained many inaccuracies of argument and statistics'. Hewins, W. A. S. op cit, ii, 163. *The Times*, 9 January 1906

32 As reported in a letter from Carrington to Burns, 9 January 1906. *Burns Papers*, Add MS 46299, ff 15–16

33 Hudson to Burns, 12 January 1906. *Burns Papers*, Add MS 46200, ff 18–19

34 *Balfour Papers*, Add MS 49735, ff 216–17

35 Campbell-Bannerman to Asquith on 5 January and Asquith's reply of 7 January 1906. *Asquith Papers*. *Campbell-Bannerman Papers*, Add MS 41210, f 258

36 *Asquith Papers*

37 *Burns Papers*, Add MS 46324, f 2

38 *Clarion*, 13 January 1906

39 *Birmingham Daily Post*, 3 January 1906

40 *Liverpool Daily Post*, 17 January 1906

41 *Manchester Guardian*, 8 January 1906

42 *Barrow News*, 30 December 1905 and 6 January 1906

43 'As for Mr Cairns [the Liberal candidate] he has said that he will regard it as a lifetime of misfortune if he and Mr. Hudson do not go in together.' The *Tribune*, 15 January 1906

44 *Labour Leader*, 15 and 22 December 1905. *Irish News* and *Belfast Morning News*, 18 January 1906
45 *The Times*, 11 January 1906; and *The Tribune*, 15 January 1906
46 *The Times*, 15 July 1905
47 *The Times*, 27 December 1905 and 11 January 1906
48 *Cork Examiner*, 29 January 1906
49 National Liberal Club Folio I, 125
50 Ervine, St John. *Craigavon, Ulsterman*, 125 and 129
51 *Dundee Catholic Herald*, 5 January 1906
52 *The Freeman's Journal*, 15 January 1906. 'I hold the cause of Ireland and the cause of Labour to be identical', he wrote in his election address. National Liberal Club, Folio I, 122
53 *The Times*, 16 January 1906
54 *Irish Times*, 3 January 1906
55 National Liberal Club Folio I, 121
56 *Irish Times*, 10 January 1906

Chapter 5 PLATFORM AND PRESS: THE CONDUCT OF THE ELECTION (pages 125–44)

1 Amery, Julian. *The Life of Joseph Chamberlain*, vi, 452
2 Cary, Joyce. *Prisoner of Grace*, 104
3 *Burns Papers*, Add MS 46324, ff 1–2
4 Cited in Green, Roger Lancelyn. *A. E. W. Mason*, 97
5 *The Times*, 19 December 1905; *Manchester Guardian*, 2 January 1906; *Croydon Advertiser*, 6 January 1906; et al. F. William Birrell in A. E. W. Mason's novel, *The Turnstile* (p 115), who decided that it was a good thing in a city of artisans keen on football to 'give them a football song'
6 *Spectator*, 20 January 1906
7 Cavendish, Richard, to Devonshire, 28 January 1906, and *Devonshire Papers*, 340, f 3178
8 *Daily Telegraph*, 2 January, and *Daily Mail*, 3 January 1906. *Evening Standard and St. James Gazette*, 15 January 1906
9 *Observer*, 14 January 1906
10 *The Motor*, 17 January 1906. See also *The Car*, 17 January 1906, 'The General Election—Motor Cars Everywhere in Use'
11 See eg *The Times*, 26 December 1906
12 *Devonshire Papers*, loc cit
13 *The Car*, 10 January 1906
14 Snowdon, Viscount. *An Autobiography*, i, 309–10
15 Spender, J. A. *Campbell-Bannerman*, ii, 219
16 Hocking, Silas. *My Book of Memory*, 206. Sir George Bartley at North Islington, *The Times*, 17 January 1906
17 'The Coming of the New Demos', *Punch*, 24 January 1906

18   *The Times*, 5 January 1906; also the *Sunday Times*, 7 and 14 January 1906

19   *The Times*, 27 January 1906

20   *Dundee Catholic Herald*, 20 January 1906; and *Manchester Guardian*, 5 January 1906; Rosebery on the 1900 election, 'I never remember dirtier work done' Crewe. *Rosebery*, ii, 568

21   Memorandum by Iwan-Muller. *Balfour Papers*, Add MS 49797, ff 115–59

22   *Worcester Election Petition*; *Parliamentary Accounts and Papers*, 1906, XCV, 481

23   *Great Yarmouth Election Petition*; *Parliamentary Accounts and Papers*, 1906, CXV, 5–21

24   *Campbell-Bannerman Papers*, Add MS 41221, ff 87–8

25   *Viscount Gladstone Papers*, Add MS 46023, ff 197–8

26   *Great Yarmouth Election Petition*, loc cit

27   Excluding petitions voided on grounds of personal ineligibility for election, ie on account of holding a particular office. *Parliamentary Accounts and Papers*, *1874*, LIII, 115–16; *1875*, LX, 413–17; *1883*, LIV, 287–91; and *1893–1894*, LXX, 805–911. *Journals of the House of Commons*, *1874*, vol 129, pp 82, 104–5, 115, 119, 123, 132, 142, 145–6, 148, 169, 186, 198, 209–10, 226, 236, 249–51, 254, 271, 295 and 321; *1875*, vol 130, p 4; *1893–1894*, vol 148, pp 3–7, 49, 348 and 501; and *1906*, vol 161, pp 131, 180, 197, 244, 295 and 296

28   *Journals of the House of Commons*, *1906*, vol 161, pp 255–6

29   *Yorkshire Post*, 11 January 1906

30   *Parliamentary Accounts and Papers*, XCVI, 255–6

31   *National Review*, February 1906

32   *Daily News*, 9 December 1906

33   *The Newspaper Directory*, 1850, 1880, 1906 and 1958; see also Wadsworth, A. P. 'Newspaper Circulations 1880–1954', *Transactions of the Manchester Statistical Society* 1954–5

34   £500,000, cf £15,000

35   Curzon to Spender, 28 December 1905. *Spender Papers*, Add MS 46391, f 7

36   *National Review*, November 1905

37   *The Times*, 13 February 1906

38   *The Times*, 22 January 1906

39   Campbell-Bannerman to Herbert Gladstone, 10 June 1905. *Campbell-Bannerman Papers*, Add MS 41217, ff 223–5

40   Muller's comment. *Balfour Papers*, Add MS 49797, ff 115–59

41   *National Review*, January 1906

42   *Balfour Papers*, loc cit

43   *Balfour Papers*, Add MS 49806, ff 100–1

44   The *Standard*, 25 November 1905

45   The *Observer*, 7 January 1906

46   *Asquith Papers*

47 *Campbell-Bannerman Papers*, Add MS 41223, ff 164–7
48 *Labour Leader*, 6 January 1906
49 Iwan-Muller—Memorandum. *Balfour Papers*, loc cit. Author's italics
50 *The Life and Times of Henry Lord Brougham written by himself*, iii, 149–50; Ostrogorski, M. *Democracy and the Organisation of Political Parties*, ii, 410; Milne, K. S., and MacKenzie, H. C. *Marginal Seat 1955*, 98–9
51 Mill, H. S., to Bryce, 30 January. *Bryce Papers*
52 Lowell, A. Lawrence. *The Government of England*, ii, 63
53 *Scotsman*, 11 January 1906
54 *Daily News*, 4 January 1906
55 *Hastings and Bexhill Independent*, 18 January 1906

Chapter 6 THE POLL AND THE RESULTS (pages 145–71)

1 Lucy, Henry. 'The next Liberal Ministry', *19th Century*, October 1904
2 Balfour to Devonshire, 27 October 1905. *Devonshire Papers*, 340, f 3155
3 Hicks-Beach, Lady Victoria. *Life of Michael Hicks Beach*, ii 220
4 Lucy, Henry, op cit
5 Taylor, H. A. *Jix, Viscount Brentford*, 55–6
6 Horne, C. Silvester. *Pulpit, Platform and Parliament*, 196
7 *The Times*, 15 January 1906
8 *The Times*, 16 January 1906
9 Channing, Francis. *Memories of Midland Politics, 1885–1910*, 329
10 Horne, C. Silvester. *Pulpit, Platform and Parliament*, 196–7
11 Kay Shuttleworth to Campbell-Bannerman, 14 January 1906. *Campbell-Bannerman Papers*, Add MS 41221, ff 87–8
12 *Campbell-Bannerman Papers*, Add MS 41217, ff 291–2
13 Speech at Glasgow. *The Times*, 16 January 1906
14 Mrs Courtney to Bryce, 22 January 1906. *Bryce Papers*
15 *The Times*, 17 January 1906
16 *The Times*, 5 January 1906
17 *The Speaker*, 20 January 1906
18 Mrs Courtney to Bryce, 22 January 1906. *Bryce Papers*
19 Snowden, Viscount. *Autobiography*, i, 309–10
20 *Bryce Papers*
21 Campbell-Bannerman to Asquith, 21 January 1906. *Asquith Papers*
22 *Campbell-Bannerman Papers*, Add MS 41210, f 260
23 'What a debacle at home, stupendous, but not it seems to me, wholly undeserved'. Curzon to Devonshire, 22 January 1906. *Devonshire Papers*, 340, f 3185
24 'What a marvellous sweep it is'. Ponsonby to Albert Gladstone on 23 January—adding wryly, 'it really alarms me'

25 Martin, Sir Richard Biddulph. 'The Electoral Swing of the Pendulum', *Journal of the Royal Statistical Society*, 31 December 1906, LXIX, Part IV, 657
26 Spender, J. A., and Asquith, Cyril. *Asquith*, i, 177
27 *The Autobiography of Margot Asquith*, ii, 81
28 Corbett, J. Rooke. 'Recent Electoral Statistics', *Journal of the Manchester Statistical Society*, December 1906. See also the Report of the 1910 Royal Commission on electoral systems (Ed 5163) which recommended adoption of the second transferable vote. *Parliamentary Accounts and Papers*, 1910, XXVI, 335

Chapter 7   ANALYSIS (pages 172–207)

(Where not otherwise indicated, citations are taken from *The Times*, the *Manchester Guardian*, and other leading dailies)
1   Cox to Bryce, 23 January 1906, *Bryce Papers*
2   *Barrow News*, 25 January 1906
3   *Manchester Guardian*, 15 January 1906
4   *Manchester Guardian*, 6 January 1906
5   Manners Sutton to Devonshire, 11 August 1904. *Devonshire Papers*, 340, f 3103
6   Figures based only on seats which were contested in 1900 and 1906; the small Welsh sample for which this comparison is possible accounts for the high negative correlation coefficient in that area, which cannot be regarded as typical. Acknowledgement is due to Dr P. Woolliams of Dial EMI for help with the computer programming necessary for the calculation of the correlation coefficient
7   Bulmer, L. F. 'Rural England from Within', *Independent Review*, August 1905
8   *The Times*, 4 January 1906
9   *Balfour Papers*, Add MS 49858, ff 31–2
10 M. S. Stewart to Balfour, undated. *Balfour Papers*, Add MS 49868, ff 36–7; and Porritt, Edward, 'Party Conditions in England . . .', *Political Science Quarterly*, June 1906
11 *Balfour Papers*, Add MS 49797, ff 115–59
12 *Spectator*, 13 January 1906
13 Lowell, A. L. op cit, ii, 15
14 *Daily Telegraph*, 19 January 1906
15 Biggs-Davison, John. *John Wyndham. A Study in Toryism*, 221
16 See F. A. Channing. *Memories of Midland Politics, 1885–1910*, 332; and the *Spectator*, 20 January 1906
17 J. Fell to Devonshire. *Devonshire Papers*, 340, f 3188
18 Sir Edward Clarke to Balfour, 20 January 1906. *Balfour Papers*, Add MS 49858, ff 167–73
19 Cited in the *Tribune*, 15 January 1906
20 O'Connor, T. P. *Sir Henry Campbell-Bannerman*, 83

21 *Balfour Papers*, Add MS 49858, f 204
22 *The Times*, 15 January 1906
23 Horne, C. Silvester. *Pulpit, Platform and Parliament*, 72
24 *The Times*, 4 January 1906
25 See *Clarion*, 3 and 20 November 1905 and 8 January 1906; NB The *Methodist Recorder* commented on 11 January 1906 that the ILP would presumably have no saints at all
26 Brogan, D. W. *The English People, Impressions and Observations*, 121
27 *Connexional Magazine*, cited in Wearmouth, R. F., op cit, 233
28 *Croydon Guardian*, 20 January 1906
29 Victor Cavendish to Devonshire, 19 January 1906. *Devonshire Papers*, 340, f 3182
30 *Devonshire Papers*, 340, f 3183
31 The *London Signal*, January and February 1906; *The Times*, 6 January 1906; and Selbie, W. B., *The Life of Charles Silvester Horne*, 196–7
32 *The Times*, 4 January 1906
33 *The Times*, 19 December 1906
34 *Kent Times and Chronicle*, 6 January 1906; *Church Times*, 5 and 12 January 1906. The Bishop of Hereford, on the other hand, openly attacked the Unionists over Chinese labour and Tariff Reform. *The Times*, 22 December 1905, and *Church Times*, loc cit
35 Gwynn, Dennis. *The Life of John Redmond*, 118
36 *The Tablet*, 19 and 20 December 1905
37 Snowden '. . . suggested that the Archbishop of Canterbury would by and by find a solution for the stretching of his conscience in the subscriptions to the Church from the mine-owners out of their increased dividends from Chinese Labour'. *Report of the Twelfth Annual Conference of the Independent Labour Party*, 25
38 *Manchester Guardian*, 1 January 1906, and *Freeman's Journal*, 15 January 1906
39 *Liverpool Catholic Herald*, 12 January 1906. Salvidge, Stanley. *Salvidge of Liverpool. Behind the Political Scene 1890–1928*, 66
40 *Viscount Gladstone Papers*, Add MS 46107, ff 28ff
41 Including a sizeable number where the Irish held the balance— among them Central Edinburgh, Midlothian, East Lothian, West Lothian, Perth, 4 seats in Glasgow and 6 in Lanarkshire—and about 20 more where the Liberals would not rest easy without Irish support. *The Scotsman*, 3, 6 and 9 January 1906
42 H. Cox to Bryce, 23 January 1906. *Bryce Papers*
43 *The Times* and the *Freeman's Journal*, 15 January 1906
44 *The Scotsman*, 6 January 1906
45 H. Cox to Bryce, 23 January 1906. *Bryce Papers*
46 Muller to Balfour, 13 February 1906. *Balfour Papers*, Add MS 49797, ff 115–59
47 *Reynolds News*, 7 January 1906

P

48   Dugdale, Blanche. *Arthur Balfour*, i, 433–6
49   See Rabinowicz, Oskar K. *Winston Churchill and the Jewish Problem*, 80
50   Eg South-West Manchester and Newton; see MacDonald, Ramsay. 'The Labour Party and its Policy', *Independent Review*, March 1906
51   Campbell, Persia Crawford. *Chinese Coolie Emigration*, 204–6
52   O'Connor, T. P. *Sir Henry Campbell-Bannerman*, 88
53   Wallas, Graham. *Human Nature in Politics*, 107
54   Masterman, Lucy. *C. F. G. Masterman, A Biography*, 64 ff
55   *Balfour Papers*, Add MS 49797, ff 115–59
56   Gooch, G. P. *Under Six Reigns*, 103
57   Spender, J. A. 'The new Government and its Problems', *Contemporary Review*, April 1906
58   *Report of the Fourteenth Annual Conference of the Independent Labour Party*, 16
59   *Clarion*, 26 January 1906
60   *Campbell-Bannerman Papers*, Add MS 41217, ff 294–5
61   *Clarion*, 2 February 1906
62   *Independent Review*, March 1906
63   Hugh Cecil to Devonshire, 19 January 1906. *Devonshire Papers*, 340, f 3181
64   Herbert Gladstone to Campbell-Bannerman, 21 January 1906. *Campbell-Bannerman Papers*, Add MS 41217, ff 294–5
65   The Liberals, he said, 'used that card and Burns himself used it to trump the Labour lead'. Burgess, Joseph. *John Burns. The Rise and Progress of a Right Honourable*, 196–7
66   Lansbury, George. *Looking Backwards—and Forwards*, 95
67   *Campbell-Bannerman Papers*, Add MS 41217, ff 291–2
68   Bealey, F. 'The Electoral arrangement between the LRC and the Liberal Party', *Journal of Modern History*, December 1956
69   Wallas, Graham. op cit, 71
70   Sandars to Balfour, 21 January 1906. *Balfour Papers*, Add MS 49764, f 146

Chapter 8 EPILOGUE: THE ELECTION AND AFTER (pages 208–13)

1   *The Times*, 24 January 1906
2   '. . . let loose in a flood by the Standard', wrote Gibson Bowles to Devonshire on 6 February 1906, 'and in trickles by the Times, Morning Post, and other papers'. *Devonshire Papers*, 340, f 3193
3   Hugh Cecil to Devonshire, 19 January 1906. *Devonshire Papers*, 450, f 3181
4   *Balfour Papers*, Add MS 49735, ff 216–17
5   *Report of the Sixth Annual Conference of the Labour Party*, 67

6 *Hull Daily Mail*, 19 January 1906
7 *The Autobiography of Margot Asquith*, ii, 81
8 Campbell-Bannerman to Asquith, 17 January 1906. *Asquith Papers*
9 Herbert Gladstone to Campbell-Bannerman, 21 January 1906. *Campbell-Bannerman Papers*, Add MS 41217, f 293
10 *Report of the Proceedings of the 39th Annual Trade Union Congress*, 45
11 Gretton, R. H. *A Modern History of the English People*, ii, 259
12 *Independent Review*, February 1906
13 *SLA Minutes, 1903–1906*, 249; see also the *Independent Review*, February 1906
14 *Report of the Sixth Annual Conference of the Labour Party*, 41
15 Morton, A. L., and Tate, George. *The British Labour Movement, 1770–1920*, 223–4
16 Burgess, Joseph. *John Burns: the Rise and Progress of a Right Honourable*, xvi
17 *Spender Papers*, Add MS 46388, f 111
18 Masterman, Lucy. *C. F. G. Masterman, a Biography*, 65

APPENDIX
Statistical Analysis of the Results

(a) DEFINITION OF REGIONS
Arabic numerals refer to Map 2 (p 165)

A LONDON:

Including the whole of the LCC area, plus 14 constituencies wholly or partly suburban

1 *Inner area*
The East End and the docks
    Bermondsey
    Bethnal Green (2)
    Deptford
    Greenwich
    Haggerston
    Hoxton
    Rotherhithe
    Tower Hamlets (7)—Bow, Limehouse, Mile End, Poplar,
      St George's, Stepney, Whitechapel
    West Ham (2)
    Woolwich
The central 'business' area
    City (2)
    Finsbury (3)
    St George's, Hanover Square
    Strand
    Westminster
The remainder of the LCC area
    (see Map 1, p 156)

2   *The outer suburbs*
Middlesex (7)—Brentford, Ealing, Enfield, Harrow, Horn-
sey, Tottenham, Uxbridge
Essex (2)—South Essex/Romford, SW Essex/Walthamstow
Kent (2)—Dartford, Sevenoaks (both of which ran up to
the boundary of the LCC area (see Map 1)
Surrey (3)—Kingston, Wimbledon, and the county borough
of Croydon

B THE SOUTH-EAST:

3   The Home Counties (i.e. Hants, Sussex, Kent, Surrey,
Berks, Oxon, Bucks, Herts, Essex, less those constituencies
included in the London area)

C THE SOUTH-WEST:

4   Devon and Cornwall
5   The rest: Gloucestershire, Wiltshire, Dorset, Somerset

D THE WEST MIDLANDS:

6   Shropshire, Herefordshire, and those parts of Worcestershire
not included in the Black Country (see 9 below)

E THE EAST:

7   Norfolk and Suffolk
8   The rest: Bedfordshire, Huntingdon, Cambridgeshire, Rut-
land, and Lincolnshire

F THE MIDLANDS:

9   The Black Country: Birmingham (7); the Handsworth and
Kingswinford divisions of Staffordshire, and the county
boroughs of Walsall, West Bromwich, Wednesbury, and
Wolverhampton (3); the South-Eastern division of Warwickshire, and the county boroughs of Aston Manor and Coventry; and the Mid, Eastern, and Northern divisions of

Worcestershire and the county boroughs of Dudley and
Kidderminster
10 The Potteries: Stoke, Newcastle-under-Lyme, and Hanley
11 Derbyshire and Nottinghamshire
12 Leicestershire, Northamptonshire, and the remainder of
Warwickshire
13 Staffordshire—less the constituencies listed at 9 above and 14
below, and Cheshire less the constituencies listed at 14 below

G THE NORTH OF ENGLAND:

14 Lancashire etc: Lancashire plus the Altrincham division of
Staffordshire and the county boroughs of Birkenhead,
Stalybridge and Stockport (2)
15 The West Riding of Yorkshire
16 Durham and Tyneside: County Durham, plus the Cleveland
division of the North Riding, the county borough of
Middlesbrough, the Wansbeck and Tyneside divisions of
Northumberland, and the county boroughs of Tynemouth
and Newcastle (2)
17 The North and East Ridings of Yorkshire less those constituencies in the North Riding listed at 16 above
18 Cumberland, Westmorland, and Northumberland less those
constituencies of Northumberland listed at 16 above

H WALES:

19 Industrial Wales: Monmouth and Glamorgan
20 The rest

I SCOTLAND:

21 The Lowlands: Ayrshire, Wigtown, Kirkcudbright, Dum-
fries, Peebles, Selkirk, Roxburgh, Berwick, East Lothian,
Midlothian and Edinburghshire
22 Clyde and Lanark: Dumbarton, Renfrewshire, and Lanarkshire
23 Firth of Forth: Stirlingshire, Clackmannan and Kinross,
and Fifeshire

24 NE Scotland
25 The Highlands

J LARGE CITIES (EXCLUDING LONDON):

(i) Glasgow	(viii) Edinburgh
(ii) Birmingham	(ix) Nottingham
(iii) Liverpool	(x) Hull
(iv) Leeds	(xi) Bradford
(v) Manchester	(xii) Newcastle
(vi) Sheffield	(xiii) Salford
(vii) Bristol	

(b) NOTES ON STATISTICAL METHOD

(i) SOURCE

All figures are based on those in *Dod's Parliamentary Companion, 1906*

(ii) NUMBER OF CONSTITUENCIES ON WHICH THE SWING FIGURES ARE BASED

Figures for the swing are based only on those 368 seats in which a contest took place both in 1900 and in 1906. The following table shows the relationship between those 368 seats and the seats won by different parties in 1906, and makes it plain that proportionately—and actually—many more Liberal and Labour than Unionist seats are included in the swing figures.

Party	Seats won in 1906	Of those won in 1906	
		Uncontested in 1900	Contested in 1900
Unionist	132	92	40 (30%)
Liberal	397	88	309 (78%)
Labour	30	11	19 (63%)
	559*	191	368

* Excluding T. P. O'Connor

Since the swing tended to be larger in 'traditionally' Unionist seats, it is unlikely that the distortion—if any—is great.

(iii) METHOD OF CALCULATING THE SWING

Except where otherwise stated, the concept of swing adopted in this work is that of a change in the percentage of votes won by one or other party (compared with the 1900 election) in a single constituency, a group of constituencies, or the whole country.

Double constituencies are treated as two separate constituencies, the winner with the highest number of votes being paired with the loser with the highest number of votes, and so on. Where only one Unionist and 2 Liberals contested a double constituency in 1906, the second Liberal is treated as if he had had an unopposed return, and no swing is calculated; and vice versa.

In constituencies where a Liberal stood in 1900 and a Labour candidate in 1906, the swing to Labour is calculated as the difference between the percentage Liberal poll in 1900 and the percentage Labour poll in 1906. Where Labour (or other candidates) stood against a Liberal in 1906, in a constituency in which the Labour (or other) candidate did not stand in 1900, the swing to the Labour (or other) candidate is calculated as the percentage polled, i.e. the increase over zero.

The votes cast for opposed Unionist or Liberal candidates are counted together for the purpose of calculating the swing.

A: LONDON

London and Suburbia: Area	Electorate in 1,000s	Average electorate	Percentage vote	Members elected										Percentage swing				No of seats on which swing is based
				Total	Unionist Total	Unionist Gain or loss	Liberal Total	Liberal Gain or loss	Labour Total	Labour Gain or loss	Other Total	Other Gain or loss	Unionist	Liberal	Labour	Other	
E. End & Docks	176	9·8	79·0	18	2	−13	13	10	3	3	—	—	−13·3	7·6	4·4[1]	1·3	17[2]
City & business	109	13·7	69·1	8	6	−2	2	2	—	—	—	—	−13·3	13·3	—	—	4
Rest	403	11·5	78·5	35	11	−19	24	19	3	3	—	—	−16·1	13·3	—	2·8	27
Total	688	11·3	77·2	61	19	−34	39	31	3	3	—	—	−15·0	11·3	1·6	2·1[3]	48
Suburbs	329	23·5	77·4	14	7	−7	7	7	—	—	—	—	−21·3	21·3	—	—	5
Total	1,017	13·5	77·3	75	26 (54·6%)	−41	46 (61·4%)	38	3 (4·0%)	3	—	—	−15·5	12·2	1·4	1·9	53

[1] NB. Large Labour gain over Liberals at Deptford of 52·1 per cent

[2] All save Woolwich, which the Unionists won unopposed in 1900. In 1906 Crooks' total vote increased by 339 votes, but his percentage poll fell by 4·6 per cent

[3] Croydon—Unionist unopposed in 1900; in 1906 Harry Stranks (LRC candidate) polled 4,112—or 21 per cent of the total

B-E: NON-INDUSTRIAL ENGLAND

Area	Electorate in 1,000s	Average electorate	Percentage vote	Total	Members elected								Percentage swing				No of seats on which swing is based
					Unionist		Liberal		Labour		Other		Unionist	Liberal	Labour	Other	
					Total	Gain or loss	Total	Gain or loss	Total	Gain or loss	Total	Gain or loss					
B SE	761	12.5	83.6	61	28	−29[1]	32	28[1]	1	1	—	—	−8.8	6.2	1.7	0.9	27
C SW: Devon & Cornwall	222	11.0	83.5	20	3	−7	17	7	—	—	—	—	−7.0	6.9	—	0.1	14
Rest	317	10.2	87.5	31	5	−18	26	18	—	—	—	—	−8.4	8.4	—	—	20
Total	539	10.7	86.1	51	8	−25	43	25	—	—	—	—	−7.8[4]	7.8	—	0.04	34
D W. Midlands	99	9.0	85.9	11	8	−3	3	3	—	—	—	—	−20.8	20.8[2]	—	—	1[2]
E East: Norfolk and Suffolk	200	11.1	85.2	18	2	−9	15	8	1	1	—	—	−8.7	6.1	[3]	2.6	12
Rest	202	9.6	70.1	21	4	−11	17	11	—	—	—	—	−8.1[4]	5.9	—	2.2	17
Total	402	10.3	81.8	39	6	−20	32	19	1	1	—	—	−8.4	6.0	—	2.4	29
Total	1,801	11.1	83.7	162	50 (30.8%)	−77	110 (68.0%)	75	2 (1.2%)	2	—	—	−8.5	6.9	0.5	1.1	91

[1] In fact the Unionists lost 31 and gained 2—Maidstone and Hastings—the Liberals gained 30 and lost these same 2

[2] Only 1 of these 11 constituencies was contested in 1900 and 1906—Shropshire Mid-Wellington; in 8 of the rest contested previously in 1892 and 1895 the swing averaged 8.6 per cent

[3] NB. G. H. Roberts stood in Norwich double constituency where he polled 11,059 votes, or 54.2 per cent of the electorate.

[4] Seeley—UFT

Area	Electorate in 1,000s	Average electorate	Percentage vote	Total	Unionist Total	Unionist Gain or loss	Liberal Total	Liberal Gain	Labour Total	Labour Gain or loss	Other Total	Other Gain or loss	Swing Unionist	Swing Liberal	Swing Labour	Swing Other	No of seats on which swing is based
F The Black Country	296	13·4	81·8	22	12	7	9	6	1	1	—	—	5·4	3·8	1·6	—	7[1]
The Potteries	40	13·3	84·0	3	—	3	3	3	—	—	—	—	17·2	17·2	—	—	3
Derby & Notts	239	15·0	85·1	16	2	4	14	4	—	—	—	—	8·4	8·4	—	—	12
Leics etc	246	13·6	84·5	18	0	9	17	8	1	1	—	—	14·7	3·7	8·3	2·9	14
Staffordshire	161	11·5	87·5	14	1	9	13	9	—	—	—	—	8·2	8·2	—	—	11
Total	982	13·5	85·6	73	15	32	56	30	2	2	1[3]	—	8·0	6·8	0·2	1·0	47
G Lancs etc	878	14·2	86·4	62	15	35	33	22[2]	13	13[2]	—	—	13·1	5·5	4·7	2·9	40
West Riding	523	13·8	85·3	38	5	11	30	8	3	3	—	—	11·8	3·9	6·0	1·9	25
Durham & Tyneside	422	18·0	81·7	24	4	6	16	4[4]	4	4[4]	—	—	14·0	7·3	6·2	0·5	18
North Riding	130	10·9	84·0	12	6	3	6	3	—	—	—	—	6·8	4·8	2·0	—	7
Northumberland	84	8·4	84·4	10	1	—	9	5	—	—	—	—	6·0	6·0	—	—	6
Total	2,037	13·9	84·7	146	31	60	94	42	20	20	—	—	12·2	5·7	4·7	1·8	96
Grand Total	3,019	13·8	85·0	219	46 (21·0%)	92	150 (68·5%)	72	22 (10·5%)	22	1	—	10·8	6·0	3·2	1·6	143

[1] Including, unfortunately, only one of the 7 Birmingham seats, Birmingham East

[2] Labour won 12 from the Unionists and one (NE Lancs Clitheroe) from the Liberals, ie the seat was Liberal in 1900; it was in fact won by Labour in August 1902. The Liberals thus won 23 and lost 1

[3] T. P. O'Connor, Irish Nationalist

[4] Labour won 2 from the Unionists and 2 from the Liberals—Barnard Castle and Chester-le-Street. The Liberals thus won 6 and lost 2

H: WALES

Area	Electorate in 1,000s	Average electorate	Percentage vote	Total	Members elected								Percentage swing				No of seats on which swing is based
					Unionist		Liberal		Labour		Other		Unionist	Liberal	Labour	Other	
					Total	Gain or loss	Total	Gain or loss	Total	Gain or loss	Total	Gain or loss					
Industrial Wales	228	16·9	91·0	14	—	−3	13	3	1	—	—	—	−3·6	1·6[1]	2·0	—	7
The rest	174	8·7	81·4	20	—	−3	20	3	—	—	—	—	−7·3	7·3	—	—	9
Total	402	12·6	86·2	34	—	−6	33 (97%)	6	1 (3%)	—	—	—	−5·6	4·7	0·9	—	16

[1] In this figure the Liberal-Labour and Liberal candidates who stood against each other are considered together as representing the Liberal vote; the Unionists contested the seat in 1906 in 1900—they did not in 1900

I: SCOTLAND

Area	Electorate in 1,000s	Average electorate	Percentage vote	Members elected Total	Unionist Total	Unionist Gain or loss	Liberal Total	Liberal Gain or loss	Labour Total	Labour Gain or loss	Other Total	Other Gain or loss	Percentage swing Unionist	Percentage swing Liberal	Percentage swing Labour	Percentage swing Other	No of seats on which swing is based
Lowlands	187	9·8	81·8	19	4	—7	15	7	—	—	—	—	8·7	—7·6	—	1·1	18
Clyde & Lanark	258	14·4	83·3	18	4	—9[1]	13	8[1]	1	1	—	—	12·6	—1·1	6·2	5·3	16
Firth of Forth	93	10·3	54·0	9	1	—2	8	2	—	—	—	—	11·6	—9·1	—	2·5	8
NE	133	11·0	76·7	12	—	—	11	1[2]	1	1[2]	—	—	14·0	—8·4	3·5	2·1	12
Highlands	77	6·4	74·3	12	1	—6	11	6	—	—	—	—	11·5	—11·5	—	—	12
Total	748	10·7	77·1	70	10 (14·3%)	—26	58 (82·8%)	24	2 (2·9%)	2	—	—	11·3	—6·9	2·1	2·3	66

[1] These figures hide the fact that the Unionists won 2 Lanark seats, (i) NW and (ii) Govan from the Liberals as a result of (i) Socialist and (ii) LRC intervention. In fact, therefore, the Unionists won 2 and lost 11, and the Liberals won 10 and lost 2

[2] Dundee (1) from Liberals; the Liberals won 2 from the Unionists

J: LARGE CITIES (excluding London)

Town	Population in 1,000s	Electorate in 1,000s	Average electorate	Percentage vote	Total	No of Libs elected 1885	Unionist		Liberal		Labour		Other		Percentage swing				No of seats on which swing is based
							Total	Gain or loss	Total	Gain or loss	Total	Gain or loss	Total	Gain or loss	Unionist	Liberal	Labour	Other	
Glasgow	67	93·5	13·3	82·1	7	7	2	−5	4	4	1	1			−15·3	3·3	11·6	0·4	7
Birmingham	52	87·7	12·3	74·5	7	7	7								−11·2		11·2		1[1]
Liverpool	62	84·1	9·3	72·2	9	—	6	−2	2	2			1		−15·7	5·5	5·7	4·5	3[2]
Leeds	42	73·8	14·7	79·4	5	2		−3	4	2	1	1			−18·4	7·7	10·7		5
Manchester	47	67·2	11·2	84·1	6	1		−5	4	3	2	2			−18·7	10·7	8·0		5
Sheffield	38	62·6	12·5	82·8	5	3	3	−1	2	1					−10·2	10·2			2
Bristol	32	52·0	13·0	83·5	4	4	1	−2	3	2					−15·5	15·5			3
Edinburgh	28	43·1	10·8	83·2	4	3	1	−2	3	2					−11·7	11·7			4
Nottingham	24	42·6	14·2	83·3	3	2			3						−10·9	10·9			3
Hull	24	42·1	14·0	80·1	3	2	1	−1	2	1					−6·2	6·2			3
Bradford	23	39·1	13·0	89·0	3	3		−3	2	2	1	1			−16·5	−3·8	13·0	7·3	3
Newcastle[3]	21	36·9	13·4	82·0	2	2		−2	1	1	1	1			−20·5	10·4	10·1		2
Salford	22	32·0	10·6	89·7	3	2		−3	3	3					−10·1	10·1			3
Total	482	756·7	12·4	80·9	61	37	21 (34·4%)	−29	33 (54·1%)	23	6 (9·8%)	6	1 (1·7%)		−14·1	7·5	5·7	0·9	44

[1] Birmingham East, where Bruce Glasier stood for Labour; there was no Liberal candidate

[2] These, conveniently enough, are the Exchange, Kirkdale and Scotland divisions where the Unionist was opposed by Liberal, Labour and Irish Nationalist, respectively

[3] Double constituency

Analysis of the swing according to type of contest

Type of contest	Unionist plus	minus	Liberal plus	minus	Labour plus	minus	Socialist plus	minus	UFT etc plus	minus
306 Unionist v Liberal	9·4		9·4							
1 Unionist v UFT[1]	1·6								1·6	
1 Unionist v Nationalist[2]	13·6								13·6	
1 Unionist v 2 Liberals[3]		17·1		17·1						
15 Unionist v Labour	16·8				16·8					
1 Liberal v Labour[4]			2·3			2·3				
15 Unionist, Liberal and Labour	15·3			16·7	32·0		19·9			
17 Unionist, Liberal and Socialist	15·1			4·8			39·7			
1 Liberal v 2 Socialist[5]			6·3							
11 other triangles[6] (chiefly UFT)		25·1	8·9							16·2
Total		10·5	7·1		2·0		0·9		0·5	

[1] Durham
[2] Scotland division of Liverpool
[3] Glamorgan West: Gower
[4] Merthyr Tydfil
[5] North-East Lancashire: Accrington, swing to two separate Socialist candidates; not included in the total
[6] 5 UFTs—Islington South, Greenwich, Kings Lynn, Lincoln, and Glasgow Tradeston
   3 Independent Liberals
   2 Independent Unionists
   1 Naval candidate—T. F. Jane at Portsmouth

SELECT BIBLIOGRAPHY

I MANUSCRIPT SOURCES

This book is based on a number of unpublished collections of leaflets, minutes and election addresses; on contemporary handbooks, Hansard, and Parliamentary Accounts and Papers; and on a wide-ranging review of the national and provincial press. The major manuscript sources used are as follows:

Arnold-Forster Papers
Asquith Papers—Bodleian, Oxford (by kind permission of Lady Violet Bonham-Carter)
Avebury Papers
Balfour Papers
Bryce Papers—Bodleian, Oxford
Burns Papers
Campbell-Bannerman Papers
Devonshire Papers—Chatsworth House (by kind permission of His Grace the Duke of Devonshire)
Dilke Papers
Viscount Gladstone Papers
Diary of Sir Edward Hamilton
Pease Collection—British Library of Political and Economic Science
Ripon Papers
Spender Papers

II PUBLISHED SOURCES

I BACKGROUND

Clapham, J. C. *An Economic History of Modern Britain* . . ., iii (London, 1938)

Ensor, R. C. K. *England, 1870–1914* (Oxford, 1936)
Halévy, Eli. *Imperialism and the Rise of Labour, 1895–1905* (London, 1951)
——. *Rule of Democracy, 1905–14* (London, 1952)
Maccoby, S. *English Radicalism, 1886–1914* (London, 1953)
Thornton, A. P. *The Imperial Idea and its Enemies. A Study in British Power* (London, 1959)

2 SOCIO/POLITICAL INSTITUTIONS AND ANALYSES

(i) General

Butler, D. E. *The Electoral System in Britain, 1918–1951* (Oxford, 1953)
Lowell, A. Lawrence. *The Government of England* (New York, 1908)
MacKenzie, Robert. *British Political Parties. The Distribution of Power within the Conservative and Labour Parties* (London, 1955)
Morris, H. L. *Parliamentary Franchise Reform in England and Wales from 1885 to 1914* (New York, 1921)
Mozley, E. N. 'The Political Heptarchy', *Contemporary Review*, April 1910
O'Leary, Cornelius. *The Elimination of Corrupt Practices in British Elections, 1868–1911* (Oxford, 1962)
Ostrogorski, M. *Democracy and the Organisation of Political Parties* (London, 1902)
Rogers, on Elections, i. *Registration, 7th Edition* (Ed Powell, London, 1909)
——. ii. *Parliamentary Elections and Petitions, 18th Edition* (Ed Williams, London, 1906)
Rosenbaum, S. 'The General Election of 1910 and the Bearing of the Results on some Problems of Representation (followed by a discussion)', *Journal of the Royal Statistical Society*, May 1910
Seymour, Charles. *Electoral Reform in England and Wales* (New Haven, Connecticut, 1916)

Wallas, Graham. *Human Nature in Politics* (London, 1908)

(*ii*) *The Unionist party*
Cecil, Lord Robert. *Conservatism* (London, 1911)
Hayter, L. H. *An Outline of the History of the Conservative Party*
    (Taunton, 1925)
Hearnshaw, F. J. C. *Conservatism in England: an Analytical
    Historical, and Political Survey* (London, 1933)
McDowell, R. B. *British Conservatism, 1832–1914* (London, 1959)
Ridgeway, West. 'The Liberal Unionist Party', *Nineteenth
    Century*, August and October, 1905
Wilson, J. Mackay. 'Ireland and the Liberal Unionists', *National
    Review*, November 1905
Woods, Maurice. *History of the Tory Party* (London, 1924)

(*iii*) *The Liberal party*
Belloc, Hilaire, Hammond, J. L., Simon, J., MacDonald, J. R.,
    and others. *On Liberalism* (London, 1897)
Blease, W. Lyon. *Liberalism. A Short History of English Liberal-
    ism* (London, 1913)
Buxton, C. R. 'A Vision of England', *Independent Review*, Octo-
    ber 1905
Lucy, Henry. 'The Next Liberal Ministry', *Nineteenth Century*,
    October 1904
Spence-Watson, R. *The National Liberal Federation, from its
    Commencement to the General Election of 1906* (London,
    1907)
Stead, W. T. *The Liberal Ministry of 1906* (London, 1906)

(*iv*) *Labour including the TUC*
Bealey, F. 'The Electoral Arrangement between the L.R.C. and
    the Liberal Party', *Journal of Modern History*, December
    1956
——. 'Negotiations between the Liberals and the L.R.C. before
    the 1906 Election', *Bulletin of the Institute of Historical
    Research*, November 1956

——, and Pelling, Henry. *Labour and Politics 1900–1906. A History of the Labour Representation Committee* (London, 1958)

Hardie, J. Keir. 'Labour and the Election', *Nineteenth Century*, January 1906

——. 'The Labour Party', *National Review*, February 1906

——, Snowden, P., and Shackleton, D. *Labour Politics, a Symposium* (Tracts for the Times, No 2, ILP, London, 1903)

Hook, A. 'Labour and Politics', *Independent Review*, June 1905

Hutt, Arnold. 'The Claims of Labour', *Independent Review*, March 1905

MacDonald, Ramsay. 'The Labour Party and its Policy', *Independent Review*, March 1906

Poirer, Philip P. *The Advent of the Labour Party* (London, 1958)

Roberts, B. C. *The Trade Union Congress, 1868–1921* (London, 1955)

Snowden, P. 'The Labour Party and the General Election', *Independent Review*, August 1905

(*v*) *The Nationalists*

Lyons, F. S. L. *The Irish Parliamentary Party, 1890–1910* (London, 1951)

(*vi*) *The Suffragettes*

Fulford, Roger. *Votes for Women. The Story of a Struggle* (London, 1947)

Pankhurst, Dame Christabel. *Unshackled* (London, 1959)

Pankhurst, E. Sylvia. *The Suffragette. A History of the Women's Militant Suffrage Movement 1905–1911* (London, 1911)

——. *The Suffragette Movement. An Intimate Account of Persons and Ideals* (London, 1931)

(*vii*) *The churches and politics*

Clark, H. W. *History of English Nonconformity, from Wyclif to the close of the Nineteenth Century* (London, 1911)

Q*

Horne, C. Silvester. *Pulpit, Platform and Parliament* (London, 1913)

Payne, Ernest A. *The Free Church Tradition in the Life of England* (London, 1951)

Taylor, E. R. *Methodism and Politics* (Cambridge, 1935)

Vickers, J. *History of Independent Methodism* (London, 1920)

Wearmouth, R. F. *Methodism and the Struggle of the Working Classes, 1850–1900* (Leicester, 1954)

(*viii*) *The press*

Dunlop, Andrew. *Fifty Years of Irish Journalism* (London, 1911)

Fisher, W. J. 'The Liberal Press and the Party', *Nineteenth Century*, July 1904

The History of the Times. *The Twentieth Century Test, 1884–1912* (London, 1914)

Jones, Kennedy. *Fleet Street and Downing Street* (London, 1920)

Strachey, J. St Loe. *The Ethics of Journalism* (London, 1908)

Symon, J. D. *The Press and its Story* (London, 1914)

Wadsworth, A. P. 'Newspapers' Circulations, 1800–1854', *Transactions of the Manchester Statistical Society*, 1954–5

(*ix*) *The House of Commons*

King, C. T. *The Asquith Parliament, a Popular History of its Men and its Measures* (London, 1910)

Thomas, J. A. *The House of Commons, 1832–1901, a Study of its Economic and Functional Character* (Cardiff, 1939)

——. *The House of Commons, 1901–1911* (Cardiff, 1959)

3 ISSUES

(*i*) *The fiscal issue*

Balfour, A. J. *Economic Notes on Insular Free Trade* (London, 1903)

Berard, V. *British Imperialism and Commercial Supremacy* (London, 1906)

Chapman, S. D. *A Reply to the Report of the Tariff Commission on the Cotton Industry* (London, 1905)

Cobden Club, The. *Fact versus Fiction: the Cobden Club's Reply to Mr. Chamberlain* (London, 1904)

Gould, F. Carruthers, and Saki. *The Westminster Alice* (London, 1904)

MacDonald, R. *Facts for the Workers about Free Trade, Protection and Monopoly* (Tracts for the Times, No 3, ILP, London, 1904)

Porritt, E. *60 Years of Protection in Canada, 1846–1907. Where Industry Leans on the Politicians* (London, 1908)

Semmel, Bernard. *Imperialism and Tariff Reform* (London, 1960)

Snowden, Philip. *The Chamberlain Bubble, Facts about the Zollverein with an Alternative Policy* (Tracts for the Times, No 1, ILP, London, 1903)

Vince, C. A. *Mr. Chamberlain's Proposals: what they mean and what we shall gain by them* (London, 1903)

(*ii*) *Social conditions and policies*

Booth, Charles. *Life and Labour of the People of London* (London, 1903)

——. *Old Age Pensions: the Aged Poor. A Proposal* (London, 1899)

Hammond, J., and others. *Towards a Social Policy: or Suggestions for Constructive Reforms* (London, 1905)

Hardie, J. Keir. *The Unemployment Problem, with some suggestions for solving it* (ILP, London, 1904)

Higgs, Mary. *Glimpses into the Abyss* (London, 1906)

——. *How to deal with the Unemployed* (London, 1904)

Masterman, C. F. G. *The Heart of the Empire* (London, 1900)

Money, L. G. Chiozza. *Riches and Poverty* (London, 1905)

Rees, J. Aubrey. *Our Aims and Objects* (National League of Young Liberals Pamphlet No 1, London, 1903)

Rowntree, Seebohm. *Poverty: A Study of Town Life* (London, 1901)

(*iii*) *The Chinese labour issue*

Birnbaum, Doris. 'Chinese Labour in the Transvaal', *Independent Review*, May 1905

Campbell, Persia Crawford. *Chinese Coolie Emigration to Countries within the British Empire* (London, 1923)
Cooke, Kinloch. 'The Chinese Labour Question', *Empire Review*, December 1905–April 1906

(iv) The education issue
Allen, Bernard M. *Sir Robert Morant. A Great Public Servant* (London, 1934)
Eaglesham, Eric. *From School Board to Local Authority* (London, 1956)
MacNamara, T. J. 'The State and Secondary Education', *Independent Review*, May 1905

(v) Intemperance and the licensing problem
Carter, Henry. *The English Temperance Movement* (London, 1933)
Rowntree, Joseph, and Sherwell, Arthur. *The Temperance Problem and Social Reform* (London, 1899)
Snowden, Philip. *Socialism and the Drink Question* (ILP, London, 1908)
Wilson, George B. *Alcohol and the Nation (A Contribution to the Study of the Liquor Problem in the United Kingdom from 1800 to 1935)* (London, 1904)

(vi) The problem of Irish government
Dunraven, Lord. 'Moderate Reform in Ireland', *Nineteenth Century*, January 1906
Green, Alice Stopford. 'The Case of Sir Antony MacDonnell', *Independent Review*, June 1906
Ker, S. P. 'Stands Ulster where it did?', *Contemporary Review*, January 1906
Philips, Alison. *The Revolution in Ireland, 1906–1923* (London, 1923)

4 BIOGRAPHY AND AUTOBIOGRAPHY

(i) Unionists

Amery, The Rt Hon Leo. *My Political Life, Vol. I* (London, 1953)
Dugdale, Blanche. *Arthur James Balfour, First Earl of Balfour* (London, 1936)
Raymond, E. T. *Mr. Balfour. A Biography* (London, 1920)
Birkenhead, Earl of. *Life of Frederick Edwin, Earl of Birkenhead* (London, 1933)
Blake, Robert. *The Unknown Prime Minister: the Life and Times of Andrew Bonar Law, 1858–1923* (London, 1955)
Hyde, H. Montgomery. *Carson. The Life of Sir Edward Carson, Lord Carson of Duncairn* (London, 1953)
Petrie, Sir Charles, Bt. *The Life and Letters of the Right Hon. Sir Austen Chamberlain, K.G., P.C., M.P.* (London, 1939)
Garvin, J. A., and Amery, Julian. *The Life of Joseph Chamberlain*, vols 2, 3, 4, 5 and 6 (London, 1933 and subsequently)
Macintosh, Alexander. *Joseph Chamberlain. An Honest Biography* (London, 1906)
Boyd, Charles W. (ed). *Mr. Chamberlain's Speeches, etc.* (London, 1914)
Ervine, St John. *Craigavon: Ulsterman* (London, 1949)
Holland, Bernard. *The Life of Spencer Compton, 8th Duke of Devonshire* (London, 1911)
Elliot, The Hon Arthur R. D. *The Life of George Joachim Goschen, First Viscount Goschen, 1831–1907* (London, 1911)
Hamilton, Lord George. *Parliamentary Reminiscences and Reflections, 1896–1906* (London, 1917)
Hewins, W. A. S. *The Apologia of an Imperialist* (London, 1929)
Hicks-Beach, Victoria. *Life of Sir Michael Hicks Beach* (London, 1908)
Askwith, Lord. *Lord James of Hereford* (London, 1930)
Taylor, H. A. *Jix, Viscount Brentford. Being the authoritative and official Biography of the Rt. Hon. William Joynson-Hicks, First Viscount Brentford of Newark* (London, 1933)
Newton, Lord. *Lord Lansdowne. A Biography* (London, 1929)

Long, Viscount, of Wraxall. *Memories* (London, 1923)
Petrie, Sir Charles. *The Life and Times of Walter Long* (London, 1936)
Lyttleton, Edith. *Alfred Lyttleton: An Account of his Life* (London, 1917)
Salvidge, Stanley. *Salvidge of Liverpool. Behind the Political Scene, 1890–1928* (London, 1934)
Mill, Hugh Robert. *The Life of Sir Ernest Shackleton, C.V.O., O.B.E.* (*Mil*), LL.D. (London, 1923)
Winterton, Earl. *Orders of the Day* (London, 1953)
Davidson, John Biggs. *George Wyndham: A Study in Toryism* (London, 1951)

(*ii*) *Liberal*
McCallum, R. B. *Asquith* (London, 1936)
Oxford and Asquith, The Earl of, KG. *Memories and Reflections, 1852–1927* (London, 1928)
Spender, J. A., and Asquith, Cyril. *Life of Herbert Henry Asquith, Lord Oxford and Asquith* (London, 1932)
Asquith, Margot. *The Autobiography of Margot Asquith*, ii (London, 1922)
Speaight, Robert. *The Life of Hilaire Belloc* (London, 1957)
Symons, Julian. *Horatio Bottomley: A Biography* (London, 1955)
Fisher, H. A. L. *James Bryce: Viscount Bryce Dechmont, O.M.* (London, 1927)
Burgess, Joseph. *John Burns. The Rise and Progress of a Right Honourable* (Glasgow, 1911)
Stewart, William. *John Burns and the Common People* (London, 1925)
Burt, Thomas. *Pitman and Privy Councillor. An Autobiography* (London, 1924)
Meech, Thomas Cox. *From Mine to Ministry. The Life and Times of the Right Hon. Thomas Burt, M.P.* (Darlington, 1908)
De Bunsen, Victoria. *Charles Roden Buxton. A Memoir* (London, 1948)
Anderson, Mosa. *Noel Buxton. A Life* (London, 1952)

Spender, J. A. *Life of the Right Hon. Sir Henry Campbell-Bannerman, G.C.B.* (London, 1923)

O'Connor, T. P. *Sir Henry Campbell-Bannerman* (London, 1908)

Channing, Francis Allston. *Memories of Midland Politics, 1885–1910* (London, 1918)

De Mendelssohn, Peter, *The Age of Churchill. Heritage and Adventure, 1874–1911* (London, 1961)

Pope-Hennessy, J. *Lord Crowe; 1858–1945. The Likeness of a Liberal* (London, 1955)

Gwynn, Stephen, and Tuckwell, Gertrude. *The Life of the Right Hon. Sir Charles Dilke, Bart. M.P.* (London, 1917)

Murray, Arthur C. *Master and Brother. Murrays of Elibank* (London, 1945)

Mallet, Sir Charles. *Herbert Gladstone, a Memoir* (London, 1932)

Gooch, G. P. *Under Six Reigns* (London, 1958)

Trevelyan, G. M. *Grey of Falloden. Being the Life of Sir Edward Grey, afterwards Viscount Grey of Falloden* (London, 1957)

Grey, Edward, Viscount Grey of Falloden. *Twenty-five Years, 1892–1916* (London, 1925)

Maurice, Gen Sir Frederick. *Haldane. The Life of Viscount Haldane of Cloan, 1856–1915* (London, 1937 and 1939)

Haldane, Richard Burdon. *An Autobiography* (London, 1929)

Gardiner, A. G. *The Life of Sir William Harcourt* (London, 1923)

Hocking, Silas K. *My Book of Memory. A String of Reminiscences and Reflections* (London, 1923)

Isaacs, Gerald Rufus, 2nd Marquess of Reading. *Rufus Isaacs, First Marquess of Reading* (London, 1942 and 1945)

Thompson, Malcolm, *David Lloyd George. The Official Biography* (London, 1948)

Owen, Frank. *Tempestuous Journey. L.G., his Life and Times* (London, 1954)

Green, Roger Lancelyn. *A. E. W. Mason* (London, 1952)

Masterman, Lucy. *C. F. G. Masterman. A Biography* (London, 1939)

Bolitho, Henry. *Alfred Mond. 1st Lord Melchett* (London, 1933)

Morley, John, Viscount. *Recollections* (London, 1917)
Wolf, Lucien. *Life of the First Marquess of Ripon, etc.* (London, 1921)
Crewe. *Lord Rosebery* (London, 1931)
Hammerton, J. A. *Lord Rosebery* (London, 1901)
Raymond, E. T. *The Man of Promise. Rosebery, a Central Study* (London, 1923)
Samuel, Viscount. *Memoirs* (London, 1945)
Bowle, John. *Viscount Samuel* (London, 1957)
Seely, Maj-Gen the Rt Hon J. E. B. *Adventure* (London, 1930)
Rhondda, Viscountess, and others. *D. A. Thomas: Viscount Rhondda* (London, 1921)
Corder, Percy. *The Life of Robert Spence Watson* (London, 1914)

(iii) Labour
Barnes, G. N. *Workshop to War Cabinet* (London, 1924)
Thompson, Laurence. *Robert Blatchford. Portrait of an Englishman* (London, 1957)
Clynes, J. R. *Memoirs* (London, 1938)
Stewart, William. *J. Keir Hardie—A Biography* (London, 1921)
Hamilton, M. A. *Arthur Henderson. A Biography* (London, 1938)
Hodge, J. *Workman's Cottage to Windsor Castle* (London, 1938)
Gould, F. J. *Hyndman. Prophet of Socialism, 1842–1921* (London, 1928)
Tsuzuki, Chushichi. *H. M. Hyndman and British Socialism* (Oxford, 1961)
Lansbury, G. *Looking Backwards—and Forwards* (London, 1928)
Snowden, Philip, Viscount. *An Autobiography* (London, 1934)
Tillett, B. *Memories and Reflections* (London, 1931)
Turner, B. *About Myself* (London, 1930)
Webb, Beatrice. *Our Partnership* (ed Barbara Ward and Margaret Cole; London, 1948)

(iv) Nationalist
Blunt, Wilfred Scawen. *My Diaries. Being a Personal Narrative of Events, 1884–1914* (London, 1919)

Fyfe, Hamilton. *T. P. O'Connor* (London, 1934)
Gwynn, Denis. *The Life of John Redmond* (London, 1932)

(v) Clerical
Marchant, Sir James. *Dr. John Clifford, C.H., Life, Letters and Reminiscences* (London, 1924)
Bell, G. K. A. *Randall Davidson, Archbishop of Canterbury* (London, 1935)
Selbie, W. B. *The Life of Charles Silvester Horne* (London, 1920)

(vi) Journalists and writers
Mills, F. Saxon. *Life of Sir Edward Cook* (London, 1921)
Gissing, George. *Letters of George Gissing to his Family* (London, 1927)
Ryan, A. P. *Lord Northcliffe* (London, 1953)
Hammond, J. L. *C. P. Scott of the Manchester Guardian* (London, 1934)
Spender, J. A. *Life, Journalism and Politics* (London, 1927)
Strachey, J. St Loe. *The Adventure of Living* (London, 1922)
Strachey, Amy. *St. Loe Strachey: his Life and Paper* (London, 1930)

5 THE ELECTION AND AFTER
Belloc, Hilaire, and Chesterton, Cecil. *The Party System* (London, 1911)
Cosby, D. A. 'The Conservative Victory and what it Signifies', *Westminster Review*, March 1906
Dangerfield, George. *The Strange Death of Liberal England* (London, 1936)
E.K.F. 'The Age of the Ostrich', *Westminster Review*, April 1906
Hammond, J. L. 'The Opportunity of the Next Government', *Independent Review*, March 1905
Hobson, J. *The Crisis of Liberalism: New Issues of Democracy* (London, 1909)
Massingham, H. W. 'Victory and What to Do with It', *Contemporary Review*, February 1906

Porritt, Edward. 'Party Conditions in England and the Cause of Liberal Success in England, 1906', *Political Science Quarterly*, June 1906

Spender, J. A. 'The new Government and its Problems', *Contemporary Review*, April 1906

Thompson, Alex. *Here I Lie* (London, 1937)

Wallas, Graham. 'Remember 1880', *The Speaker*, 27 January 1906

Wells, H. G. *An Experiment in Autobiography* (London, 1934)

6 NOVELS

Belloc, Hilaire. *Emmanuel Burden* (London, 1904)

Carey, Joyce. *Prisoner of Grace* (London, 1956)

Galsworthy, John. *The Forsyte Saga* (London, 1956)

Gissing, George. *In the Year of the Jubilee* (London, 1894)

——. *New Grub Street* (London, 1891)

Mason, A. E. W. *The Turnstile* (London, 1902)

Sackville-West, Victoria. *The Edwardians* (London, 1952)

Tressell, Robert. *The Ragged Trousered Philanthropists* (London, 1955)

Wells, H. G. *The New Machiavelli* (London, 1911)

INDEX